FLOWER SEEDS

EDITED BY
JULIET BINGHAM
TATE PUBLISHING

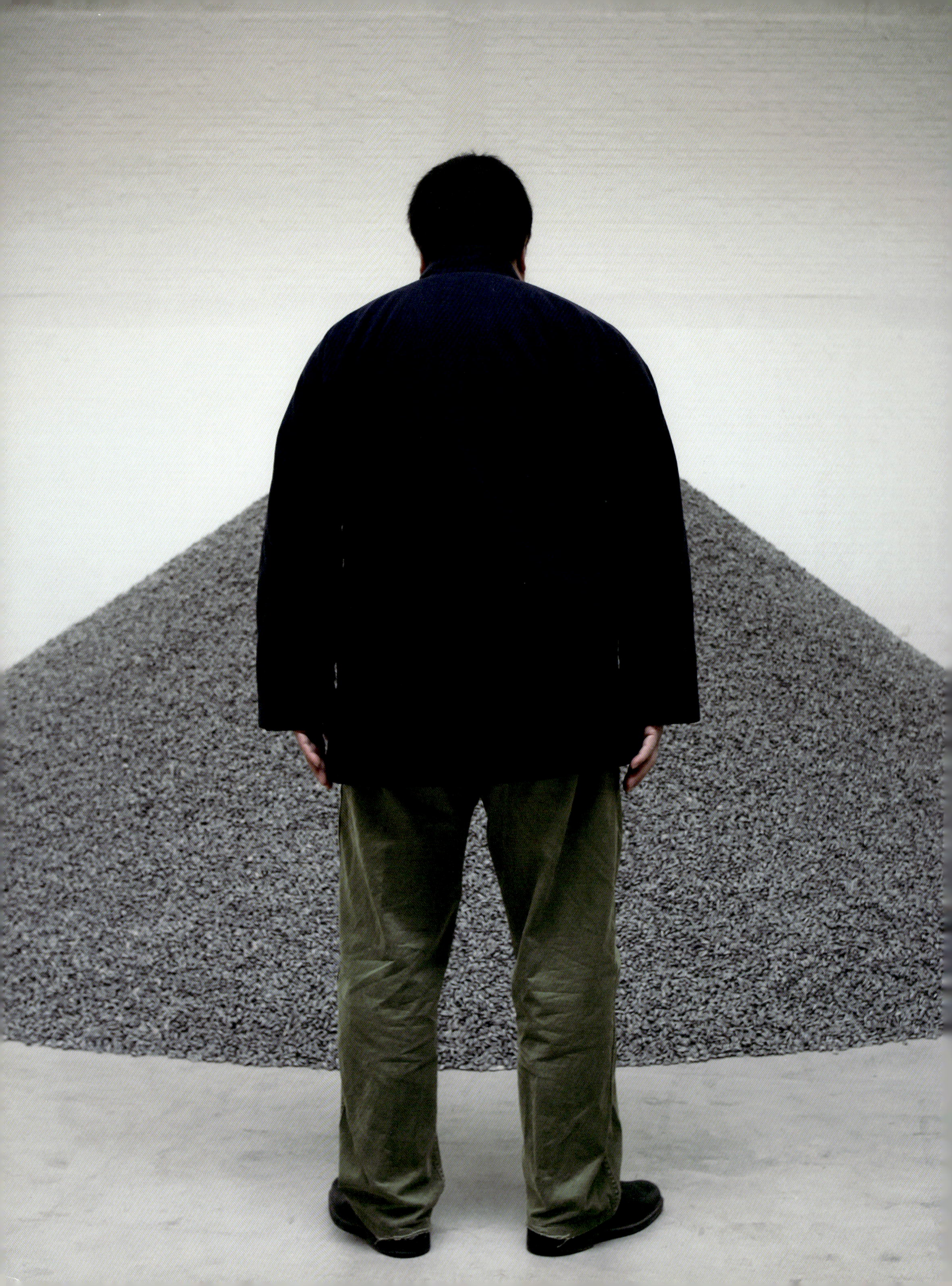

AI WEIWEI

SUN-FLOWER SEEDS

The Unilever Series:
an annual art commission
sponsored by Unilever

Unilever

Published by order of the Tate Trustees on the occasion of the exhibition at Tate Modern, London
12 October 2010 – 2 May 2011

This exhibition is the eleventh commission in The Unilever Series

First published 2010 by Tate Publishing,
a division of Tate Enterprises Ltd,
Millbank, London SW1P 4RG
www.tate.org.uk/publishing

A catalogue record for this book is available from the British Library

ISBN 978 1 85437 884 2

Designed by Rose
Printed in the United Kingdom by PUSH

Cover: *Sunflowers Seeds* 2010 (details)
Frontispiece: Ai Weiwei in his studio with pile of seeds, March 2010

Cover and pp.122–6, 127 (top, middle), 128–35: photography by Andrew Dunkley and Marcus Leith, Tate Photography
All other images are courtesy Ai Weiwei unless otherwise stated

CONTRIBUTORS
Juliet Bingham is Curator at Tate Modern
Carol Yinghua Lu is an art critic and curator based in Beijing and contributing editor for *frieze* magazine
Brendan McGetrick is an independent writer, editor, and designer
Marko Daniel is Curator: Public Programmes at Tate Modern

The opinions expressed here are those of the authors and do not necessarily represent the views of Tate

CONTENTS

SPONSOR'S FOREWORD

The Unilever Series brings some of the world's greatest artists to the unique setting of Tate Modern's Turbine Hall. Undertaking the eleventh commission in the Series, Ai Weiwei has responded with a beautiful yet disquieting work which poses questions about contemporary society. His thought-provoking installation *Sunflower Seeds* continues the tradition of innovation and experimentation established by previous artists in the Series.

2010 marked the tenth anniversary of not only the opening of Tate Modern, but the launch of The Unilever Series. This makes it one of the most enduring and successful arts sponsorships. Since 2000, over twenty-four million people have come to view and experience some truly remarkable installations.

Unilever's partnership with Tate also extends to an online education programme called turbinegeneration. Now in its third year, this project encourages children from around the world to explore and share their thoughts on a range of cultural issues through a variety of art forms. Turbinegeneration has not only inspired children from many different countries to engage with art, but has served to improve their knowledge of other cultures.

We hope that you enjoy and are inspired by Ai Weiwei's work.

Paul Polman
Group Chief Executive, Unilever plc

Unilever

FOREWORD

When Tate Modern opened in 2000, The Unilever Series of annual commissions for the Turbine Hall was launched with Louise Bourgeois' poignant sculptural towers *I Do, I Undo, I Redo* 2000. In the ensuing ten years, we have seen increasingly complex and memorable responses to the iconic space of the Turbine Hall by leading international artists. Each year artists have taken new and unexpected approaches to this vast, public environment, from Bruce Nauman's audio installation *Raw Materials* 2005, in which sound was presented as sculptural material, to Doris Salcedo's *Shibboleth* 2008, a subterranean chasm that literally broke open the fabric of the building, and most recently, Miroslaw Balka's, *How It Is* 2009, a cavernous steel structure with a vast, dark interior chamber. We were delighted therefore to be able to invite Ai Weiwei, widely regarded as one of China's most active and creative Conceptual artists, as the eleventh to participate in the series. His spectacular solo exhibition *So Sorry* at Munich's Haus der Kunst in autumn 2009 under the Directorship of Chris Dercon – who joins Tate Modern as the new Director in spring 2011 – was an important factor in our decision to extend the invitation for a new commission, confirming our belief in his ability to create installations that are both thought-provoking and awe-inspiring. His installation *Remembering* 2009 on the building's facade, composed of thousands of children's backpacks, commemorated the thousands of young people who perished in the 2008 Sichuan earthquake disaster. *Soft Ground* 2009, a rug measuring 380 square metres, which recreated in minute detail the tiled floor of the Haus der Kunst that lay beneath it, implicitly referred to the building's vexed and complex history.

Unlike previous commissions, in which the entire Turbine Hall space has been made available to visitors, Ai's installation is conceived specifically for the east end of the Turbine Hall. This is due to the Transforming Tate Modern building work, for which part of the west end of the Turbine Hall has been sectioned off as engineers prepare to lay the foundations of Tate Modern's new annex on the south landscape, the first part of which begins with the renovation of the massive underground oil tanks. These are challenges to which Ai has more than ably responded, producing a work that is subtle yet extremely powerful. His *Sunflower Seeds* 2010 is a landscape made up of what appear to be millions of sunflower seed husks, apparently identical but actually unique. Although they look realistic, each seed is made out of porcelain. And far from being an industrially produced, 'readymade' or a found object, each individual seed has been intricately hand-crafted by one of a number of skilled artisans. *Sunflower Seeds* is a vast sculpture which can be gazed upon from the vantage point of the Turbine Hall bridge, or contemplated at close range. To attempt to quantify such a vast seedscape is impossible, yet each piece is a part of the whole, a poignant commentary on the relationship between the individual and the masses.

Ai's extraordinary artistic achievements, which span three decades, encompass sculpture, installations, architecture, publishing, photographs, documentaries, films and extensive writings in the form of personal blogs and commentaries on social-networking sites. Tate has an ongoing commitment to his work. In 2008, with the support of its Asia Pacific Acquisitions Committee 2007, the gallery acquired his sculpture *Table and Pillar* 2002. It is our ambition to continue to build on our collection of works from the Asia Pacific area, and to represent it within the programme as well as developing our expertise and research into artists living and working in this region. This commission has proved an important step in this endeavour.

We would like to express our sincere thanks to Ai for accepting this commission and for engaging so thoughtfully in the process. It has been a great honour for Tate Modern's Curator, Juliet Bingham, to work with him and his studio team at FAKE Design in realising this project and we thank her most particularly for her dedication and intelligent curatorial guidance. In addition, we would like to thank Ai's assistants, Nadine Stenke, E-Shyh Wong, Inserk Yang, Zhao Zhao, Jiang Li, Gui Nuo, Wen Tao, Lucas Lai, Ragna van Doorn and Gao Yuan for handling every aspect of the complex organisation and installation, the publication and for facilitating smooth communication with the various departments at Tate. Most emphatically, we thank the artisans of Jingdezhen for creating such beautiful objects.

We wish to thank the authors – Juliet Bingham, Marko Daniel, Carol Yinghua Lu and Brendan McGetrick – each of whom has contributed an insightful essay to the catalogue, exploring a different facet of Ai Weiwei's practice. In addition, we are grateful to Wenny Teo for assisting with research for the catalogue, and to Jennifer Ng for her language and cultural translation skills. Rose Design adeptly conveyed the artist's vision of a casual and open publication. Sincere thanks are due to Judith Severne for her editorship, and to Roanne Marner for the catalogue production.

At Tate Modern, Assistant Curator Kasia Redzisz has given invaluable organisational support. Stephen Mellor, Coordinator: Exhibitions & Displays, has provided perceptive advice and technical support during the process. Registrar Stephanie Bush has negotiated insurance and all aspects of sea and land transportation. Phil Monk has carefully planned the systematic installation of the work with his team. Special thanks go to other Tate colleagues who have supported the project including: Marko Daniel and Gabriela Salgado in Public Programmes; Annie Bicknell for turbinegeneration; Duncan Holden in the Press Department; Livia Ratcliffe and Pete Gomori in Marketing and Communications; Marina Busse and Emilie Janvrin in Development and Alison Kennedy in the Director's Office. Many thanks to Helen Sainsbury, Julian Bird, Adrian Harwicke and Dennis Ahern, for their advisory role on financial and logistical aspects of the project. Kate Vogel, Tate Media, has produced an engaging and informative documentary about Ai's practice and thought processes leading up to the commission. Kirstie Beaven, Digital Programmes, has managed and coordinated a microsite project, *One-to-One with the Artist*, which specifically relates to Ai's own use of the internet.

For support in shipping the sunflower seeds by sea from China to the UK and then returning them to China at the close of the commission, we warmly thank Hanjin. Equally warm thanks go to Hiscox for insuring the sunflower seeds for transit and display. We are also grateful to Cogapp for its work and support in realising the *One-to-One with the Artist* project.

Finally, we would like to express deep appreciation to Unilever, and to Group Chief Executive Paul Polman, for continuing to provide essential support for this ambitious and world-renowned programme of commissions. The Unilever Series has inspired over twenty-four million visitors to Tate Modern since its inception in 2000, enabling Tate to continue to invite artists to make innovative responses to this monumental and unique space.

Sheena Wagstaff
Chief Curator, Tate Modern

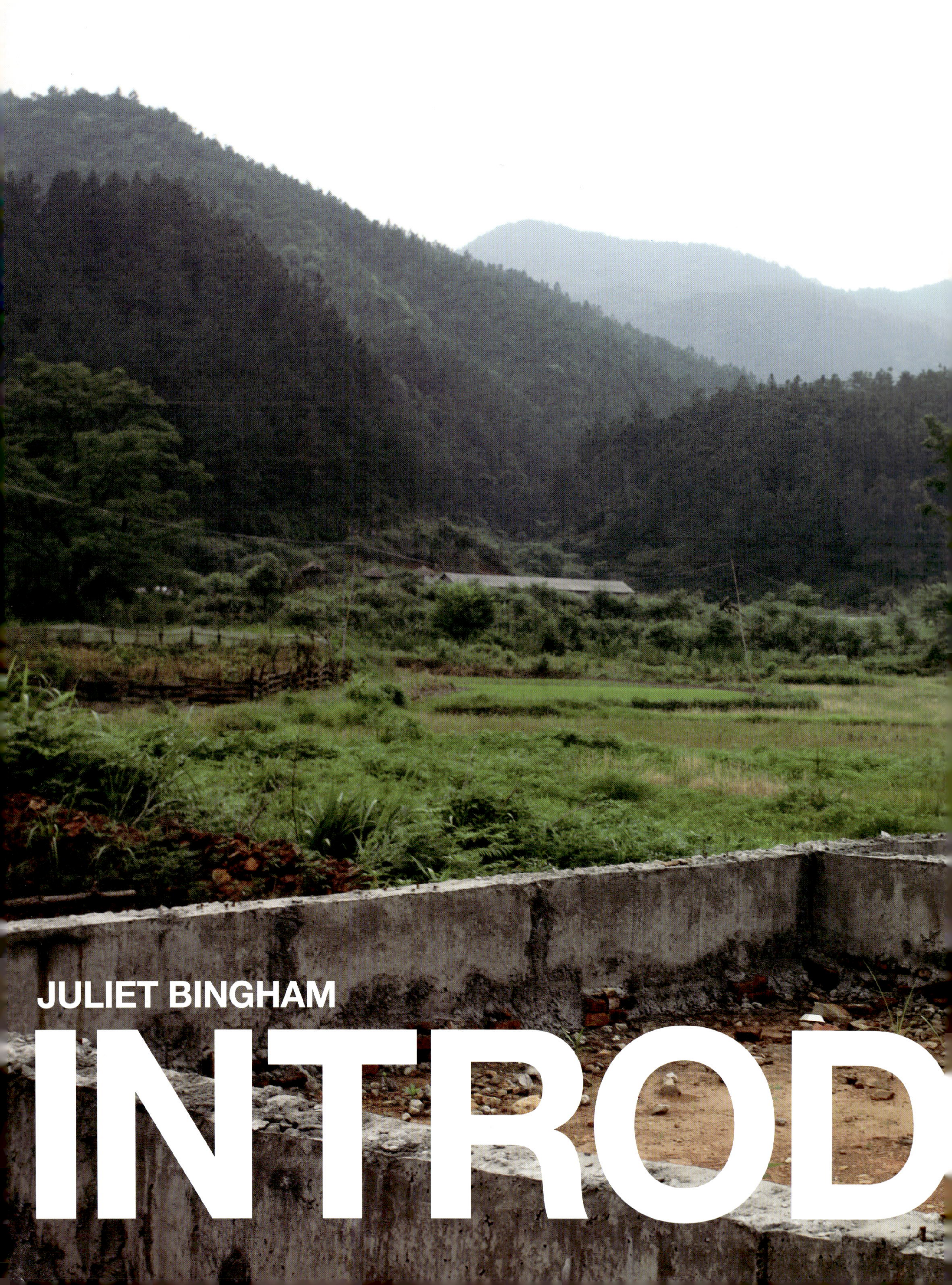

JULIET BINGHAM

INTROD

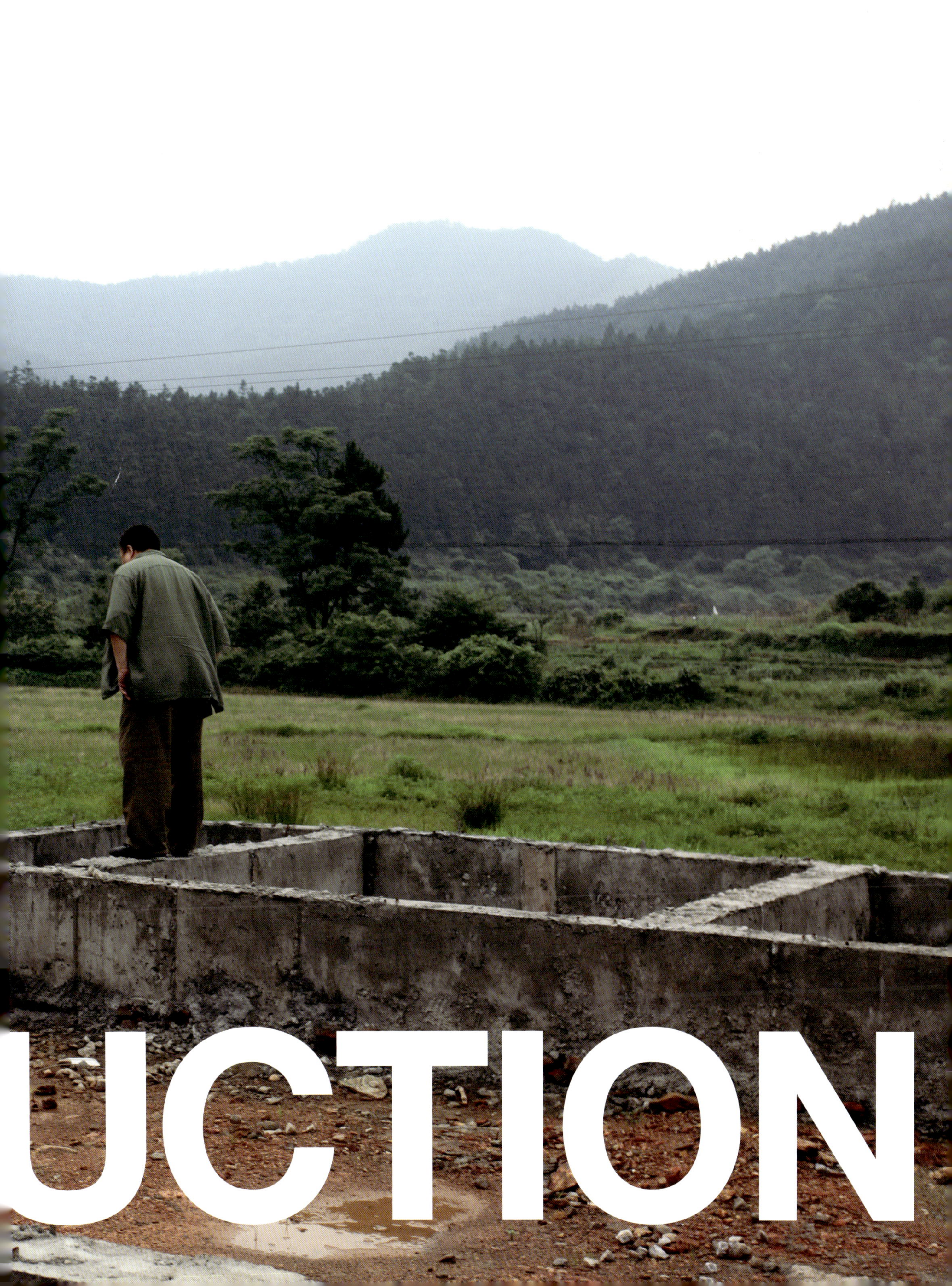
UCTION

Previous spread: Ai Weiwei in Jingdezhen, southern China, 2010

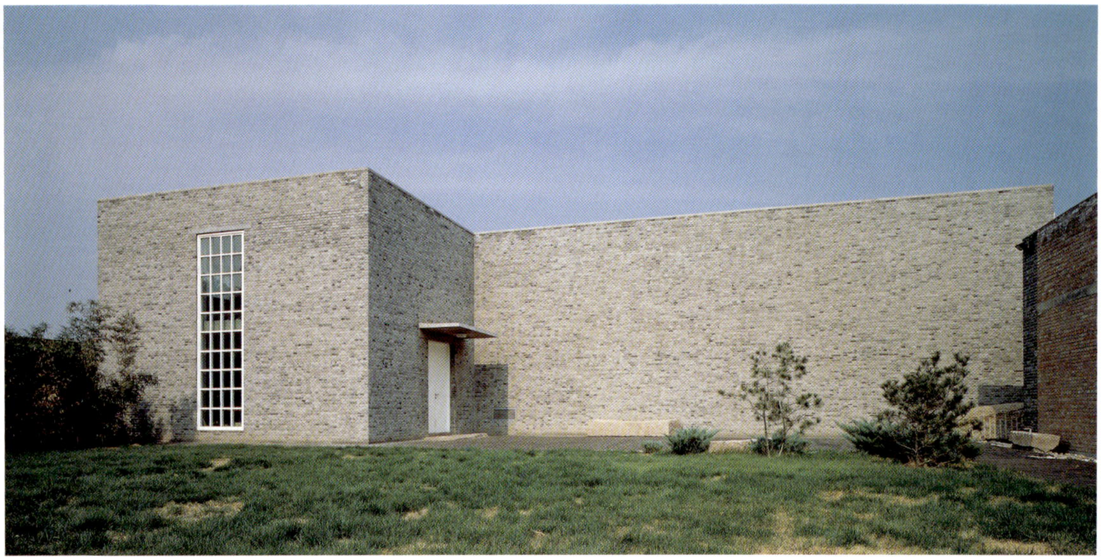

1
Studio House, Beijing 1999

Instead of putting a personal mark on something as an artist, you set up a structure, you make room for possibilities.[1]

Ai Weiwei's house and studio complex, FAKE Design, is located in Beijing's northeast Caochangdi district, a semi-industrial area near the city's fifth ring road and not far from Beijing Capital International Airport. The studio bustles with activity day and night, while at its centre Ai's nonchalant presence belies his radical thinking and incessant output. The constant stream of visitors to the studio includes musicians, actors, collectors, curators, architects, academics, fashion designers, journalists and film crews, many of whom are informally photographed by Ai and their images posted directly onto the internet, part of his approach to making his life and art transparent.

Before it was shut down by the Chinese authorities in May 2009, Ai had a popular blog on which he posted thousands of documentary images of his life alongside poignant social and political commentaries. He now avidly uses Twitter, on which he currently has over fifty thousand followers, to communicate his philosophical and political views.[2] A number of assistants live within the studio compound in their own apartments, while others arrive each day to work on various projects, from Ai's ongoing citizen's investigation into the thousands of children who were killed in the Wenchuan Earthquake in Sichuan Province on 12 May 2008 (a disaster compounded by the collapse of inadequately built schools) to preparations for myriad international exhibitions, commissions and biennales. The studio has a cook, vegetable garden, chickens, ducks and idle dogs, not to mention the many 'rescue' cats. In fact, cat welfare is the subject of the Studio's most recent hard-hitting documentary distributed via the internet, *San Hua*, which reveals the cruelty of the Chinese cat-trafficking trade.[3] Ai's other, larger studios are located further outside the city, and accommodate skilled craftsmen who produce his 'dysfunctional' sculptures using ancient Chinese furniture and complex temple-wood structures. Ai also has his own kiln and a dedicated team in Jingdezhen, the 'porcelain city' in southern China's Jiangxi Province, producing his varied ceramic works and continually experimenting with new ceramic forms.

Ai has recently been threatened with eviction from his Caochangdi studio, as have other artists and gallerists in the area; the surrounding small-holdings are currently being demolished in order for rapid reconstruction to take place as part of China's frenetic urbanisation. In the late 1990s, with no prior architectural training, Ai designed his studio complex 'in an afternoon' and had it built in less than two months, using a common brick to create a minimal style (figs.1, 2) that has since generated many architectural commissions for his Studio – from designing a monument for the Jinhua Architecture Park in Zhejiang (fig.3) to the Three Shadows Photography Art Centre in Beijing – as well as many imitators. Ai's own architectural endeavours were inspired by a house that the philosopher Ludwig Wittgenstein had built for his sister in Vienna, of which Ai has commented: 'He's so articulate in his expression. He tried to crack the absolute truth there. The effort, the repeated effort, made all his practice become one – just one act.'[4] We can see a similar effort continually repeated in both Ai's art and his architectural projects. The Studio House was the beginning of some sixty architectural projects, interior design and architectural collaborations, culminating most publicly in his role as artistic consultant for the Beijing 'Bird's Nest' Stadium with architects Herzog & de Meuron. For the Ordos Project (2008), Ai created a curatorial framework, inviting Herzog & de Meuron to select 100 young international architects who were each asked to design a villa for the site in Inner Mongolia, China.[5] Providing a 'structure', such as enabling 100 individual approaches to architecture, is a strategy that Ai has used and continues to use in his work, from his conceptual anthology books of the 1990s (the *Black*, *White* and *Grey Cover* books); curatorial projects, most notably *Fuck Off* (2000); participatory works like *Fairytale* for Documenta 12 (which enabled 1,001 individual experiences in Kassel) to the challenges that he continues to set for his artisans working with carpentry and ceramics.

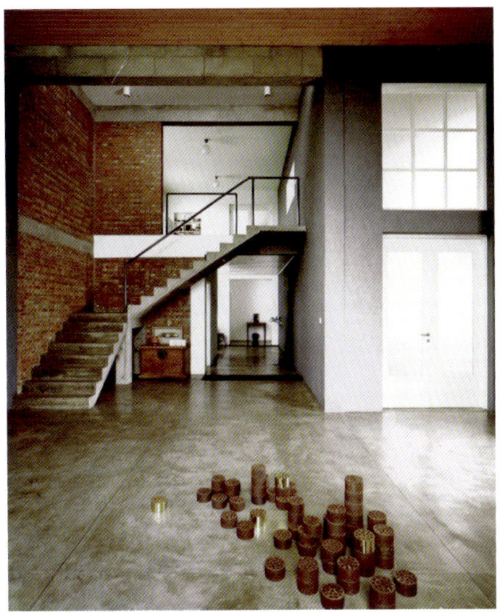

2
Studio House,
Beijing 1999

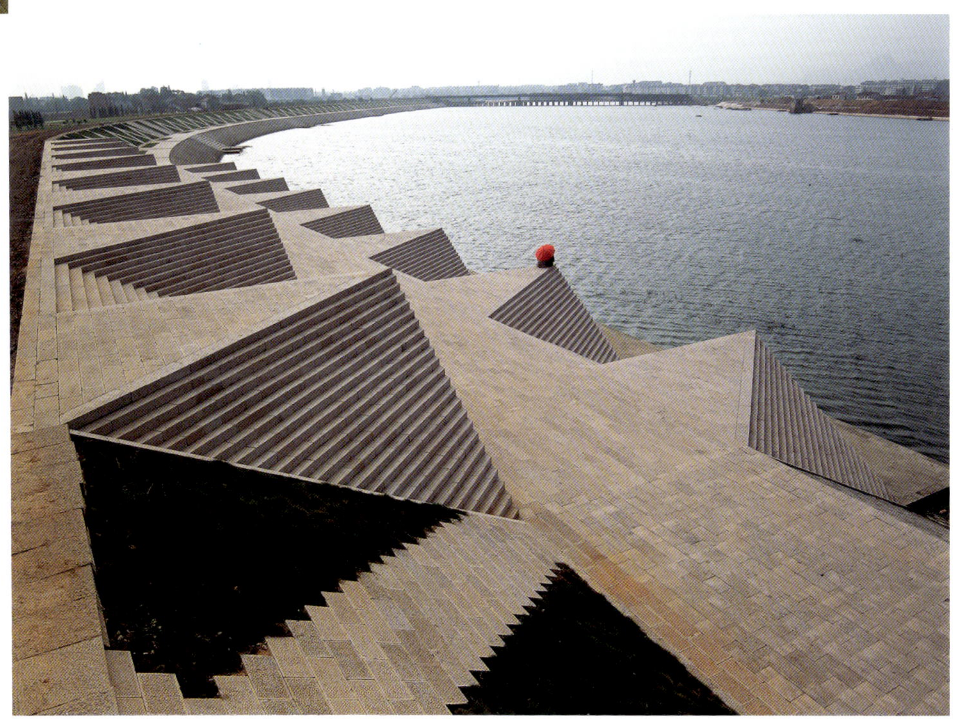

3
Yiwu Riverbank,
Jinhua, China 2004

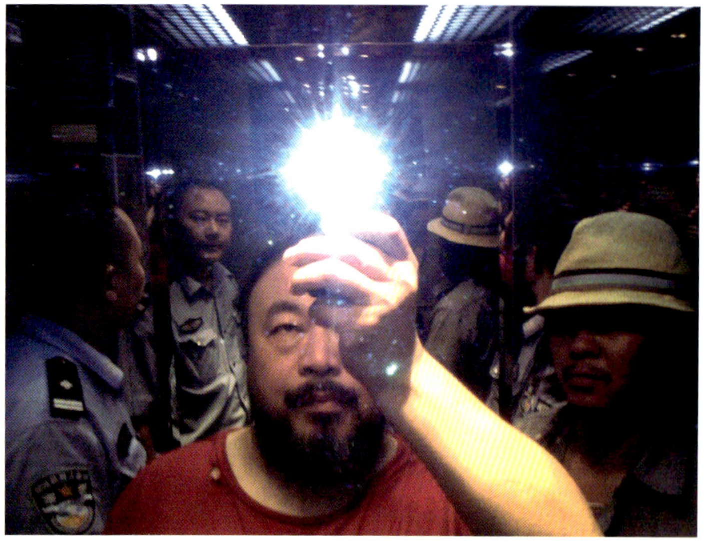

4
Ai Weiwei with rock star Zuoxiao Zuzhou in the elevator when taken into custody by the police, Sichuan, China, August 2009

Ai's journey to his current position of cultural influence and international acclaim as a Conceptual artist and architect has involved a long struggle: a childhood of poverty, a father who was excluded from society during Mao's regime; his own aimlessness and anonymity during a decade in New York in the 1980s as a young man; and a sense of alienation from the Chinese art world upon his return to Beijing in the early 1990s. Even now his situation is in certain senses an unstable one, with not only the threat of eviction hanging in the air but continued official 'interest' in his outspoken comments on Chinese society via his internet activism, spontaneous protests and campaigning activities for human rights and freedom of expression in China.[6] Within Beijing, this has resulted in surveillance of his studio, his emails being hacked, his bank account monitored and his blog shut down. Outside of Beijing, Ai has come to physical harm. In 2009, he and several other activists were detained in Chengdu (the capital of Sichuan province in south-west China) to prevent them attending the trial of a campaigner investigating the children's deaths in the Sichuan earthquake (fig.4). Ai was assaulted by provincial police, leading to haemorrhaging and emergency brain surgery, which took place in Munich during the installation of his solo exhibition there last autumn.[7] In August 2010, while in Chengdu to persuade the authorities to investigate his repeated formal allegations of police misconduct, his attempt to go through the proper channels was met with violence once again as Ai, his assistant and his lawyer were harassed by plain-clothes police from the Public Security Bureau.[8]

Ai's life and art are entwined to the extent that, quoting Marcel Duchamp, he has referred to himself as a 'readymade'.[9] Equally, he takes contemporary China as a readymade, as well as the various cultural artifacts that he challenges and subverts.[10] Ai has been the protagonist in various 'iconoclastic' performance actions, most notably *Dropping a Han Dynasty Urn* 1995 (fig.44), and provocative gestures including the *Study in Perspective* series of photographs from 1995–2003 (figs.5–7) in which he 'gives the finger' to various cultural and political symbols of power. Though he takes a conceptual approach, Ai engages directly with objects – often culturally specific – from his lamps, chandeliers and lanterns (see *Descending Light* 2007; fig.8), which evoke overtly ostentatious forms found in official Chinese buildings, to installations using tables, beams and pillars from dismantled temples of the Qing dynasty (for example *Fragments* 2005 (fig.9) and *Through*

2007–8;) or variations of 'rectified' readymades and more recently, mobilisations of the public (*Fairytale* 2007; figs. 11, 12, 13).

Given the diversity of Ai's practice, his various styles, media and approaches, we were open-minded as to what form his project for the Turbine Hall might take, but we knew that his philosophy of advocating both the freedoms and responsibilities of individuals would be central. The result is a work of extraordinary beauty and subtle power. Titled *Sunflower Seeds* 2010, it leaves the fabric of the building undisturbed. His intervention is reminiscent, in both its subtlety of form and its labour-intensive nature, to his floor-based, site-specific carpet-piece *Soft Ground* 2009 (figs. 10, 11), created for his recent solo exhibition at Haus der Kunst. *Sunflower Seeds*, in striking contrast to the monumentality of Bankside's former power station, is composed of millions of small objects. These have been poured into the interior of this vast industrial space to form a seemingly infinite landscape made up of an innumerable quantity of tiny objects. Contained in the east end of the Turbine Hall, and bounded by the east and south walls, the seeds are

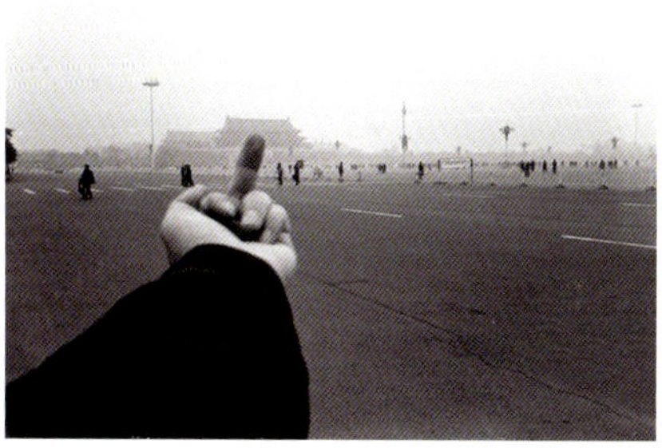

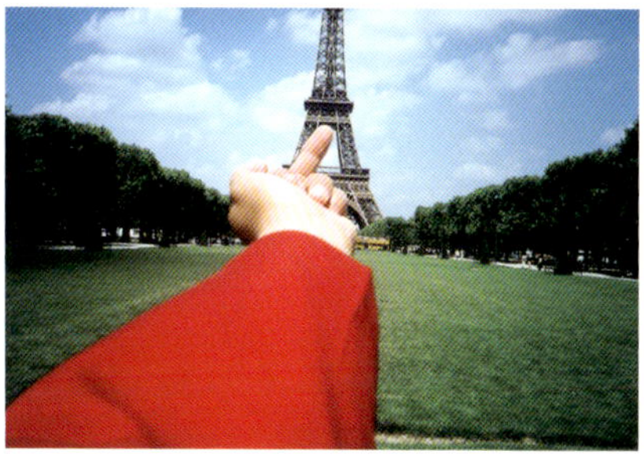

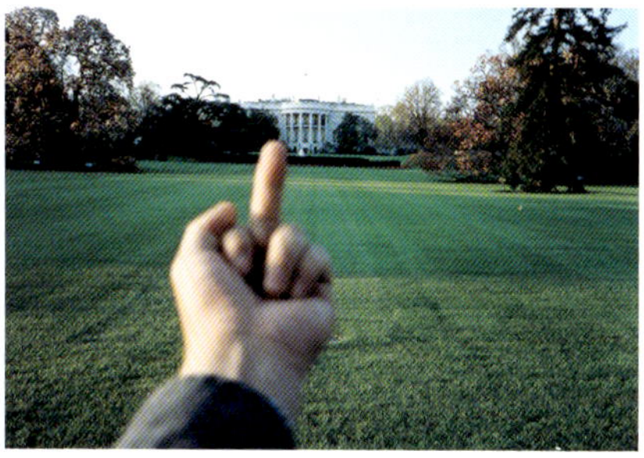

5
Study of Perspective – Tiananmen
from the *Study of Perspective* series of photographs 1995–2003, black and white print

6
Study of Perspective – The Eiffel Tower
from the *Study of Perspective* series of photographs 1995–2003, c-print

7
Study of Perspective – The White House
from the *Study of Perspective* series of photographs 1995–2003, c-print

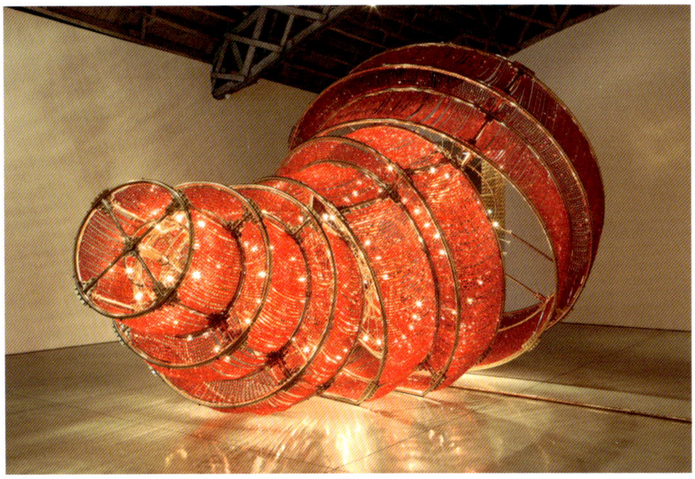

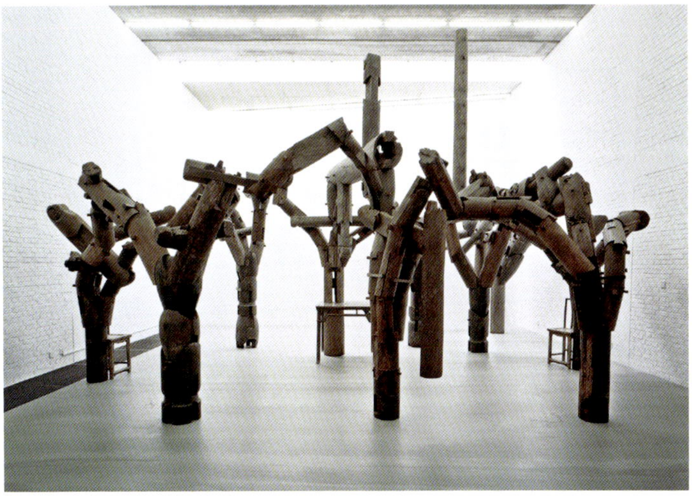

8
Descending Light 2007
Glass crystal, lights and metal
400 x 663 x 461 cm
Installation at Mary Boone Gallery, New York, 2008
(Photo: Adam Reich, courtesy Mary Boone Gallery)

9
Fragments 2005
Ironwood (Tieli wood), Qing dynasty (1644–1911) table, chairs, parts of beams and pillars from dismantled temples of the Qing dynasty (1644–1911) 500 x 850 x 700 cm
Installation at Galerie Urs Meile, Beijing-Lucerne, Beijing 2006

shaped into a gently tapering form facing the entrance to the Turbine Hall on the west and to the river to the north. The delicately patterned grey and white seeds blend almost into invisibility next to the muted grey tones of the Turbine Hall's concrete floor. However realistic they may seem, this is in fact an illusion: each object is intricately handcrafted from porcelain, the effort of hundreds of individuals. The appearance of the work thus challenges the spectator's first impression and automatic perceptual response: what you see is not what you see, and what you see is not what it means. The precious nature of the material, the effort of production and the narrative and personal content make this work a powerful commentary on the human condition and the struggle for the universal human values of freedom and open society.

As Ai comments in the interview within this catalogue, 'individualism' is a recent phenomenon in China: previously, every person identified with another. It is interesting to note that in the Chinese language there is no direct translation of the word 'individualism': the literal translation is *geren zhuyi*, meaning 'individual-ism', which has the connotation of 'me-first-ness' and the negative implication of selfishness or self-centredness.[11] The role of the individual in society is a concept that has preoccupied Ai's thinking:

> Modern Chinese cultural history is one that scorns the value of the individual; it is a history of suppressing humanity and spirituality. Intellectuals are invariably attacked from all directions; powerful Western culture represented by aggression and decaying cognitive structures represented by feudalistic influences have placed Chinese intellectuals in an embarrassing predicament.[12]

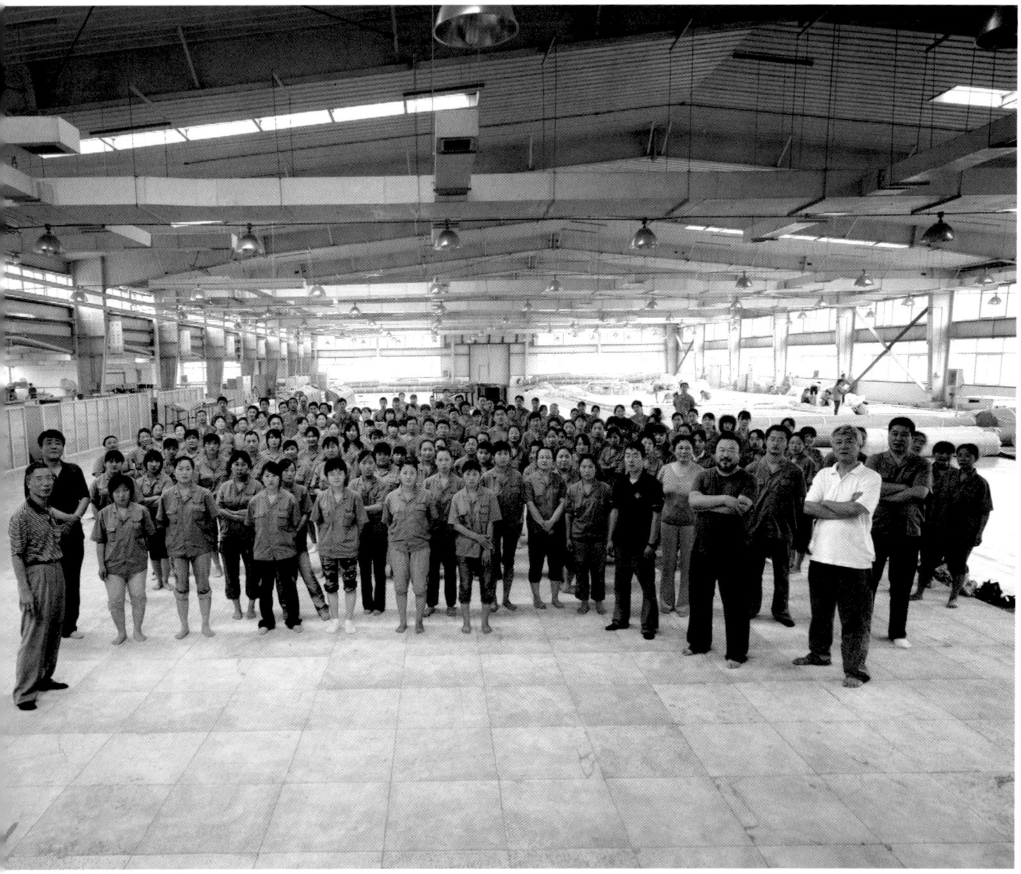

10
Making of *Soft Ground*
2009

The uneasy place of the individual in China can be located historically in factors such as the long tradition of kin-focused collectivism and the authoritarian family structure. Accordingly, China's ruling class welcomed Confucianism, since its hierarchical ideology met the needs of the feudal rulers and served the feudal system well. Depending on the personality of each ruler, this led either to a highly centralised state with absolute control over the individual, or to a situation of chaos, as seen though the collapse of one dynastic house and its replacement with another. Before the Chinese Communist Party (CCP) came to power in 1949, 'collectivism' was stressed as part of military discipline. China's history of denying the value of individualism enabled a cultural climate that was conducive to the Marxist criticism of individualism. Under Mao, state-focused collectivism predominated and Maoist China became deeply hostile to individualism, denouncing it as contrary to the new socialist society. The Great Proletarian Cultural Revolution (1966–76) saw the individual entirely stripped of personal freedom; everything – home life, work units, movement, education – was controlled by the Party. 'Individuals' were expelled from the party, or labelled as negative elements. In the post-Cultural Revolution era, writers and critics started to criticise the revolution by appealing to universal humanity, although such criticisms were eventually quashed.[13] Chinese philosopher and journalist Wang Ruoshui argued that society should be seen as the aggregation of individuals, not as something more important than individuals, in contrast to the position still promoted by the Party, in which the people are subordinate to society, which itself is represented by the Party. Wang proposed that the rejection of humanism was a key cause of the brutality and chaos of the Cultural Revolution and advocated that the CCP, rather than

11
Rooted Upon, Soft Ground and *Fairytale* 2009
Rooted Upon: 100 pieces of tree trunks, installation size 3600 x 1300 cm;
Soft Ground: wool 3560 x 1060 cm;
Fairytale: 1,001 Chinese visitors, wallpaper from digital photographs of black and white prints
Installation at Haus der Kunst, Munich 2009

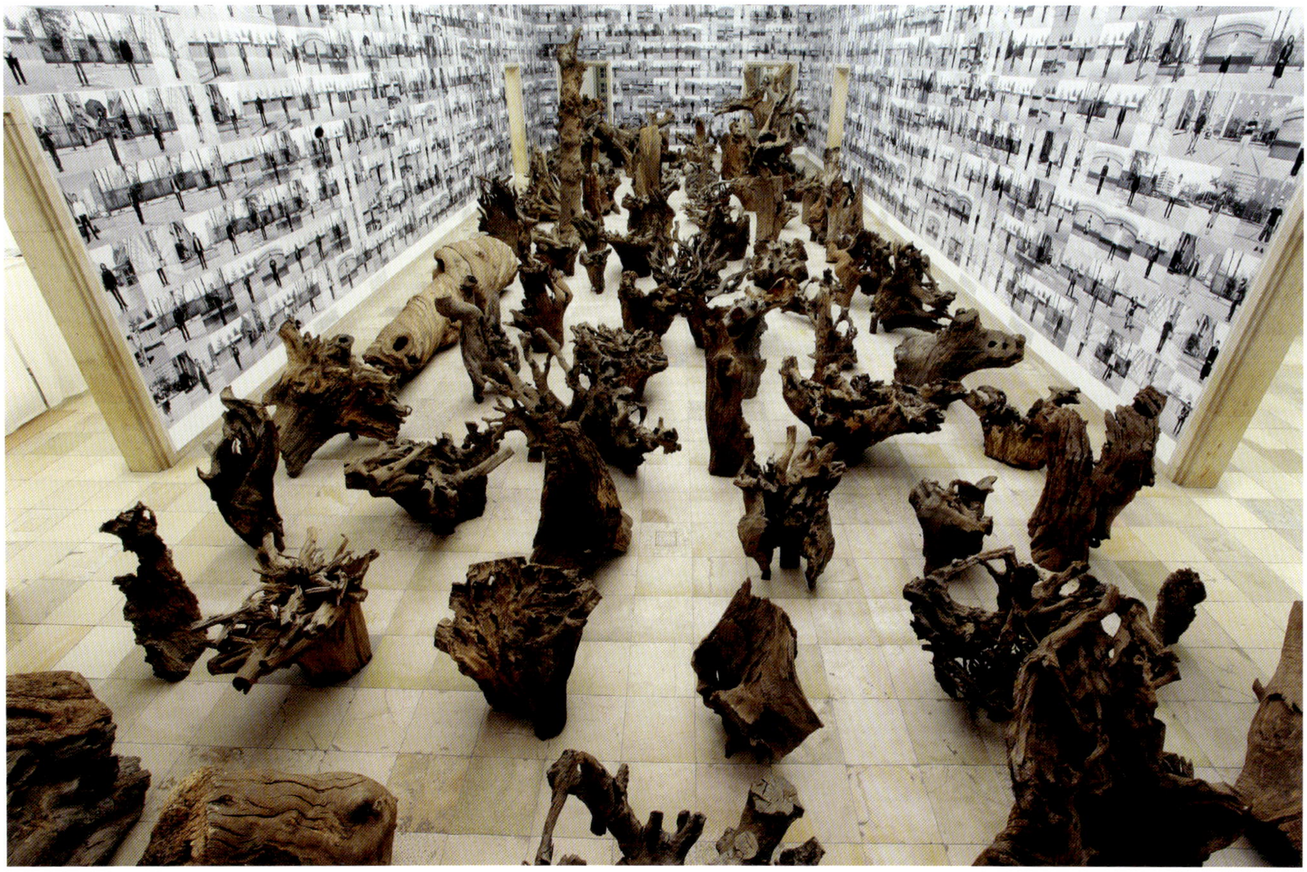

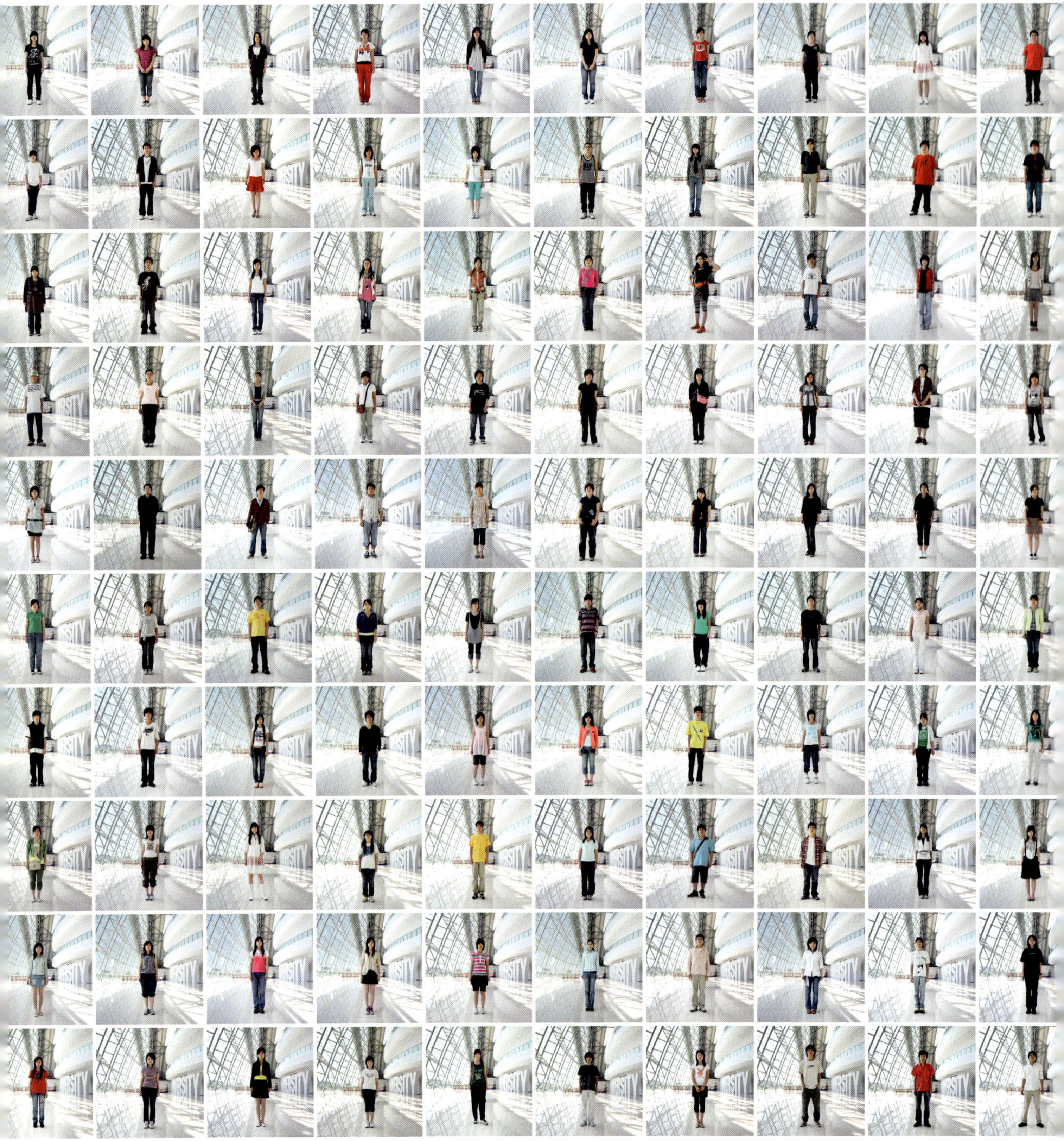

12
Fairytale 2007
1,001 Chinese visitors, 1,001 c-prints
Project for Documenta 12, Kassel, Germany 2007

dismissing humanism as a 'bourgeois concept', should embrace the universality of human rights. In 1983, leading to his denunciation by the CCP, he wrote: 'There is a ghost haunting the vast expanse of China. "Who are you?" "I am humanity."'[14]

Sunflower Seeds is a powerful metaphor for the precarious nature of individualism and collectivism: each seed is a unique object among the 100 million seeds, yet one seed is identical to or synonymous with the whole. In the work, Ai seems to pose multi-faceted questions: are we trying to achieve a single collective way of thinking? Do we really want the state of individual freedom that people make so much of today? What are our shared human values? What does it mean to be an individual in today's society in which television, computing and information networks have changed the way people relate to each other so that there are fewer 'individual attitudes and methods or unique attributes'?[15] Are we actually insignificant, or powerless, unless we act together? What do our increasing desires, materialism and number mean for society, the environment and the future? What is the modern condition?

Asked on Twitter in June this year why he sleeps so little and has so much energy to communicate, Ai responded: 'As soon as I think that one fifth of the world's population are still not considered to be individuals, I am unable to sleep.'[16] For Ai, the value of life lies in 'the interpretation of and act of interpreting both liberty and rights'. He questions a system of government in which there is no public transparency and which projects a false image of peace and prosperity – in Ai's words, a 'fake smile'.

Shortly after the Sichuan earthquake, Ai posted this statement on his blog: 'Totalitarian crimes originate from denying individuals the value of their lives, avoiding reality and refusing responsibility.'[17] A number of his artworks and socially engaged projects have since called for the direct participation of individuals in an attempt to take small steps to change China's embedded structure. For example, every year, on the anniversary of the birthdays of each child who perished in the Sichuan earthquake, Ai's team posts the students' details on Twitter as an act of remembrance. *Nian* is a recent large-scale audio work related to this, in which Ai recruited thousands of on-line participants via Twitter to recite, record and up-load the names and details of those children and young people. For Ai, the least everyone can do is to remember one name. Earlier this year, on Twitter, he asked Chinese internet users to 'say out your name' rather than sending anonymous tweets. Although it is potentially dangerous for Chinese Twitter users to put their real identities in the public sphere, the response was overwhelming.

Fairytale 2007 is another significant work that centres on the individual (figs.11–13). Ai invited 1,001 Chinese 'tourists', as he referred to them, to 'colonise' Kassel, Germany, for the 2007 Documenta.[18] Asked about the choice of the number of participants, Ai Weiwei responded:

> The choice is due to the fact that what we really want to emphasize is '1', not '1001'. Each participant is a single person, and that's why our logo is 1=1000 – that means that in this project 1001 is not represented by one project, but by 1001 projects, as each individual will have his or her own independent experience.[19]

But there is also a paradoxical element to *Sunflower Seeds*. What does it mean to be an individual in China's current political and economic situation in which materialism seems to be growing at the expense of humanistic values? How can people cope with the duality of capitalist liberalism and a very old Communist structure? Global capitalism, which celebrates the freedom of capital and the new liberalism within China, has emphasised economic success over fundamental values such as the environment, education, social standards and morals. Political slogans like 'scientific development', 'harmonious society' and 'advanced socialist culture'[20] are widespread in contemporary China and used by the CCP to help maintain a stable social order in which the economy can grow.[21] As Chinese scholar Richard Baum has recently noted, the CCP is a party whose 'ideology is one of power, the defense of power and by extension, the defense of the existing system'.[22] However, this desire for 'harmony' and defence of power in China comes at the cost of an open and transparent society, one in which 'human values … not Western values, but values developed from human struggle', as Ai speaks of them, are not openly discussed or allowed to freely exist.[23]

As Ai often remarks, he is a Chinese citizen with strong feelings for his country and does not criticize it without reason. He has lived through the past thirty years of 'Reform and Opening Up' in China that began in 1979 with Deng Xiaopoing's economic reforms, although he states that politically there have not been significant changes.[24] As the Chinese government continues to maintain a one-party system, Ai has dedicated his life to questioning such power structures, seeking increased liberty and encouraging individuals to take active responsibility: 'society quickly develops into two levels: a higher level who just want to maintain stability and make a bigger profit and be stronger, and the general public who don't feel capable of being involved'.[25]

The expanding population, the increasing wealth and the desire this spawns, the limited natural resources and the environmental consequences, are all pressing issues for Ai, as are the effects of materialism and commercialism. The new economic liberalisation in China may be changing the way in which people live and shape their lives, but without freedom of expression, at what cost?

Given China's rapid economic expansion, growing affluence in certain levels of society (although equally, growing disparity), it is poignant that for Ai sunflower seeds represent a common street snack shared with friends, a minimal ingredient that 'constituted the most essential needs and desires' during a childhood of extreme poverty under Mao's regime: 'The empty shells or husks were the ephemeral traces of social activity: the least common denominator for human

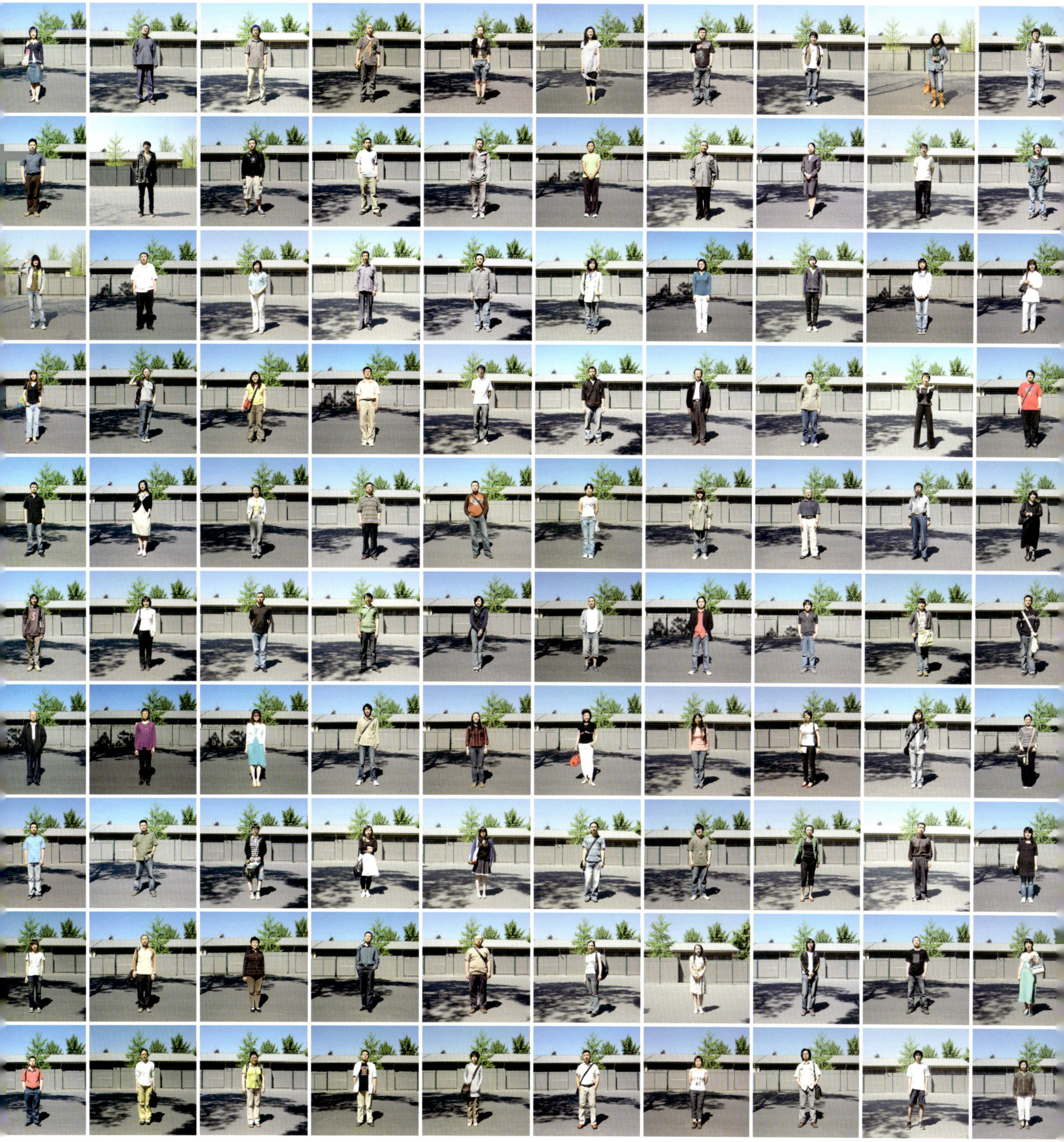

13
Fairytale 2007
1,001 Chinese visitors, 1001 c-prints
Project for Documenta 12, Kassel,
Germany, 2007

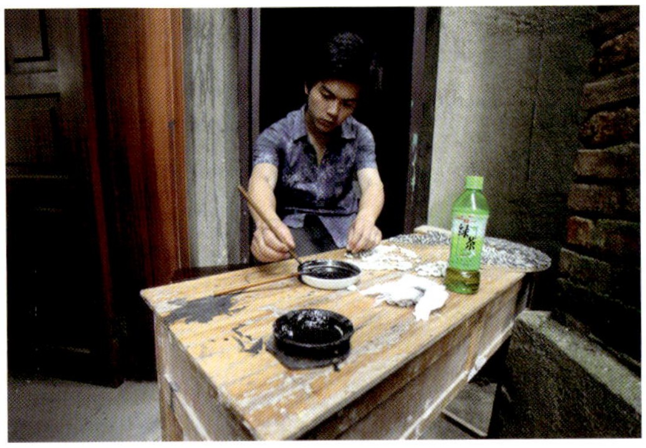

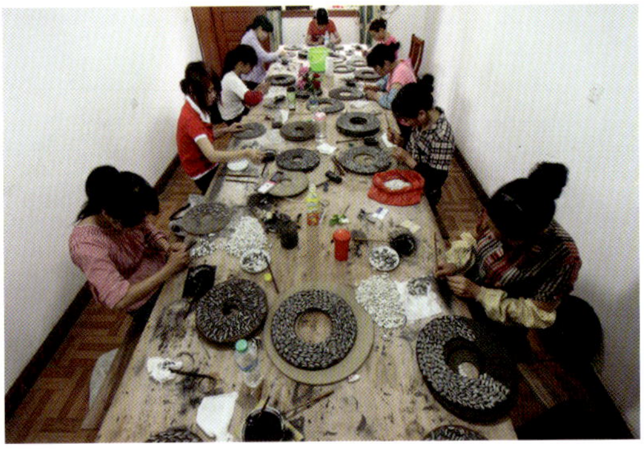

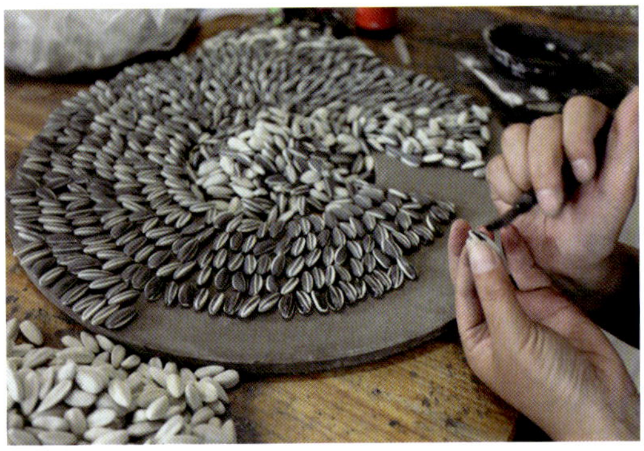

Production of sunflower seeds in Jingdezhen, southern China, 2010

satisfaction. I wonder what would have happened without them?'[26] Although born in Beijing in 1957, Ai spent his childhood first in rural Dongbei and later in Xinjian in remote Northwest China. His father Ai Qing, a famous poet and at one time connected to Mao, had been denounced as a 'rightist' and endured a severe regime of 're-education through labour' during the Cultural Revolution. Mao, in his attempt to abolish the anti-revolutionary 'Four Olds' (Old Customs, Old Culture, Old Habits and Old Ideas) used violence, persecution and the Red Guard youth movement to execute the severe repression of intellectuals, artists and educators. The slogan of the Cultural Revolution was 'smash the old world; establish a new one'. During this time, merely reading certain books could have led to imprisonment or death. As Ai recalls:

> I had to help my father burn all the books and destroy all the artifacts. Anything related to humanity was destroyed. We are in a new world, and this new world offers the opportunity for us to reconnect our knowledge and to start anew. We are learning from the past. You have to know it to destroy it. You can only destroy something by being an expert in it.[27]

China is a country whose people, in Ai's words, have been 'cut off from our own past'. He has increasingly responded to China's current political and social situation in his efforts to understand and 'adjust to the new condition'. All of this clearly has a bearing on his thinking. The street-like character of the Turbine Hall provides an opportunity for an event in which the work, the audience and the place combine 'for the creation of a singularity in which masses are confronted under temporary conditions that allow a re-evaluation of our paradigms'.[28]

Ai's porcelain sunflower seeds, as well as his various works in the same material including children's and women's dresses, pillars, oil spills, watermelons and exact replicas of vases in the style of various dynasties, are produced in a specialist region in China famed for its porcelain production. Each life-size ceramic sunflower seed has been patiently hand-sculpted and hand-painted by specialists working in small-scale workshops. The quantity and scale of the work echoes the scale of industrial mass production, yet the seeds have been produced in 'cottage industry' workshops using materials and techniques that have a long history in China. As Ai has commented:

> In the classical sense, porcelain in China is the highest art form, and belongs to the Imperial Court. In fact, it's almost synonymous with Chinese culture. My work has always focused on how to bring older craftsmanship into a contemporary context and how to create or to use a new language. At the same time, I try to reinterpret artifacts from Chinese traditions and manipulate items from the country's everyday modern culture. This has many layers of meaning, but in the end, the appearance of the work is the most important aspect. The appearance can, of course, be very misleading or fake, and yet the work always has to be attractive. But it also has to be natural and people need to feel naturally attracted by it.[29]

Painted porcelain sunflower seeds, or *Kui Hua Zi*, first appeared in sculptural form in Ai's oeuvre in 2006. They were tipped and piled up by hand to form a conical mound weighing 1 tonne (fig.14). Ai's interest in working with ceramics, however, started when he returned to Beijing from New York in 1993 and began scouring Beijing's antiques markets with his younger brother, developing an eye for Yuan, Ming and Qing dynasty ceramics and the variations in

14
Kui Hua Zi 2010 (detail)
Pile of porcelain seeds in
Ai Weiwei's studio

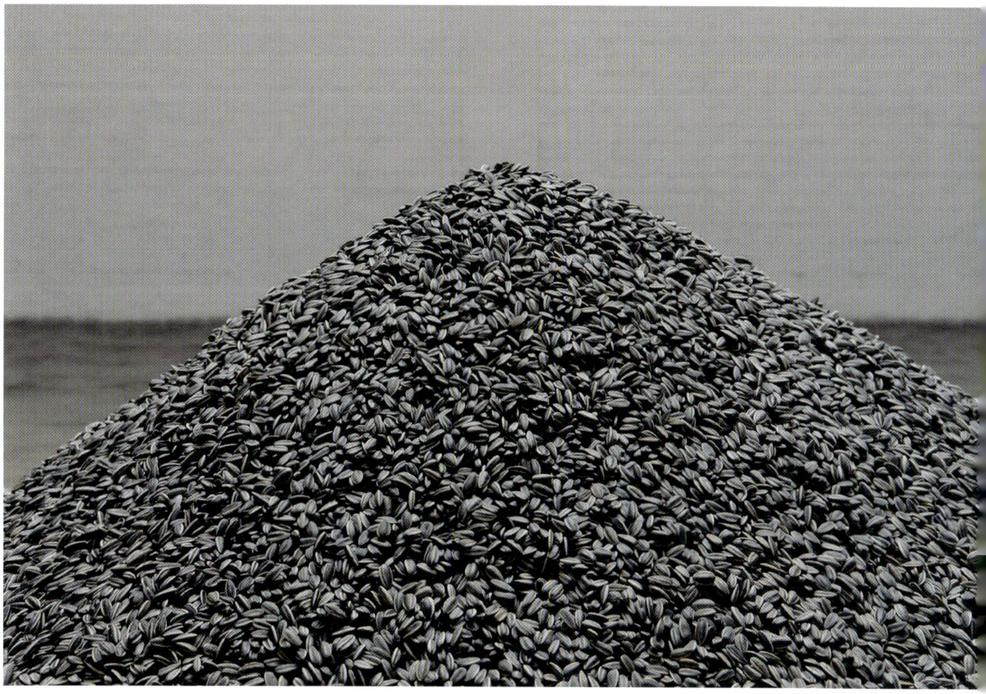

15
Han Dynasty Urn with Coca-Cola Logo 1994
Urn, Western Han dynasty (206BC–24AD) and paint
25 x 20 cm (diameter)

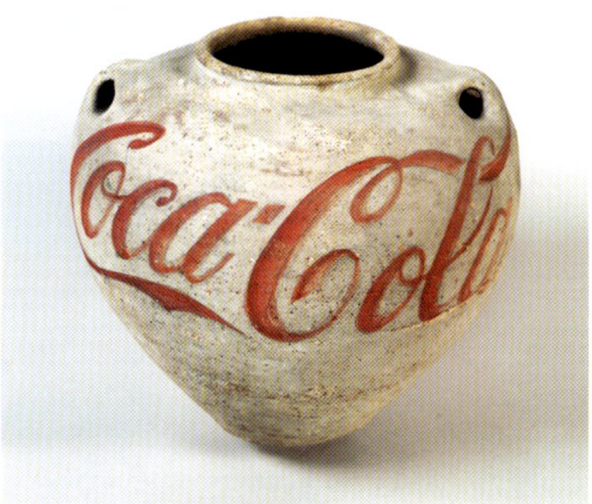

aesthetic judgments – form, colour, scripts – made in each. This was followed by a series of rectified ceramic readymades such as *Han Dynasty Urn with Coca-Cola Logo* 1994, the first in a series of such Coca-Cola vases that he continues to make today (fig.15). More recently, Ai has used vases from the Neolithic age (5000–3000 BC), dipping them in industrial paint (figs.16, 17). His efforts to destabilise notions connected to the meaning and value of cultural artifacts has led to him shattering valuable historical objects by dropping them (*Dropping a Han Dynasty Urn* 1995; fig.44), smashing two Kangxi era (1661–1722) bowls with a hammer (*Breaking of Two Blue-and-White Dragon Bowls* 1996), and grinding Neolithic pottery to dust (*Dust to Dust* 2009). He has also kept alive the historical techniques of firing and controlled glazing by commissioning Jingdezhen craftsmen to create replicas of the instantly recognisable 'blue-and-white' porcelain (for example, in the style of the Qing dynasty, 1736–95), and abundantly producing useless organic forms, such as watermelons and sunflower seeds.

The principle of critical mass and multiplication are leading Chinese concepts. Historically, the Chinese have produced works of art in huge quantities, from fifth-century entombed bronze artifacts; some seven thousand terracotta army warriors; eleventh-century timber pagodas constructed from over thirty thousand separately carved wooden parts; and in the seventeenth and eighteenth centuries, the export from China to the West of several hundred million pieces of porcelain.[30] As Lothar Ledderose points out: 'Because of their methods of production, the Chinese were well prepared to flood the entire world with porcelain … for the first time, Europeans experienced the ramifications of mass production in China'.[31] For the Turbine Hall, over 100 million seeds, with a combined weight of some 150 tonnes, have been transported in container ships from China to the UK. The seeds cover an area of the Turbine Hall

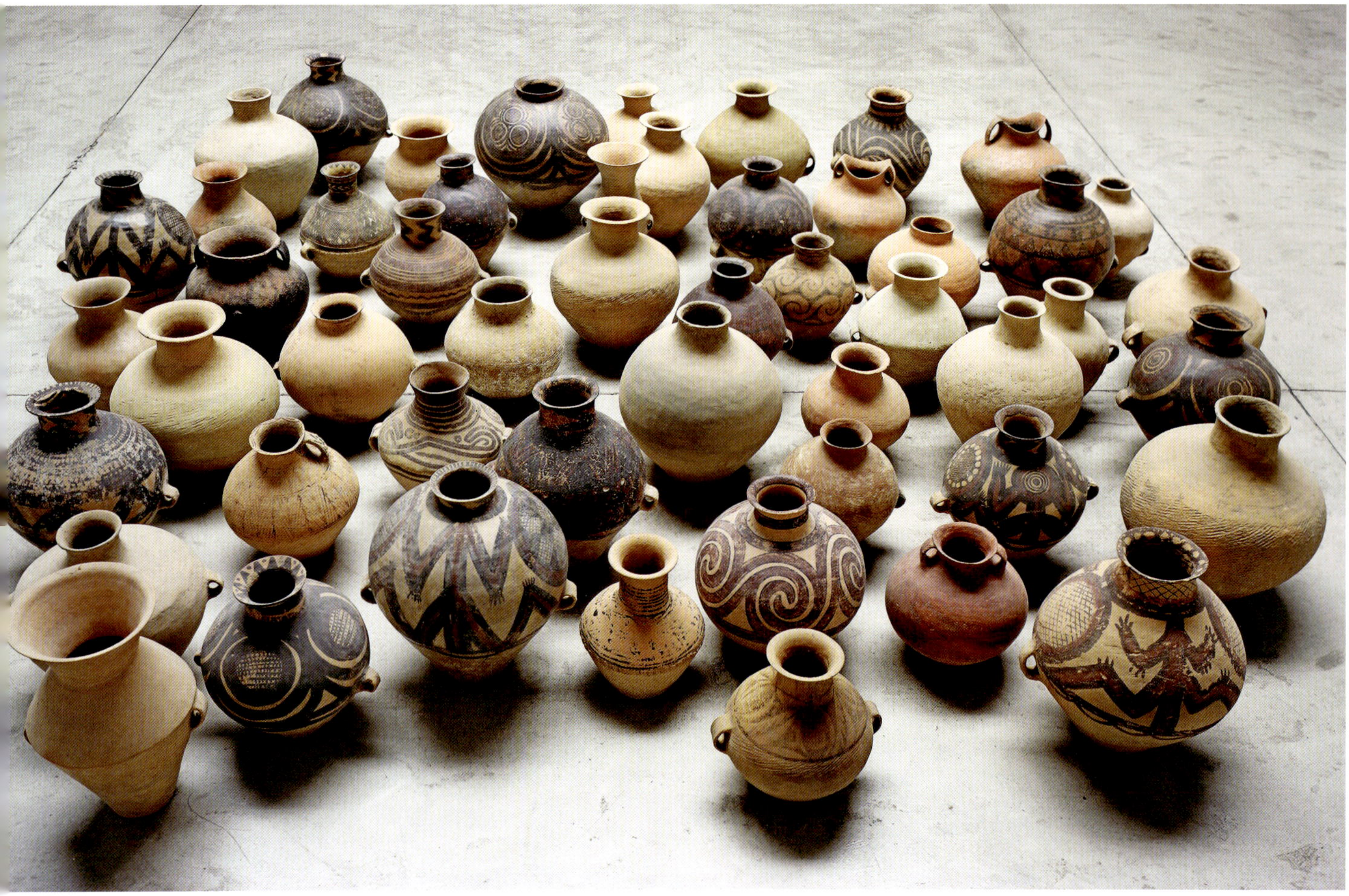

16, 17
Coloured Vases 2006
Neolithic vases (5000–3000 BC)
and industrial paint, 51 pieces,
dimensions variable

measuring approximately 1,000 square metres and have a depth of 10 centimetres. These vast quantities clearly reference China's capability for mass production and distribution, but there is an underlying commentary, as Ai notes:

> China is blindly producing for the demands of the market … My work very much relates to this blind production of things. I'm part of it, which is a bit of a nonsense. The sunflower seeds can never be planted and can never grow, but the process of continuously doing something that's not really useful in such a massive way and takes such a long time and with so many people involved reflects those conditions.[32]

Ai talks of the 'useless' condition of the seeds, that they have no purpose and that such effort has been expended in creating them. 'Uselessness' is an interesting concept in terms of resistance to prevailing power structures and can be traced back through Ai's experiences and work. Of his furniture work, for example, he remarked: 'You don't know its usage, but it's made to such a high quality that you can't ignore its purpose. But what the purpose is, you don't know. I feel

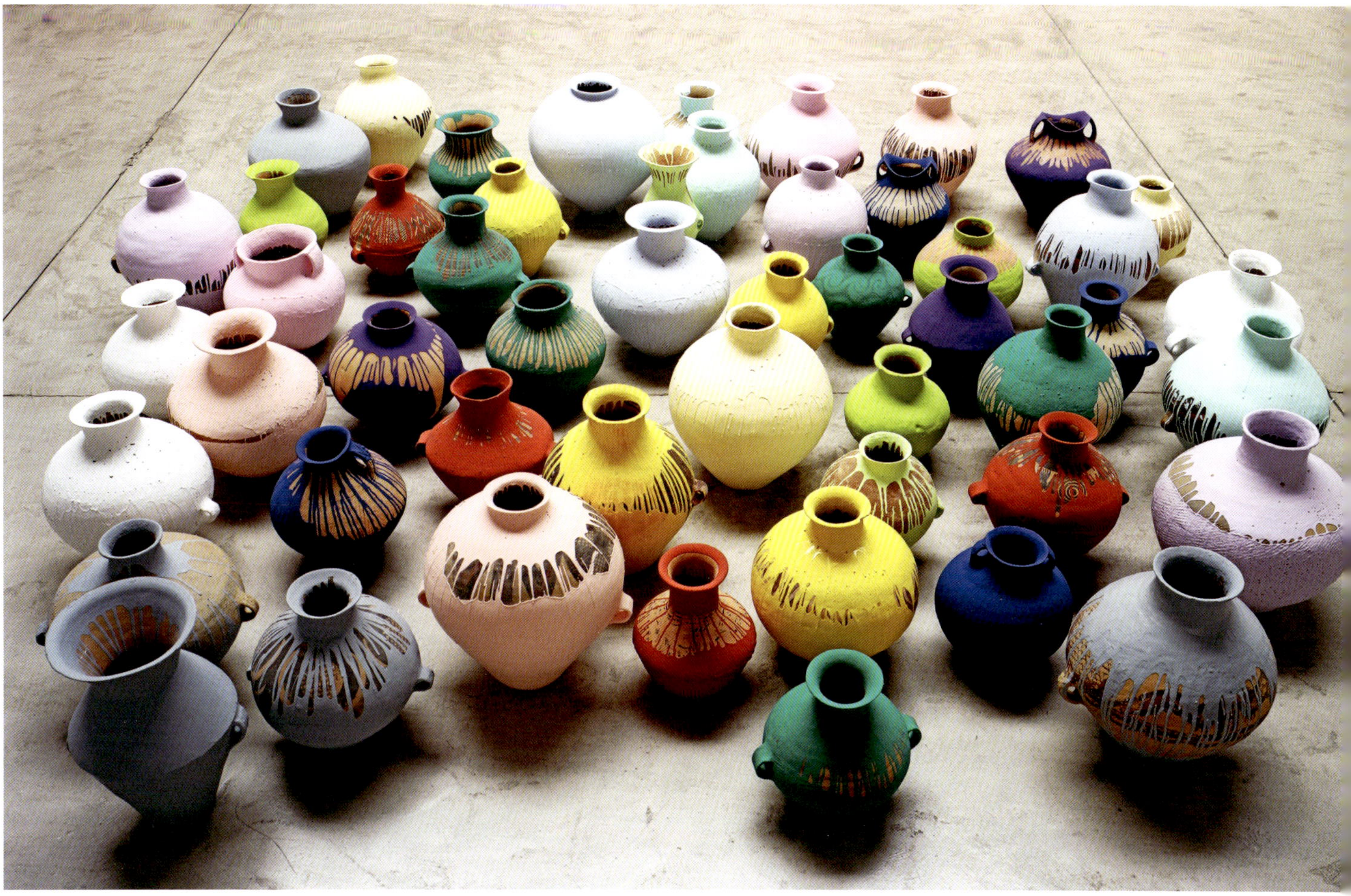

it's very interesting to put a tremendous effort or art or craftsmanship into something useless or even nameless'.[33] Prominent intellectuals and artists were denounced as enemies of the state and their skills rendered useless during the Cultural Revolution. Ai has often taken objects and rendered them useless; for example, a violin that turns into a shovel or China's once ubiquitous 'Forever' bicycles melded together in an eternal circular form, their functionality gone (fig.18). In the production of his exquisitely made 'fake' ceramic vases and now in the careful production of the sunflower seeds, Ai brings traditional skills that are deemed useless to modern technological society back into contemporary practice. The seeds themselves are functionally 'useless' since nothing can be grown from them and they cannot offer sustenance, yet metaphorically, they suggest human compassion.

Over the past thirty-five years, Ai has continually sought to develop 'structures', whether conceptual frameworks, collaborative processes, curatorial devices, participatory events, anthology publications or internet networks – within which philosophical or theoretical ideas can be reconsidered, examined and challenged. This critical line of enquiry runs through a practice that includes photography and film, sculpture, installation, performance, as well as curating, architecture, publishing

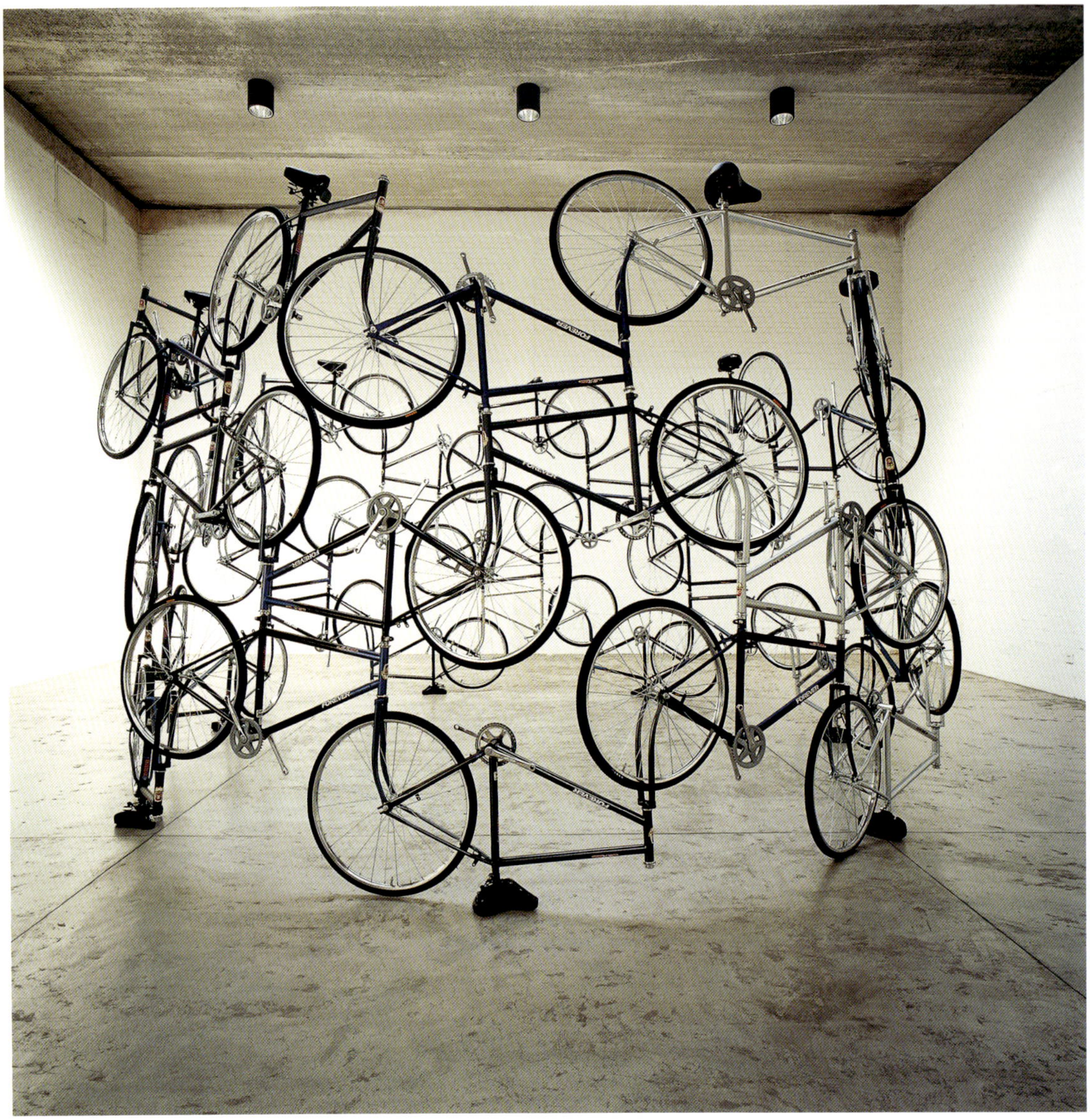

18
Forever 2003
42 bicycles, overall
275 x 450 cm (diameter)

and activism. Ai uses all of these different platforms in order to investigate and challenge perceived truths in relation to art, artifacts, history, culture, society and politics. His subversive strategies all point towards the basic aims of questioning reality and challenging power in order to change the structure of society and to encourage individual responsibility under the massive condition of contemporary society. As Ai has commented:

> Art's power is a psychological power. It is not about how big a work you can make, or how many years you spend on a work, or how far you have travelled. The question instead is how these things take effect in our psyche … In a rational society the artist should play the role of a virus, like a computer virus. A very small design is capable of effecting change throughout the entire world, and this change brings about chaos, so it is actually a process of eliciting the vigilance of the rational world … This consciousness of cultural and psychological subversion is where the power of a work of art lies.[34]

NOTES

1 *Art and Cultural Policy in China: A Conversation between Ai Weiwei, Uli Sigg and Yung Ho Chang, Moderated by Peter Pakesch*, ed. Cristina Bechtler, Vienna and NewYork 2009, p.109.

2 See Ai Weiwei's Twitter in Chinese at http://twitter.com/AIWW or see in English (beta) community-based translation co-ordinated by Jennifer Ng and An Xiao at http://aiwwenglish.tumblr.com

3 The link for *San Hua* was tweeted by Ai's Studio on 4 July 2010. At the time of writing, the link had received more than one hundred thousand hits. Footage from the sixty-eight-minute documentary, filmed between December 2009 and April 2010, shows how cats are captured in China's major cities and transported for the exotic food trade in the southern city of Guangzhou, Guangdong Province, enduring great cruelty. For Ai, such brutality is indicative of society's inability to empathise: 'Abuse and torture happens in this society because you don't care about suffering that you don't feel yourself.' (http://www.globaltimes.cn/www/english/metro-beijing/update/society/2010-07/554272.html)

4 Ai Weiwei, interview with Hans Ulrich Obrist, in Karen Smith, Hans Ulrich Obrist, Bernard Fibicher et al., *Ai Weiwei*, London 2009, pp.22–3.

5 See http://www.ordos project.com/

6 In 2009, Ai protested online and instigated a public event against Green Dam, which was a plan by the government to install an information filtering system on every computer in China.

7 Ai has produced an eight-part documentary about his trip to Chengdu in August 2009 to testify on behalf of imprisoned activist Tan Zouren. The video, which is on YouTube, can also be viewed with English subtitles at the following link and includes footage of the incident in which Ai was beaten by security guards. He later underwent emergency brain surgery while travelling in Germany, due to injuries sustained during the beating. In 2010 he had a T-shirt designed and printed with the image of his brain scan. http://chinadigitaltimes.net/2010/04/ai-weiwei-艾未未-laoma-tihua-老妈蹄花-video

8 See footage of the incident at: http://www.guardian.co.uk/artanddesign/2010/aug/10/chinese-artist-police-attack, http://vimeo.com/14085678 and http://www.youtube.com/watch?v=eZzIVdg3A1A. As Ai noted on Twitter: 'In China, following procedures is a way to seek repeated injuries' (12 August 2010, 2.12am; translated into English on http://aiwwenglish.tumblr.com/page/2).

9 Ai Weiwei: 'I put myself as a readymade in order to carry out investigations. Using yourself as an example becomes a purpose in life.' Quoted in Ai Weiwei and Mark Siemons, *Ai Weiwei: So Sorry*, Munich, Berlin, London, New York 2009, p.28.

10 Ai Weiwei: 'Duchamp had the bicycle wheel. Warhol had the image of Mao. I have a totalitarian regime. It is my readymade.' From a conversation between Ai Weiwei and Philip Tinari, 2 December 2009, Miami Beach, in *Ai Weiwei: Dropping the Urn. Ceramic Works, 5000 BCE – 2010 CE*, exh.cat., Arcadia University Art Gallery, Pennsylvania 2010, p.039); MONO Culture: Ai Weiwei: 'I take the constitution and the political situation in China as a readymade', p.8.

11 Song Jia commenting at *On the Eve: China Symposium '89*, Bolinas, California, 27–29 April 1989, http://www.tsquare.tv/film/Bolinas1.html

12 Ai Weiwei, posted on blog 23 February 2006, from the *Grey Cover Book*, November 1997, trans. Lee Ambrozy for *Ai Weiwei: So Sorry*, p.101.

13 Querying of the socialist state ideology and the goals of Communism prompted the Chinese Communist Party to launch two political counteroffensives: the 'Anti-spiritual Pollution' movement in 1983 and the 'Antibourgeois Liberalisation' movement in 1987–8.

14 See John Gittings, 'Wang Ruoshui: Persecuted, but still Hopeful, Chinese Intellectual', *Guardian*, 8 February 2002, http://www.guardian.co.uk/news/2002/feb/08/guardianobituaries.china.

15 From Ai Weiwei and Feng Boyi (eds.), *White Cover Book*, Beijing 1995; interview between Zhuang Hui and Ai Weiwei (trans. Philip Tinari) in *Ai Weiwei: Dropping the Urn. Ceramic Works, 5000 BCE – 2010 CE.*

16 14 June 2010, see Tumblr translation.

17 Ai Weiwei, posted on blog 21 June 2008, translated in *Ai Weiwei: So Sorry*, p.13.

18 The exhibition Documenta 12, held in Kassel, Germany, in 2007, was centred around three questions or themes: 'Is Modernity our Antiquity?', 'What Is Bare Life?' and 'What Is To Be Done?'

19 Interview with Nataline Colonnello, www.artzinechina.com.

20 Under Hu Jintao's administration.

21 See Vivienne Shue, 'Legitimacy Crisis in China', in Peter Gries and Stanley Rosen, *Chinese Politics: State, Society and the Market*, London and New York 2010, p.26.

22 Chinese scholar Richard Baum quoted in Richard McGregor, *The Party: The Secret World of China's Communist Rulers*, London 2010, Prologue, p.xii.

23 BBC Worldwide podcast, 15 July 2010, BBC World Service, Global News.

24 In 1979, former Chinese leader and economic reformist Deng Xioping's 'open door reforms' and his later implementation of the Open Door Policy in 1986, led to an era of economic and cultural liberalisation. The attempt to develop a capitalist market economy under the name of 'socialism with Chinese characteristics' has not resulted in an easy post-Mao transition, as the 'further dismantling of the old socialist system, the deepening marketisation of economic relations, and the startling redistributions of property rights' have all contributed to widespread social change, disruptions and popular unrest. See Shue 2010, p.41.

25 From Ai Weiwei, Juliet Bingham and Marko Daniel, 'A Conversation', below.

26 Ai Weiwei, 'Proposal for Tate Modern', March 2010.

27 'Interview: Ai Weiwei and David Pilling', *Financial Times*, 24 April 2010.

28 'Proposal for Tate Modern'.

29 Author?, 'Ai Weiwei', *Artforum*, 12 April 2008.

30 See Lothar Ledderose, *Ten Thousand Things: Module and Mass Production in Chinese Art*, Princeton, New Jersey 2001.

31 Ibid, p.89.

32 From the interview between Ai Weiwei, Juliet Bingham and Marko Daniel, below.

33 See Ai Weiwei, Interview with Hans Ulrich Obrist.

34 Quote taken from *White Cover Book*; interview between Zhuang Hui and Ai Weiwei (trans. Philip Tinari) in *Ai Weiwei: Dropping the Urn. Ceramic Works, 5000 BCE – 2010 CE*, p.21.

@AIWW

Selected quotes from Ai Weiwei's Twitter posts, June 2009 to July 2010
(including messages posted on *Fanfou* and *Zuosa*, both microblogging sites in China)
Translated by Jennifer Ng

@aiww Children can get kidney stones, become big-headed babies, be kidnapped and sold, be buried alive, have their virginity taken away, and be poisoned, but their purity must be maintained.
10.6.2009, 12:30:31

The reference to kidney stones and big-headed babies relates to two different incidents of tainted milk in China. In 2008, melamine-tainted infant formula killed six babies and harmed 300,000 children (news.bbc.co.uk/2/hi/asia-pacific/7614083.stm). In 2004, fake baby-milk caused such malnourishment that some babies appeared to have abnormally large heads in comparison to their bodies (news.bbc.co.uk/2/hi/asia-pacific/3648583.stm). The reference to children buried alive points to the students who perished in the Sichuan earthquake, when schools with substandard architecture collapsed (www.nytimes.com/2008/05/13/world/asia/13scene.html)

@aiww I solemnly announce that an era of scolds has begun: we need to softly scold our enemies to death.
11.6.2009, 08:00:39

@aiww Catching someone for rape was said to be anti-China; children died and queries about building quality were anti-China; the food had poison in it and exposing the news was anti-China; the revelation of beatings and killings was anti-China. Selling children, selling blood with AIDS, underground coal mines, public security, prosecutors and judiciaries violating laws, fake news, corruption, going against the constitution to invade rights, internet donkey tyrants: if you just speak about those you are anti-China. If you are not anti-China, are you still human? 14.6.2009, 08:29:18

'Internet donkey tyrants' refers to the censorship software Green Dam Youth Escort (en.wikipedia.org/wiki/Green_Dam_Youth_Escort),which the Chinese government regulated must be pre-installed in all new computers before sale. Disregarding tonal differences, the word for 'green dam' is a homophone for the word 'donkey tyrant'. The term is commonly used as a derogatory name for the software.

@aiww The Party is testing its people. You're recorded on the internet, you're duped when you go to school, you deserve it when you drop out of school, you're being cheated when you read the news, there's poison when you drink water, you die when you're unemployed, there's an explosion when you're on the bus, you're robbed of your land, houses get torn down, you're sold, buried, raped, harassed by security officers, harassed by United Defence, harassed by the armed police, abused in the name of 'maintaining stability', called mentally ill. You motherfuckers – you're quite tough.
14.6.2009, 08:47:33

@aiww For 60 years, I've seen no ballots, no education for all, no medical insurance for all, no media openness, no freedom of speech, no freedom of information, no freedom of relocation, no judicial independence, no supervision by public opinion, no independent labour unions, no army that belongs to the country, no protection from the Constitution; what's left is only 'next door to the mud horse lying in a manger'.
14.6.2009, 09:10:39

In order to counter government censorship, much slang has developed on the internet, often homophones of the original message. The seemingly nonsensical 'next door to the mud horse lying in a manger' is one such example. It is homophone of the phrase 'I fuck your mother's vagina'.

@aiww Flipping over a police car is an extreme physical exercise. I like this event. It's possibly the only event that I do like. I'll definitely participate.
15.6.2009, 18:46:59

@aiww Without question, one day we'll judge those who've persecuted the people. They include those who implemented persecutions, those who sympathised with persecutions, and the people who were oblivious to persecutions. Sometimes I naively think that the day of this festival is not too far away.
20.6.2009, 00:39:16

@aiww In this world, what could be more moving than the end of an evil and corrupt era? This is the real reason for the grass mud horse's penchant for spreading his happiness. Speaking from this perspective, we thank this era: it's the internet that's given ordinary people power and opportunity, and has proved that it's joyful and blessed to yearn for liberty and fairness. The freedom of choice and the freedom of speech are birthrights. No one should touch them; whoever touches them dies.
20.6.2009, 08:37

Although 'grass mud horse' is internet slang for 'fuck your mother', since 'mother' can refer to 'motherland', the term has developed to describe someone who stands up for their rights against hegemony.

@aiww In this country, violence is not only stripping off the ordinary people's right to live: it's also stripping off their right to expression, including the right to doubt, the right to ask for information, and the right to know. Political powers destroy all efforts made in gaining these rights without considering the price that they have to pay. Death under a violent regime has no corpse.
21.6.2009, 10:17:16

@aiww A strike on the internet is a feasible proposal: it has a time and is an event, it's a conscious action, it practices restraint and it doesn't create a disturbance. Changes have to begin with 'me'. We need to act, even with the smallest action, the most insignificant action, actions that are feasible and can be achieved. Reject empty ideals. Reject off-tangent politics.
22.6.2009, 08:04:19

@aiww Under totalitarian rule, every single day is a death anniversary, but there's no room for corpses.
22.6.2009, 10:49:21

@aiww 'Freedom has always been the freedom of those who are different from you.' With or without the freedom of others, you won't have a day of peace.
3.7.2009

@aiww The system is the rules, the regulations, and the possibility for a healthy game. What we have to say to the government is: 'It's not a problem for you to be in power, but don't cheat. It's not a problem for you to be rotten, but don't be crazy. You can steal, but not in a dignified, high-sounding manner.'
3.7.2009

@aiww Terror doesn't come from barbarianism and cruel violence; terror comes from a resounding silent approval of cruel violence. Sad.
4.7.2009

@aiww When all truths under the sun are your truths, you become an illusion; you're only an excuse for your own existence. The overall significance of freedom of speech is to say that the world isn't like this; the world has its own image in each and everyone's eyes.
5.7.2009

@aiww The concluding remarks are as follows: it's these people, who don't like to sleep at night, who ended the last dark age by hitting [the keyboard] with their fingertips in front of the screen. It should be called a miracle.
2.8.2009, 01:45:55

@aiww In China, non-governmental organisations are anti-government armour. You should just stop pretending. I saw through your spiritual armaments long ago.
2.8.2009, 23:17:25

@aiww If Tan Zuoren is guilty, then I'm at least equally guilty; if Tan Zuoren is punished, I should be punished under the same line of reasoning.
3.8.2009, 22:08:46

Tan Zuoren is a writer who initiated an investigation into the death of the students who perished during the Sichuan earthquake and was subsequently charged by the government for subversion of state power. Ai Weiwei initiated an investigation into the same issue, independent of Tan's work.

@aiww Crimes exist only to challenge our courage. Crime uses its existence to prove that we can all be humiliated, that we are the part of reality that we least hope to have. If we're all unhappy with that, then even the most arrogant and violent government must kneel before us.
3.8.2009, 22:47:32

@aiww We're no longer upset. This system has stripped us of our right to happiness, and at the same time it has stripped of our right to be upset.
4.8.2009, 21:45:08

@aiww What this country needs to do the most is to prove its innocence, to prove its legitimacy, to prove its sanity; these are also what it fears the most.
6.8.2009, 13:32:24

@aiww Skills of living under totalitarian rule: 1. Don't practice self-slavery and self-injury before being enslaved and injured. 2. Don't co-operate, don't believe in bullshit from those in power. 3. Have self-respect, speak for others. 4. Don't be a coward, don't be superstitious. 5. Be happy in the days of knowing shame. 6. Do something little every day to prove the existence of righteousness.
6.8.2009, 14:39:25

@aiww We need to end totalitarian power with our own hands. We'll use this kind of honour without hesitation to avenge our shame, for our fathers' generation and our fathers' fathers' generation, and it will be a completely new, bright, joyful and different reality when we pass it on from our hands to the generation that follows.
10.8.2009, 19:26:06

@aiww We are the most tiring sort among humankind, because we have yet to prove that we're human.
21.8.2009, 20:26:54

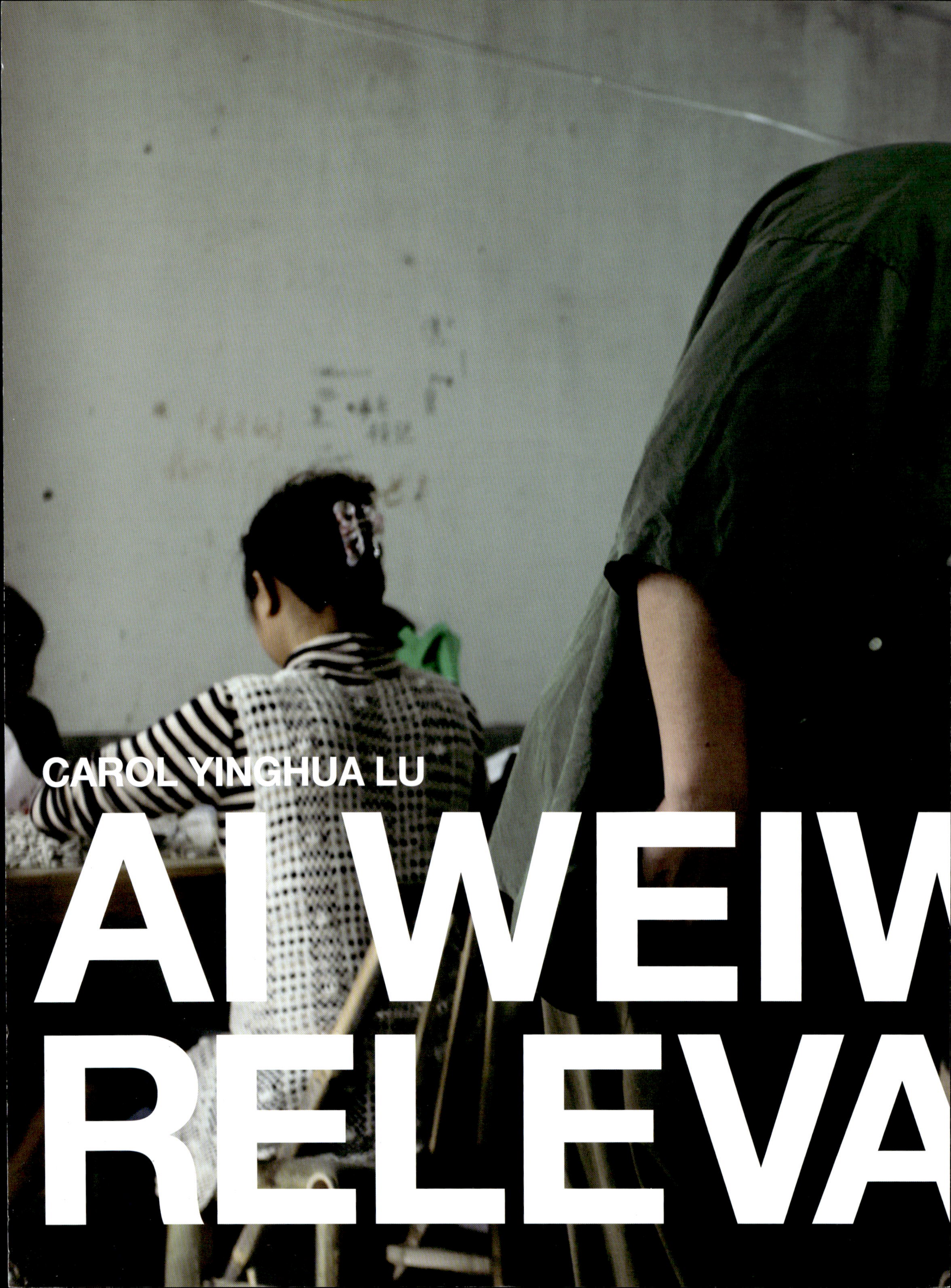
CAROL YINGHUA LU
AI WEIW
RELEVA

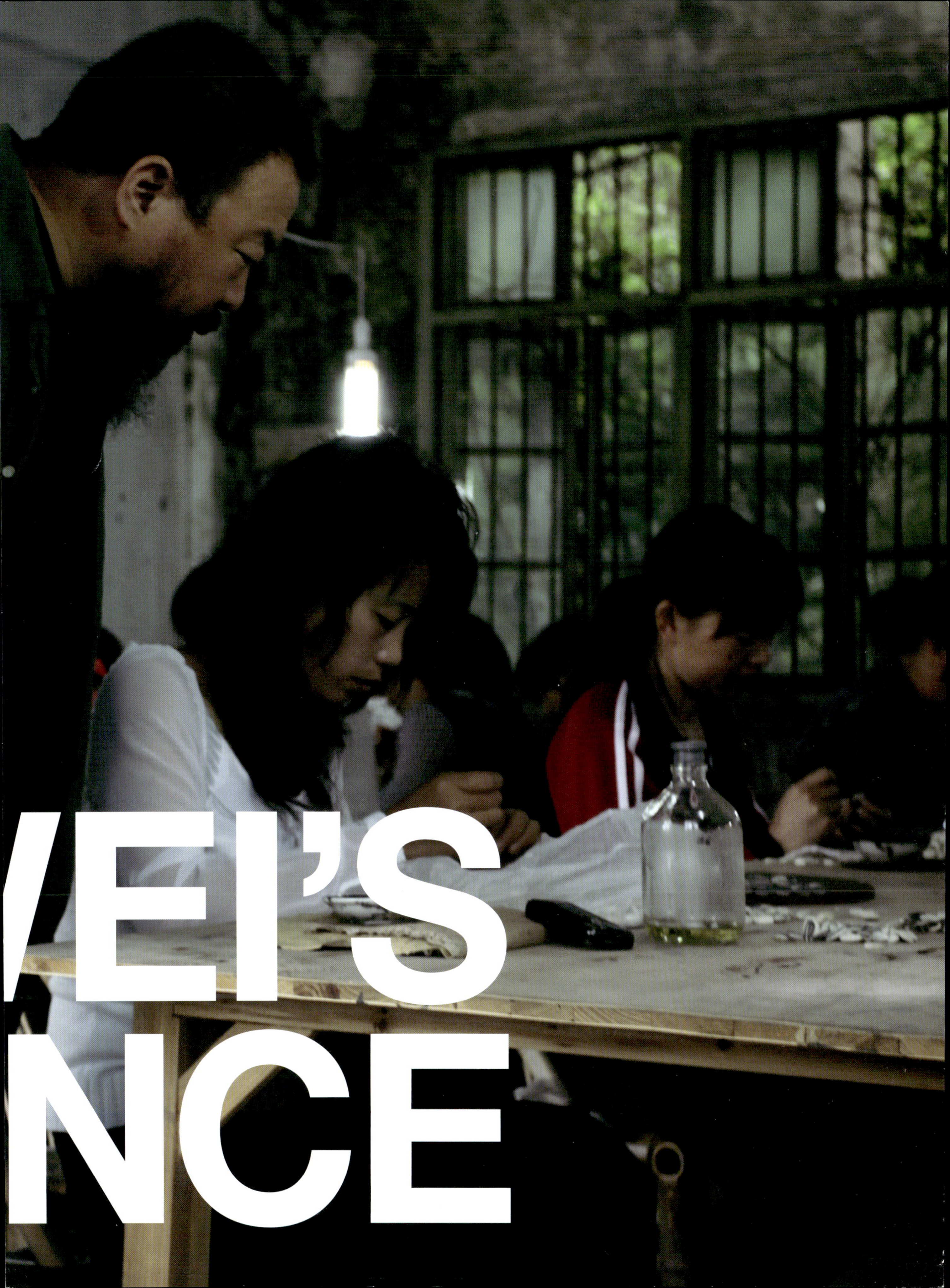

VEI'S
NCE

Previous spread:
Production of sunflower seeds in Jingdezhen, southern China, 2010

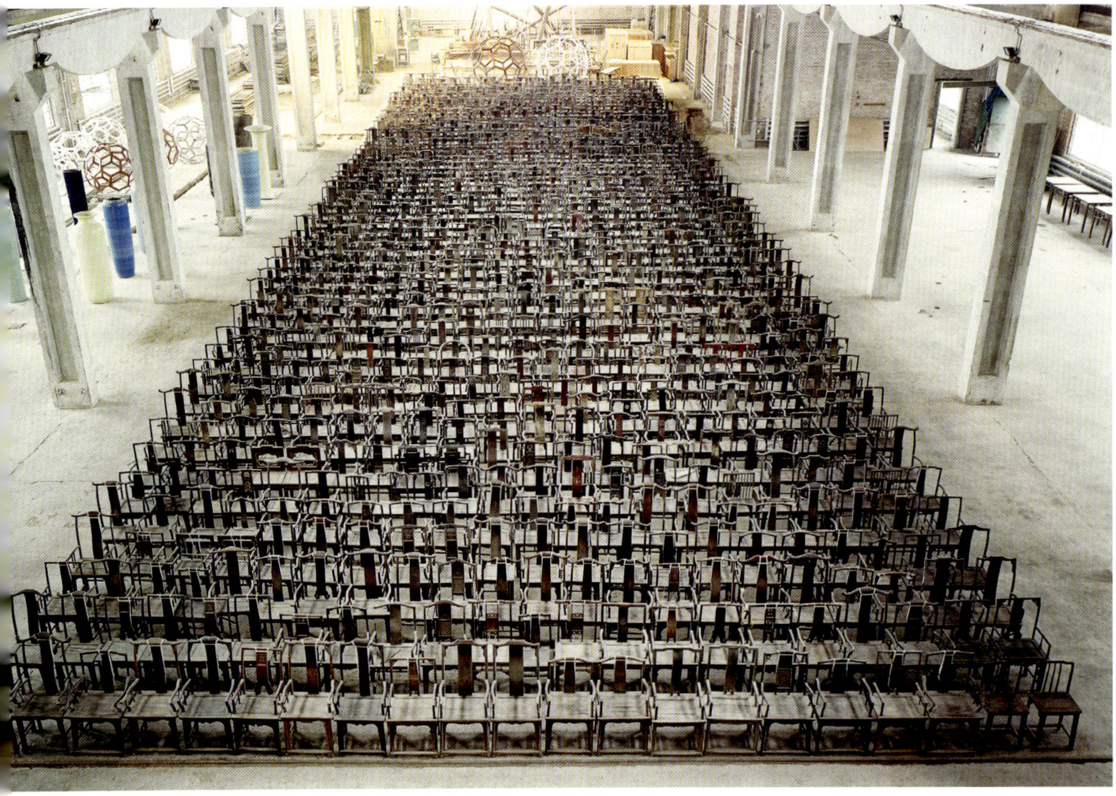

19
Fairytale 2007
1,001 Qing dynasty wooden chairs (1644–1911)
Project for Documenta 12, Kassel, Germany 2007

Despite Ai Weiwei's seemingly unstoppable popularity on the international art scene, there is still a great deal of uncertainty in terms of his relevance to the Chinese art world, its history and market. The scant recognition that he has gained in the Chinese art system is completely out of proportion to the immensity of his oeuvre, which ranges from beautiful concepts such as *Fairytale* 2007 (fig.20) to powerful objects like *Map of China* 2006 (fig.21).

For *Fairytale*, Ai's contribution to Documenta 12, he took 1,001 Chinese people, whom he recruited through his blog, to visit Kassel during the three months of the exhibition, at his own expense. The visitors were accommodated in a former textile mill that had been transformed into a communal dorm. Not only did Ai design their beds, sheets, outfits and suitcases, which he had made in China, but he also brought along his favourite local cooks to prepare daily meals for them. The project cost a mind-blowing $4.28 million. He also transported 1,001 Qing dynasty wooden chairs to Kassel, which were scattered throughout the exhibition sites (fig.19). *Map of China* was made of *tieli* wood from dismantled temples of the Qing dynasty (1644–1911), a material that Ai has used to create a number of installations and sculptural works.

But despite such accomplishments, in a recent exhibition held in Beijing entitled *Reshaping History*,[1] which was meant to be an historic survey of Chinese art produced within the last decade, Ai was conspicuously omitted from the list of over two hundred artists in the show. A partial explanation could be that Ai's practice fails to fit into the nascent narrative of recent Chinese art history, which is structured around such categories as 'cynical realism', 'political pop', 'kitschy art', 'conceptual photography' and 'cartoon art'. These 'movements' did not emerge out of any artistic or political beliefs, but were man-made by a small group of art critics, curators and gallerists whose interests were bound together in such self-

20
Fairytale 2007
1,001 Chinese visitors in Kassel
Project for Documenta 12, Kassel,
Germany, 2007
(aerial photo looking down on participants with luggage)

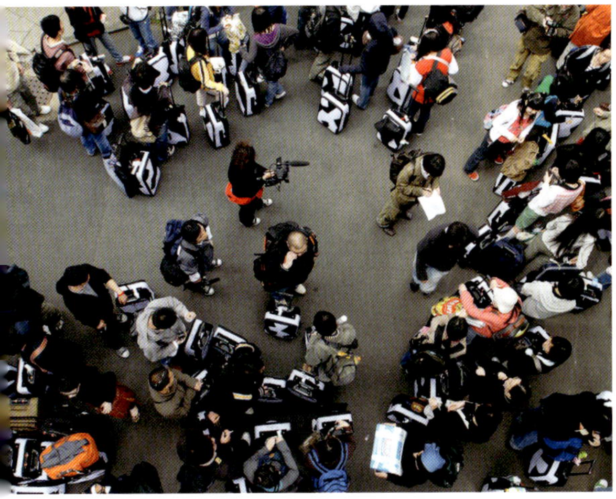

definitions. Chinese contemporary artists and critics owe a large part of their approach to the avant-garde legacy of modernity, yet such an avant-garde attitude is aimed more at ideology on a superficial level than the ideals, understanding, values and discourse of art. This rigid movement-based art-historical dogma in China tends to overstress the importance of certain groups of artists whose work can be interpreted within such a narrow framework, yet underestimates, if not completely excludes, practices that cannot be framed in such a value system. But the authority of this value system has been underlined over and over again by the dominant commercial structure in China so that it has become accepted unquestioningly by the majority.

The current historic narrative, which has largely been penned around the success stories of the art market rather than a methodology employing critical scrutiny, only serves to reaffirm those successes and leaves little room for more conceptual, contemplative and less easily defined practices. These latter practices have, however, existed all along and have been equally valuable in shaping artistic thinking. Ai's work certainly resists easy categorisation within those 'trends' that have been identified and packaged for market consumption. Although he was a member of the Stars group, which is generally considered one of the key starting points for the rise of contemporary art in China at the end of 1970s, he left the country in the early 1980s before getting a chance to benefit from its success.[2] Between then and his return to Beijing

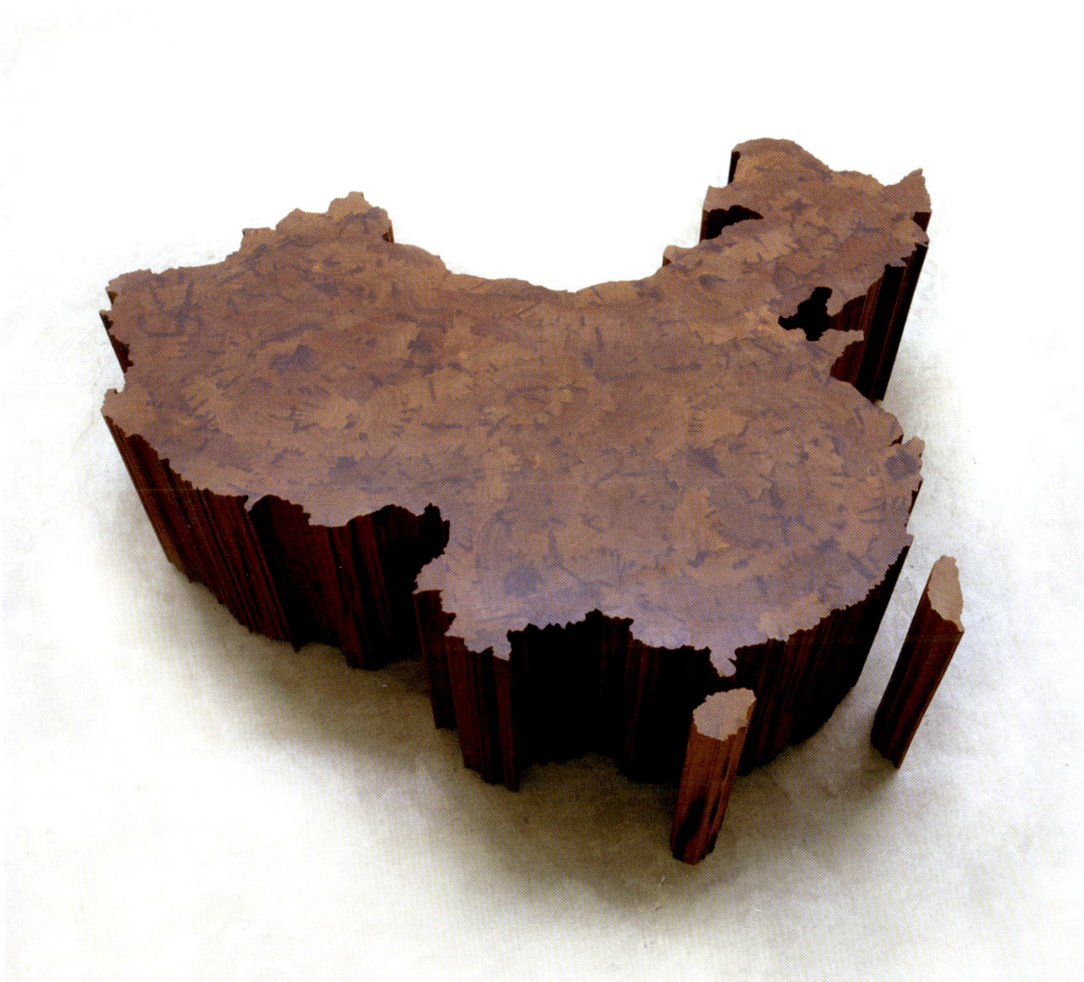

21
Map of China 2004
Ironwood from dismantled temples of the Qing dynasty (1644–1911)
51 x 200 cm (diameter)

22
The Black Cover Book 1994
160 pages, 23 x 18cm

23
The White Cover Book 1995
160 pages, 23 x 18cm

24
The Grey Cover Book 1997
160 pages, 23 x 18cm

in 1993, the basic shape of the art world and the circles of friends and foes within it had already been formed. Upon his return, Ai had to search for a new entry point into the local art world, which didn't come easily. The mid-1990s saw the peak of the so-called 'avant-garde artists' whose work was interpreted in a political and ideological light and was gaining widespread popularity and recognition. Following the *China/Avant-garde* exhibition[3] and the student movement in 1989, there was scant official support, in terms of access to exhibition spaces and funding, for more conceptual contemporary art practices The social climate was conservative and alert to anything that did not conform to the ideological hegemony of the state, creating a heightened level of tension between the contemporary art circle and the state throughout the 1990s.

Ai chose not to subscribe to the existing rules, but slowly developed his own individual system that was logistically, artistically and intellectually independent of mainstream preferences and practices. He funded his own productions through antique-dealing, helped establish an art space, self-published his works, built his own team, created a circle of artist friends whom he supported with work and funding, and courted attention for himself through actively creating contexts in which to act and be visible. From 1994 to 1997, he co-edited the *Black Cover*, *White Cover* and *Grey Cover* books, three independently published compilations of artist interviews, proposals, texts and theoretical references (figs.22–4). These gave visibility not only to Ai's thinking and work, but also to that of his peers, including Xu Bing, Huang Yong Ping, Geng Jianyi and Qian Weikang.

In 1997, Ai joined the Dutch artist and curator Hans van Dijk to establish the China Art Archive and Warehouse (CAAW) in Beijing. CAAW continued Van Dijk's diligent work of building up an archive of materials relevant to the artists with whom CAAW worked, and supported and organised exhibitions featuring a younger generation of artists from different parts of China who otherwise received little exposure. Since Van Dijk's death in 2002, Ai has been acting as CAAW's artistic director and has kept it as a space free from mainstream tastes and preferences.

In 2000, Ai co-curated with Beijing-based curator Feng Boyi the seminal exhibition *Fuck Off*, whose Chinese title literally translates as 'Ways of Non-Cooperation' or 'Uncooperative Approach'. The show was a defiant gesture of refusal to comply with the official system as represented by the Shanghai Biennale, which opened at the same

25
Spreads from *The Black Cover Book*
1994

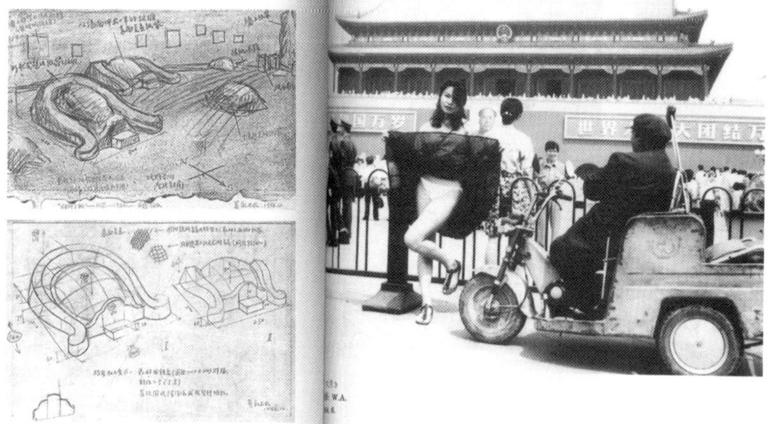
108

《爬行物》
創作草圖　1989

作品制做設計草圖

W.A.

媚笑陽臺

組一光

『愛情
是您好，再見
直到我們再次相見』

死亡
是窗口 陽臺
等到我們跳下陽臺

你哀求着有户窗口
我乞求着高高陽臺
愛情對死亡開始憐憫
我對死亡產生了愛情

一九九四年六月十日
NO樂隊作品選

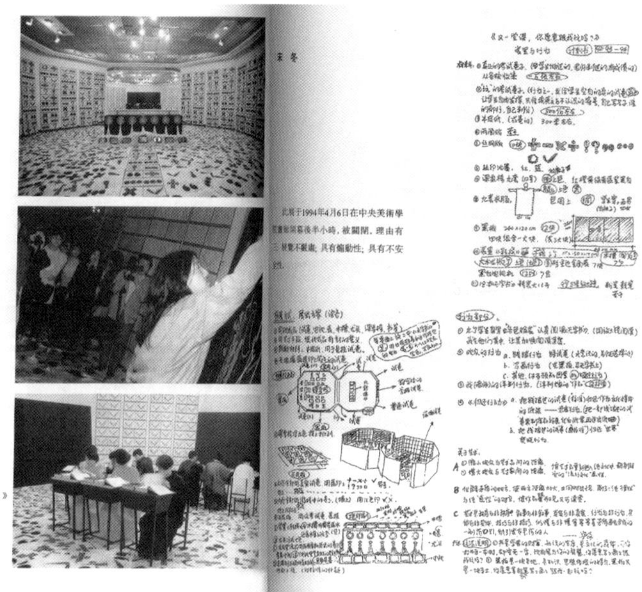
58

宋冬
《又一堂課，你願意跟我玩嗎？》
1994
中國北京

攝影：王安禾
攝影：王　虎

宋冬

此展于1994年4月6日在中央美術學
……開幕後半小時，被關閉。理由有
……不嚴肅；具有煽動性；具有不安
……性。

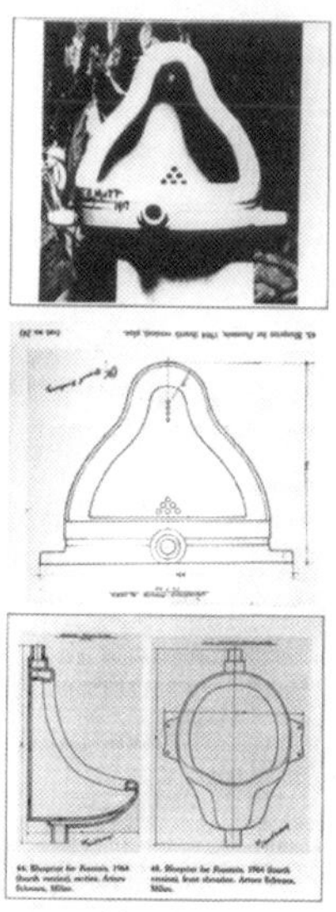
128

馬塞爾・杜香
《噴泉》設計圖
1964(第4版)
馬塞爾・杜香
《噴泉》
1917
美國紐約

創作的行爲

馬塞爾・杜香

我們來考慮一下兩個重要的因素，即藝術創造的兩個角色：一方面是藝術家，另一方面就是以後要成爲後人的觀衆。

很顯然，藝術家的行爲猶如巫士，他從超越時空的迷宮中尋找通往光明的途徑。

如果我們將媒介的屬性賦予藝術家，那麼我們就會在美學層面上否認他對自己在做什麼和爲什麼這樣做等問題擁有清醒的狀態。他在作品的藝術創造中所作出的一切決定都出于純粹的本能，並且不可能被譯解爲自我分析，無論是口頭的、文字的甚或是思考中的。

T.S.愛略特在《傳統與個人天賦》一文中寫道："藝術家越是完美，那麼在他身上肉體的人與創造的大腦之間就越是徹底分離；大腦也就越是完全地吸收和改變作爲其素材的情感。"

億萬個藝術家都在創造，只有數萬個藝術家被觀衆討論和接受，而受後人所敬仰的就更少。

在上述分析中，藝術家也許會大聲疾呼自己是天才；他會耐心等待觀衆的裁決以使自己的名聲產生社會價值，並最終使後人將他收入藝術史的入門書籍中。

我知道我的這段話不會得到很多藝術家的同意，他們不願承認巫士的角色，而是一味堅持認爲他們的創造活動中確實很清醒——然而藝術史決定一件藝術作品的價值所依據的想法與藝術家本人理性化的解釋全然無關。

如果藝術家作爲一個對自己和整個世界充滿了最美好的意圖，但對

129

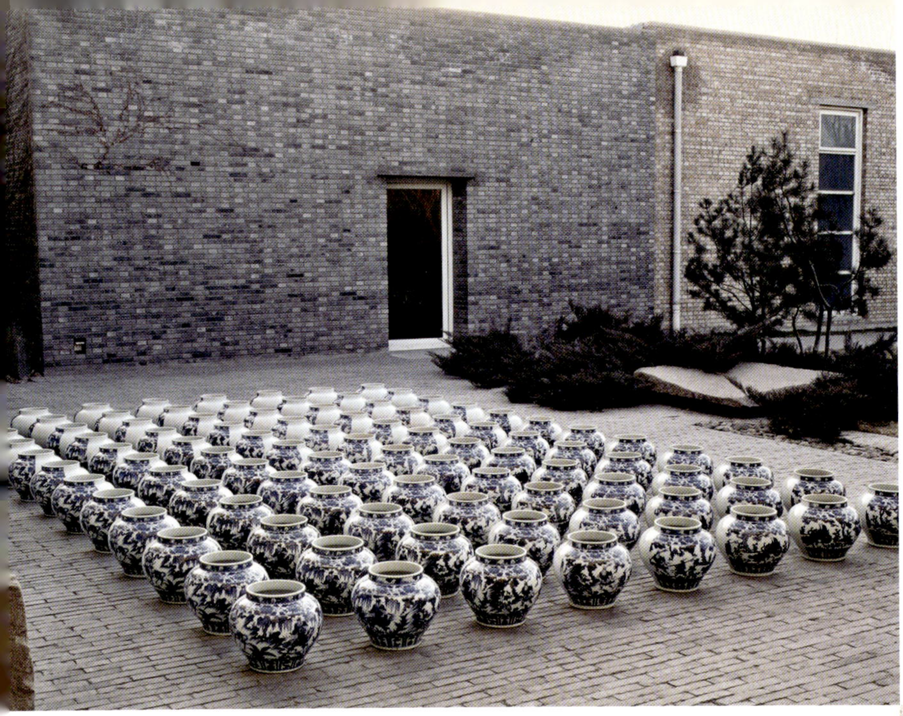

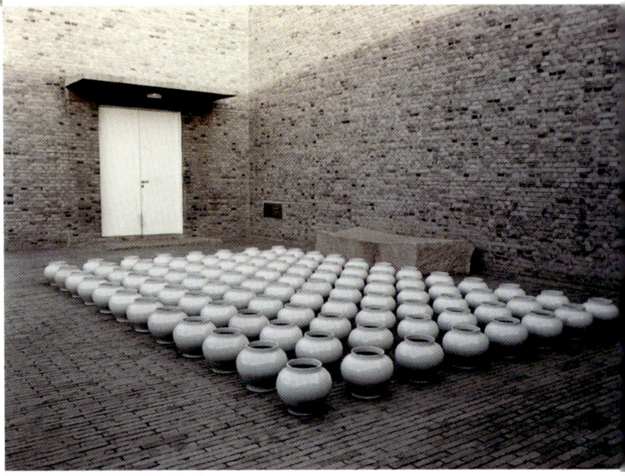

26, 27
Ai Weiwei and Serge Spitzer
Ghost Gu Coming Down the Mountain 2005
Blue and white porcelain, 96 vases, each 27 x 35 cm (diameter), edition 3/3
Installation at Ai Weiwei's studio, 2006

time and signalled a crucial turning point in the government's attitude towards contemporary art, from one of rejection and suppression to one of acceptance and assimilation. This conscious and courageous choice to resist association with established circles and powers in the art world has ensured Ai's rejection and exclusion from many exhibitions and possibilities offered by the local art system. From the very beginning, he has experienced the extreme difficulties, yet also the power, of developing his own independent platform.

It is interesting to observe how, in his approach to reasserting and legitimising his presence in the art world of his own country, Ai differs from most of his peers who have shared the same experience of living abroad and returning in recent years to China. Many have opted for certainty rather than operating on an indeterminate ground as Ai does. Most of these artists left China in the 1990s, disillusioned and distrustful of a system that has changed little since. Today, they seem so eager to comply with the system that they simply throw themselves at its mercy. Some have taken up prominent jobs in the art academies. Others make works that glorify its politics. Still more have joined the government-sponsored Contemporary Art Academy of China (CAAC), which was founded in 2009 and now has thirty members. The significance, danger and paradox of this event is far greater than it may at first appear. The fact that these 'academy experts' were unanimously among those classified as outcasts by the same government in the early 1990s should not be forgotten.[4] The seeming openness and tolerance of the government as demonstrated by this professional body should be interpreted with alarm, yet is accepted and welcomed without question by these artists who once prized their independence and critique of such a system. Far from signalling the victory of art in Chinese society, this landmark event in fact marks the further corrosion and loss of artistic autonomy to the baits of authoritarian power.

This shift in the climate makes Ai's position even more precarious and isolated, yet crucial to the health of the art system. His prolific and inexhaustible practice is in many senses a model, primarily for the importance and possibility of independent thinking. As seen in many of his works in which he collages, breaks, repaints,

28, 29
Template 2007
Wooden doors and windows from destroyed Ming and Qing dynasty houses (1368–1911), wooden base
Before collapsing:
720 x 1200 x 850cm
After collapsing:
422 x 1106 x 875 cm
Project for Documenta 12, Kassel, Germany 2007

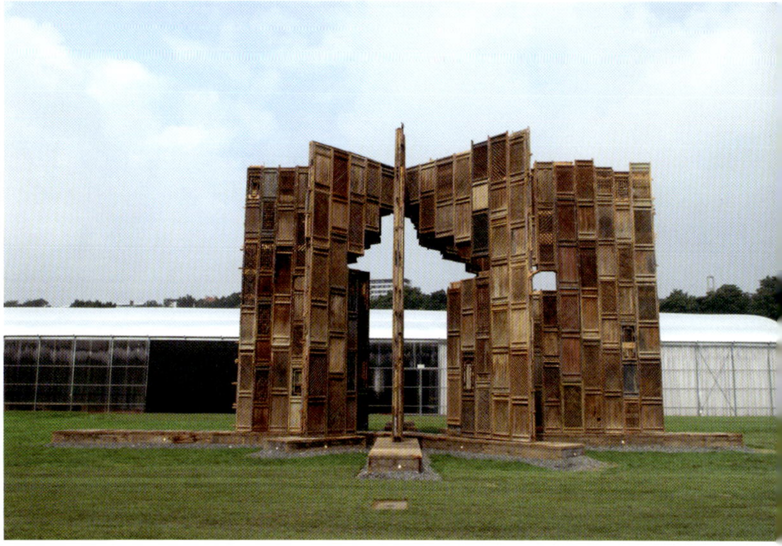

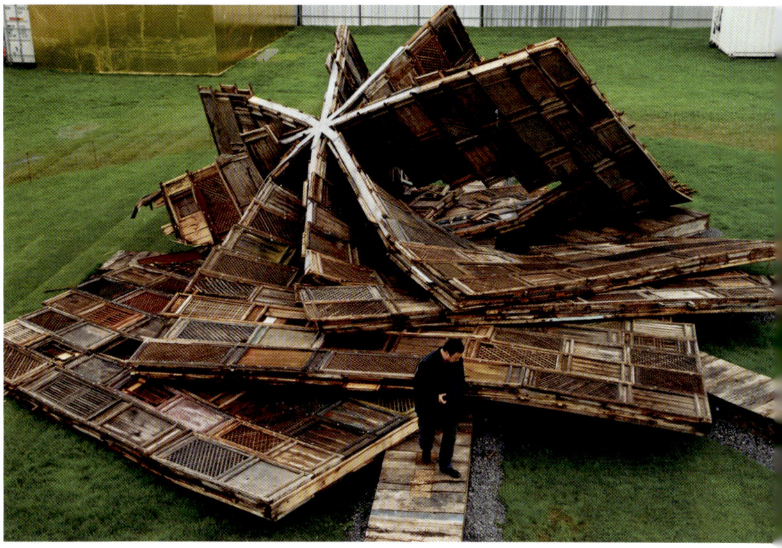

deconstructs, re-arranges and reinvents elements of traditional Chinese culture – whether antique statues or porcelain-making techniques – Ai understands, and more importantly respects, the specificities as well as the fundamental ideas behind these objects and the culture around them while at the same time continuously questioning and challenging the authoritarian power, agency and traditional values associated with them (figs.26–7). The 'readymade' he takes aim at in his works is not the object, but the fixed perceptions, ideology, myths, misunderstandings and authority attached to them. These works are about letting go of certainties and allowing new possibilities to emerge (figs.28–9).

The impression that I have formed of Ai over time, having followed his practice through his exhibitions, his writings and the documentary films produced by his studio about his recent activist campaigns, is that he seems to know more than the majority of people. On the one hand, 'knowing more' implies a certain level of authority, but authority in turn creates a hierarchy that thrives on protecting its privileged access to information, using it to intimidate the less well informed. This approach is fundamentally against Ai's worldview. On the other hand, 'knowing more', sharing such awareness and promoting a deeper understanding of our reality, can stimulate a sense of responsibility to act and an urge to make changes. This has become an important thread that runs through

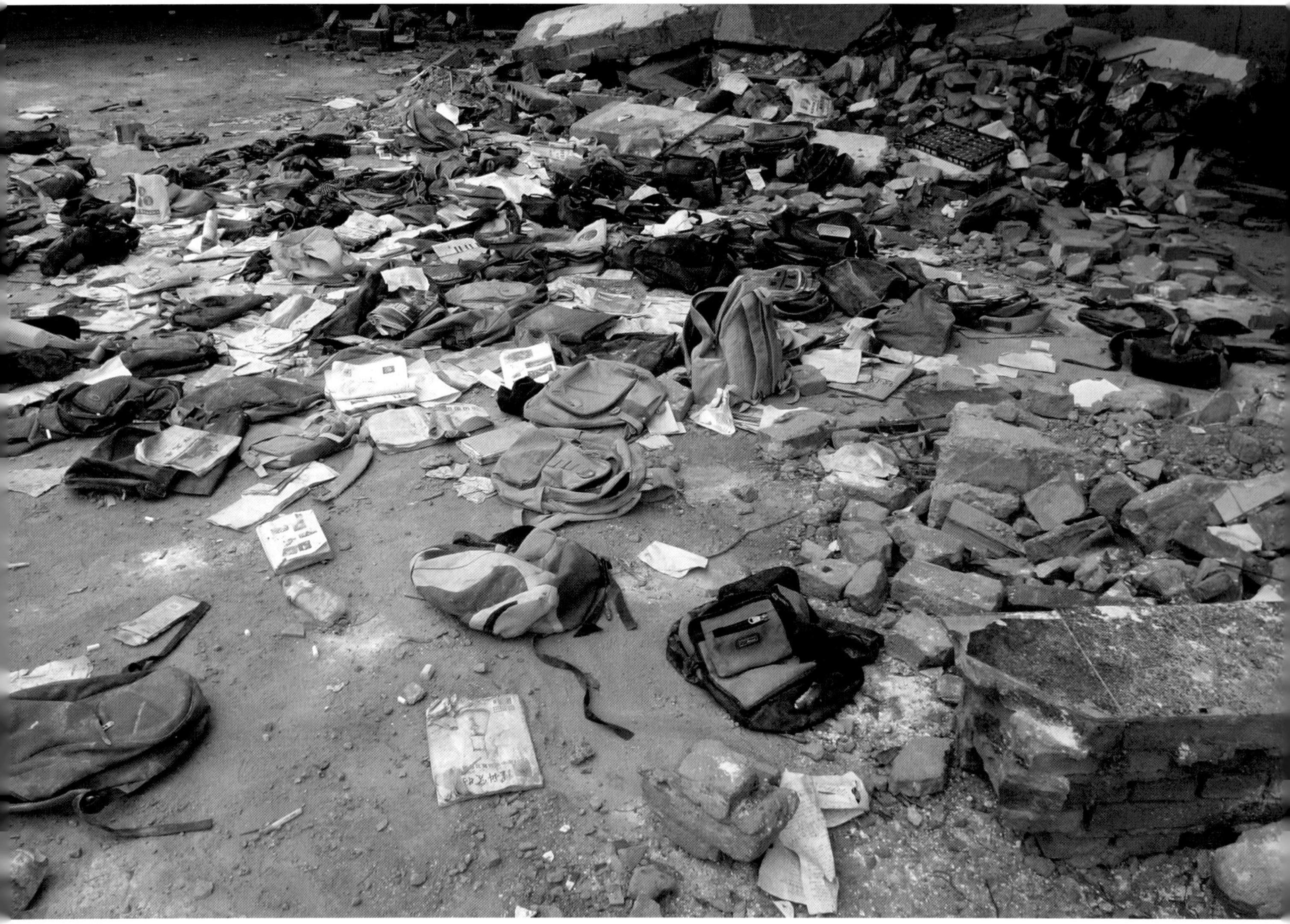

Ai's thinking and actions and has continuously prompted him to pose questions to the Chinese government, perhaps the best informed and most secretive of all.

When I first met Ai in his studio early in June this year, he remarked: 'Most people don't really know and understand what I do.' This was not false modesty, but a genuine statement that did not surprise me at all. Many people in the Chinese art world share a certain scepticism towards Ai and his multiplicity of roles and projects. In 2008, he initiated a civil investigation into the numbers and names of the five thousand or more children killed in poorly constructed school buildings during the Sichuan earthquake. However, certain Chinese artists, a number of them linked to the so-called 'cynical realism' group, asked whether Ai's investigations were being supported by a political party in order to undermine China's current government. According to this view, Ai is just a courier for another political agenda, complying with such a role in order to develop his own portfolio and social status.

It is important to realise that the Chinese social system, a system afflicted with corruption and lacking in transparency, fairness and humanity and that led to the death of those school children in the earthquake, could have had an equally devastating effect in any other context. No one is immune to the fundamental problems of corruption, inequality and disregard for human life that is apparently prevalent in

30
Sichuan Earthquake Imagos 2008
Black and white print

the system. In this context, the notion that art can change society is not just a romantic ideal, but one of significant social relevance. The incentive and courage to initiate and establish one's own system that speaks to the mainstream establishment is built on a sense of critical involvement and thus responsibility. It takes a truly independent state of mind to consider what can be done better and how one individual can contribute to such changes. Ai chose to ask legitimate questions about the identity and numbers of students who died. These facts, however, were classified as state secrets. The government wanted society to focus on the obvious: that a terrible natural disaster had taken place. What it did not want was for anybody, including those whose loved ones were hurt or killed in the earthquake, to be rational, clear-headed, or to question and reveal unpalatable truths. Yet, for the sake of understanding what actually happened and how it could be avoided in the future, Ai and his team wanted to know more. This turned them into alleged spies and therefore targets of incessant police harassment. What Ai and his teammates did in risking their own freedom and safety was not in line with how the leaders and media, controlled and shaped by the singular value system of the government, had repeatedly told the general population to respond: to mourn, to forget and to move on.

It certainly seems easier to forget than to seek more knowledge. Ai and such activists as Tan Zuoren were amongst the few people who actively questioned what had led to the collapse of so many schools. The state's quick response and much publicized reaction to the disaster, as portrayed and amplified by the media, garnered almost universal applause and gratitude, but this overshadowed the truth. This deliberately simplified and abstracted representation of the event, set up for spectacle, philanthropic outpouring and ideological brainwashing, brutally consumed those who had suffered and lost loved ones in the disaster.

One can see how cynical, agenda-based interpretations of Ai's concern regarding the earthquake have their subscribers in the spiritually deprived and materially hungry value system not only of the Chinese art world but also of society at large. After all, historically, during the Cultural Revolution, many people acted with self-interest for the sake of surviving human cruelty. Since then, there has been an almost complete loss of compassion and trust in humanity among the Chinese population. Unable to grasp the complexity of a situation, people habitually arrive at superficial conclusions based on the simplified two-fold moral stands of right or wrong. In the face of crisis, individuals often fall prey to such false moral judgments, which condemn individual decisions that fail to fulfill the collective sentiment. As Ai has pointed out, there is no clear distinction between public and private in Chinese society. For example, in the eyes of the media, and people in general, the private property of celebrities should be at the disposal of those in need, and their kind intentions are weighed only in monetary terms. The media seems to be exercising a certain monitoring function in such cases by imposing the duty of donation onto people living in the spotlight, but even then, in their charitable donations in response to large-scale natural disasters, their motivations for donating (self-publicity) or the extent of their generosity are questioned. However, the premise of such stage-managed criticism is rarely examined.

Ai is also conscious of how the blurred border between the public and the private domains could be turned to a good use. He has been very open about his troubled family history and has never shied away from revealing his present life, which he constantly and voluntarily exposes to the public through his own camera or the media. His blog

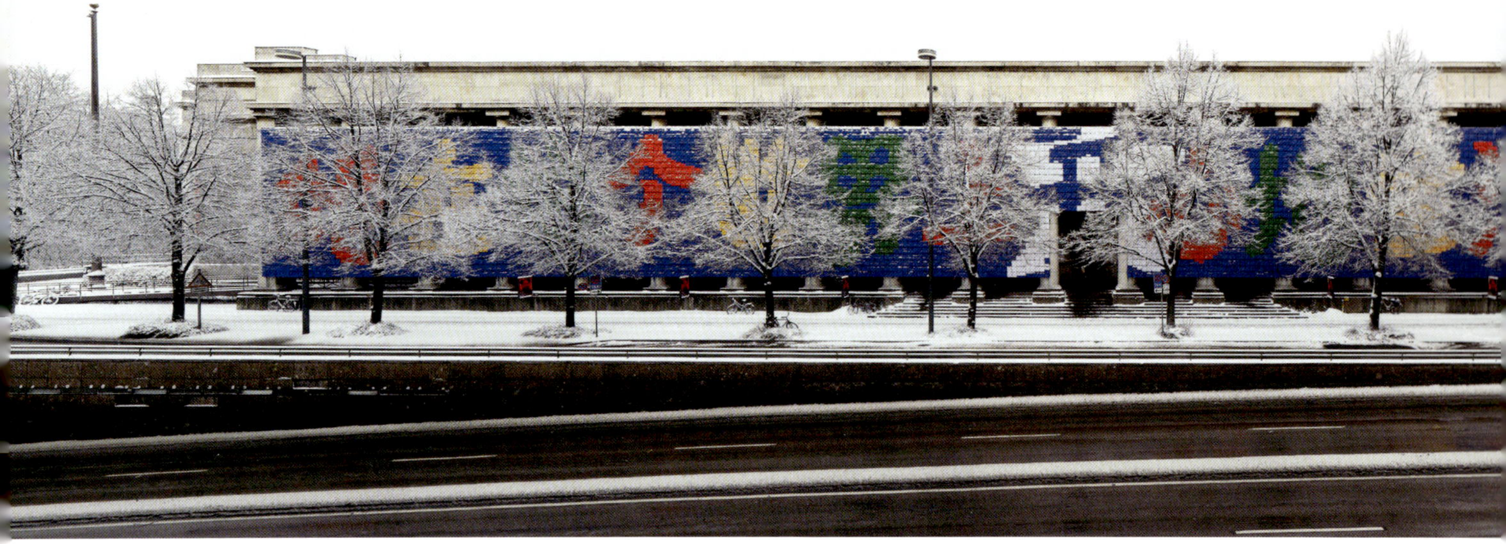

31
Remembering 2009
Backpacks and metal structure
920 x 10605 cm
Installation on facade of Haus der Kunst, Munich 2009
(Photo: Jens Weber)

entries were loaded with images from his travels, openings, meetings and gatherings with friends. To many in the Chinese art world, anything Ai does is dismissed as an opportunistic way to gain visibility for his artistic career, especially as it gathers increasing momentum and weight internationally. Many people simply stop at such an assumption without looking any closer into the actual practice and detail of Ai's work. Like the social temperament out of which it grows, the spirit of the Chinese art circle is not one of independent criticality, but is an extremely simplistic and distorted functionalist one: it recognises and identifies with success, as well as breeding professional envy and bitterness. In such a perspective, Ai's outspoken commentaries on political and social issues are viewed as feeding into the celebratory status that he enjoys in the Western media and the international art scene. Thanks to the inferiority complex of the contemporary art scene in China, whose commercialisation and industrialisation was initiated and supported by the Western market that now consumes it like a new regional cuisine, Ai's success story agonises those who long to be accepted by the West yet at the same time are deeply jealous of those who achieve this. It is no wonder that Ai should say that the art world, operating around such limited and limiting premises, is too small for him. For someone like Ai, who moves fluidly at the top level of the international art scene through exhibitions and conferences, the sky is the limit. His studio is one of the most visited destinations for the influx of curators, journalists, museum directors and collectors that arrive from everywhere in the world. The fact that the world has come to Ai and that Ai takes it so lightly is a source of frustration for those seeking similar status within the Chinese art world.

Ai also knows that there is more to the thorny and complicated relationship between art and politics than has been portrayed, defined and taken for granted in the recent history of Chinese art.

There hasn't been a single moment when art hasn't been taken hostage by politics in China. It has been modelled as an effective propaganda tool since Communist rule, and is still tightly controlled and steered towards political calculation. At the end of the Cultural Revolution, artists claimed to have taken art back into their own hands, only to unconsciously or consciously adapt it to another purpose. It was employed as an uncomplicated expression of anger, dissatisfaction and defiance towards government control, a seemingly avant-garde attitude. Yet as soon as such a critical gesture became marketable and was quickly consumed both by the market and the political machine itself, it became an empty signifier that merely made visual and thematic references to all kinds of political symbols and icons without touching upon the fundamental issues or thinking analytically. Indeed, artists seem almost to have lost their ability to think independently, habitually taking criticality as a mere posture of artistic freedom. This reality deprives art of its ability to contemplate and stand its own ground.

It also makes Ai appear excruciatingly alone in his soberness and refusal to confuse the kind of superficial political engagement and position-taking tactfully made by many Chinese artists in their artworks with the notion of true political art. Yet his persistence in communicating his views openly through the internet, first on his blog, until it was forcibly shut down by the authorities, and now through Twitter, has attracted hundreds of thousands of people, especially those of a younger generation, to his ideas.

Communicating through Twitter for eight hours a day has been described by Ai as a form of schooling that he enacts for those that follow him. This is reminiscent of the position taken by Joseph Beuys, who can be seen as an important precursor to Ai's work. As Jan Verwoert has commented:

> What does have a significant bearing on the politics of Beuys' overall practice is his adoption of a speaking position that is inextricably bound to the articulation of certain ideas precisely because this position is traditionally justified by these ideas: the position of the messianic speaker whose mythical authority is justified and authenticated by the invocation of the idea of primordial healing powers. The use of the concept of healing is thus synonymous with the creation of an unquestioned – and, by virtue of its superior justification, also unquestionable – position of power.[5]

Those who write to him on Twitter, follow him on Twitter, answer his calls for spontaneous lunch or dinner meetings with fellow Twitter users, and join his campaign for voluntary activist acts, help contribute to the formation of a network around Ai and his philosophy. Through this ever-growing network of contacts, Ai spreads his reflections on both current affairs and humanity, as well as news about his latest legal and artistic pursuits, and distributes documentary films that his studio has produced independently, which would be impossible to circulate through normal channels. The more people listen to him, the more clout he gathers. Twitter becomes an important means of social organisation that presents a formidable amount of human power and political potential. Without being endorsed by any authoritarian order, Ai occupies a position of power that many people look up to. He has single-handedly created his own system, which does not look for approval and acceptance but challenges the establishment. Through this regular manoeuvring within the establishment, now almost a staple in his everyday life, he subjects himself both to the spotlight

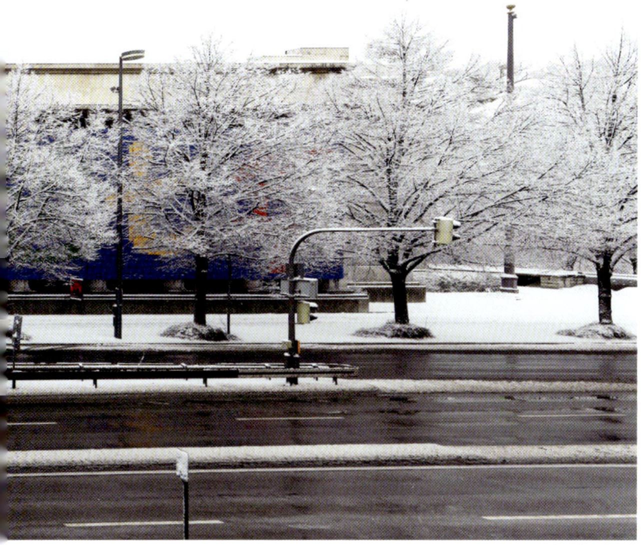

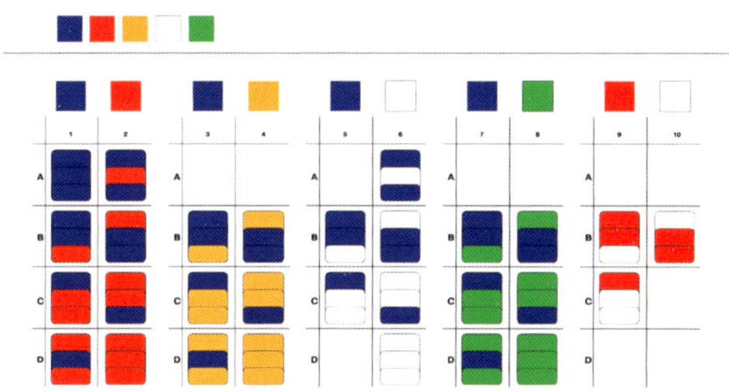

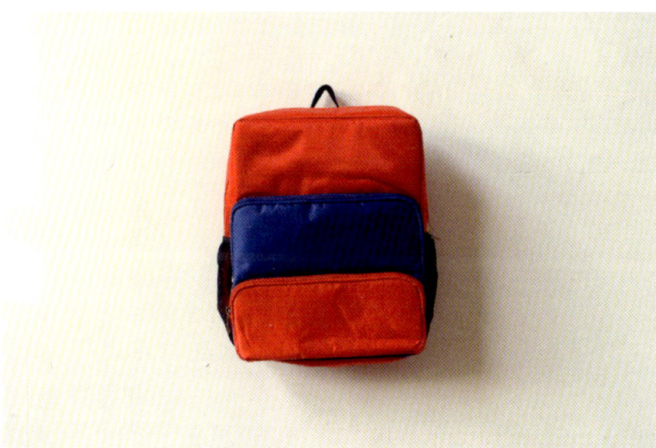

32
Render image for *Remembering*
2009

33
Detail from *Remembering* 2009

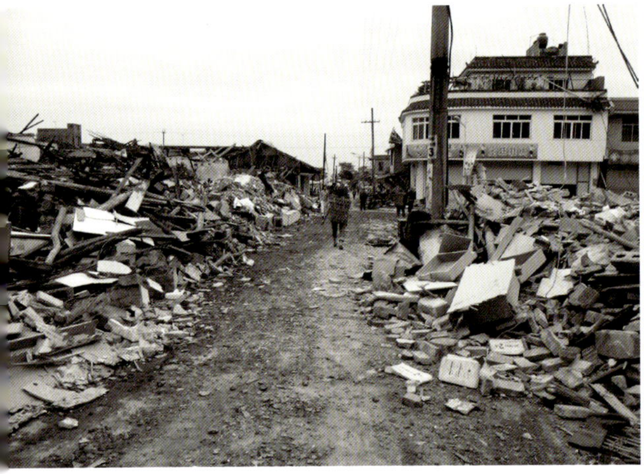

34
Sichuan Earthquake Images 2008
Black and white print

and to high risks. Simultaneously a pessimist and a romantic, he is characterised and energised by such contradictions.

Ai is a gifted and powerful writer. He exercises much self-constraint in his writing, as he does when making aesthetic decisions in his artworks, which are always concise, subtle, elegant and absolute. He writes succinctly and gracefully, employing compelling reason but igniting fiercely emotional responses. 'Emotion is a kind of adhesive', Ai told me. 'It glues everything together. Without it, an object, an event, a place or a person has no story or history and feels cold.'

With this, I understand a lot more about his works and why he refers over and over again to old wood, antique pots, past events and patterns of life – things carrying with them the weight of time and the warmth of emotion. It also sheds light on his metaphorical installation for Tate Modern's Turbine Hall. The sunflower seeds are a similar kind of adhesive. In north China in particular, no matter how difficult the conditions, people offer each other a handful of sunflower seeds for comfort. As a simple snack, they provide a space for basic pleasure, for friendship and kindness, for peace of mind, a place untouchable by and independent of external turmoil and change. The immensity of this piece illustrates, however, another hard and hopeless reality: each of us is as insignificant as the sunflower seeds. To live on and to keep going is to understand and make peace with such a realisation, yet at the same time to retain hope for the future.

A question I have often asked myself is whether I could have acted in the way Ai has without being imprisoned long ago? Many people attribute his immunity from long-term imprisonment to the influence of his father, the celebrated poet and a good friend of Mao, Ai Qing. But I think the most fundamental and permanent system of immunity that Ai has inherited from his family is his spirit of independence and belief in human dignity and integrity. Perhaps it's true that without such a privileged background others cannot push the envelope as far as Ai has. But if each of us asserts a little more and asks to know a little more, the space we can make for ourselves will grow bigger and bigger. This idea can be exercised in the social arena, as well as practised in the domain of art, by living with less certainty but with more inner security. As an independent art critic, I have been inspired by Ai to question and intersect through my writing with the power structure of an art system that is not simply about capital but has a dangerous appetite for the concentration of power and accrual of value. I call for respect and understanding of our responsibility to encourage independence, creativity and intellectuality, and by consciously advocating such ideas in my essays, I hope that my profession can be more open, more fluid and more inspirational. By changing the profession of art, I believe that we can make a contribution to society as well.

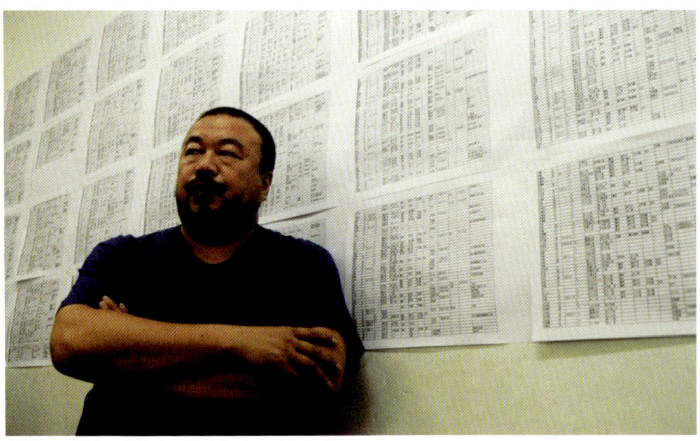

35
Ai Weiwei in his studio with the lists of earthquake victims

NOTES

1 *Reshaping History*, curated by Lv Peng, Zhu Zhu and Gao Qianhui, Beijing 4 – 21 May 2010. Subtitled 'Chinart from 2000 to 2009', the exhibition was meant to survey ten years of contemporary art produced in China and led to the production of a publication intended as a major historic account of this recent period. Co-curator curator Lv Peng is an art historian who has written some of the most widely read books on Chinese contemporary art, including *History of Chinese Contemporary Art: 1990–1999* and *A History of Art in Twentieth-Century China*. The exhibition took place in the basement of the China National Convention Centre. Although this is normally a space for fairs, the fact that it is a governmental institution was also intended to give a certain level of endorsement to the legitimisation of contemporary art in China.

2 Most members of the Stars group were not formally trained and did not affiliate themselves with any official art institution. The group exhibited works to public acclaim in a park next to Beijing's National Art Gallery in September 1979, although the event was quickly shut down by the local authorities. In 1980 the *Third Stars Art Exhibition* was the first experimental art exhibition to be held in Beijing's National Art Gallery. It was attended by more than 80,000 visitors in just over two weeks. The Stars group disbanded in 1983 although its members continued to show in Hong Kong and Taiwan.

3 *China/Avant-garde* was a large-scale exhibition of experimental Chinese art that took place at Beijing's National Art Gallery in 1989. The exhibition was conceived as colonising an official art institution. A number of radical works were included, including a 'shooting' performance, reflecting the strong sense of 'happening' associated with this exhibition and closely related to the social situation of the time.

4 See http:/news.cultural-china.com/20091123173800.html: *'The appointed CAAC artists will not receive salaries, but will get budgets for art projects'*.

5 Jan Verwoert, 'The Boss: On the Unresolved Question of Authority in Joseph Beuys' Oeuvre and Public Image', *e-flux journal* #1, December 2008.

@AIWW

@aiww If I cannot prove that my willpower and ideals have to do with your happiness, then my entire life has been unsuccessful.
21.8.2009, 20:29:39

@aiww If only you would return to us the power to vote, then you would leave our vision from that moment on, forever. What a shame, totalitarian power! We won't curse you anymore. What belongs to you is only oblivion.
21.8.2009, 22:02:21

@aiww Thinking about our reality, apart from helplessness and hopelessness, there's more excitement, an emotion of gratitude. Mankind will end trifles such as stupidity and a history of evil, softly pushing it underneath our feet. What that means is that we're watching. Bring it on! See what you can do.
22.8.2009, 17:20:55

@aiww Without judicial **, everyone is in a dire situation; without media free***, every power is sinful and rotten; without free*** of speech, every life has wasted its efforts. What we want is not much: just to gain the power of living a clean life.
23.8.2009, 18:33:20

The asterisks appear in the records as the result of censorship and stand for 'judicial independence', 'media freedom', and 'freedom of speech'. The same applies to the following tweets.

@aiww If one person has no free***, then I have no free***; if one person is humiliated, then I'm humiliated. If one person has been hurt, then I've been hurt. Have you heard and understood?
23.8. 2009, 18:38:54

@aiww All speech prisoners, thought prisoners and political prisoners must be released; otherwise you'll never be forgiven.
23.8.2009, 18:41:32

@aiww I don't believe in the so-called intellectuals because I despise their views of honour and disgrace. I despise it when actions don't catch up with thoughts, and I call those fake thoughts, which means being pretentious.
23.8.2009, 21:13:23

@aiww The for-profit corporation has already formed and has already completed its new format. It can be clearly seen, from the internationalization of a mighty economic body to the crazy splitting the spoils of every inch of land, mountain quarry and resource. What's left is a reshuffle, completing its legalisation in the shuffling process, completing the optimal moral combination, regaining a legal and reasonable political stance, silently con***ling the so-called new demo****** politics. This is an almost surefire situation that is about to happen.
23.8.2009, 21:26:09

The censored sentence should read 'silently controlling the so-called new democratic politics'.

@aiww This is why we can put our hopes on the internet. Only when we put one person's emotions and values together with everyone else's emotions and values, to grow at the same time and in the same place, can substantial kindness form. Only this kindness can battle against the omnipresent evil and win.
24.8.2009, 03:28:47

@aiww My success lies in my persistent use of the human viewpoint to see and treat everything, using human emotions to explain the relationship between you and me, even though I'm also a fairy.
24.8.2009, 22:12:18

@aiww We live in a ** system that needs to be cursed; we need to curse it furiously, and it must die before our eyes. Otherwise, there's absolutely no real happiness to speak of.
27.8.2009, 08:37:43

The censored word is probably 'despotic'.

@aiww One day, the world that surrounds you and makes you unhappy will die away. It withers away only because of your attitude and your unconscious bits of speech and actions. Can you begin to get excited about this?
28.8.2009, 08:25:28

@aiww If it could be said that what happened 20 years ago was a massacre of the students' bodies, then the celebrations prepared this time are yet another blasphemy against the students' souls. Trampling and twisting facts and truths eventually turns a generation of people into idiots. Regarding these 10,000 brain-damaged people, it's already an extraordinary performance for them to be able to get organised and march in a square.
29.8.2009, 08:41:51

'What happened 20 years ago' refers to the Tiananmen Massacre on 4 June 1989. The 'celebrations prepared this time' refers to the closing ceremony of the Beijing Olympics.

@aiww Every time we're delighted by our microblogs, it's one count of death for des/potism and totalitarian power.
3.9.2009, 08:45:53

The forward slash is not a typo but another tactic to avoid the term being filtered on the internet.

@aiww Gods, when you see fear in the eyes of your enemies, when they can no longer look you straight in the eye, but only pass you with their heads down, pretending nothing has happened, do you feel depressed by having an enemy like that?
5.9.2009, 08:04:28

@aiww Choices to make in the morning: 1. To be a part of life or a part of death 2. To want truths or to want lies 3. To be happy or to be rotten 4. To love or to be abandoned 5. To be wise or to be brain-damaged 6. To smile or to be humiliated 7. To condemn or to celebrate 8. To have more courage or to have more fear 9. Zuosa or Sina 10. To have free/dom or to be imprisoned.
5.9.2009, 08:50:36

Zuosa and Sina are both microblogging sites in China. It is interesting to note that Ai Weiwei does not call Sina by its official name, which means 'new wave'; he plays with homophones and calls it 'stinky waves'.

@aiww Imagine that this body of crime finally collapses in a field of keyboard-hitting sounds. It's your disdain that has easily ended a time of terror, ended the humiliation of mankind.
.9.2009, 10:37:20

@aiww Shouldn't a boy know what a girl likes; shouldn't an artist know what his people need? If art cannot be used, then it's rubbish.
5.9.2009, 11:05:50

@aiww In China, 320 people die every day through [lack of] work safety. 15,000 people die every year through industrial injuries and accidents. All these injuries and deaths are silently continuing and spreading across the entire society. Injustice and unrighteousness are maintained with the silent approval of all the people.
11.9.2009, 18:35:35

@aiww Will the Shanghai government apologise to the people that it has cheated? If an apology is behaviour between one human and another human, then clearly it will not. In the eyes of the government, those who are cheated are not humans but slaves, and the government sees itself as God; only this can explain the arrogance and carelessness of totalitarian power.
26.10.2009, 23:35:08

@aiww About the visit of the Americans: established power structures have all to varying extents betrayed the ideals of mankind. There's no nationality to pretentiousness, but transactions are forever. All you need to prepare are flat tiles.
3.11.2009, 19:23:22

In a northern Chinese dialect, 'flat tile' refers to a large, coarse wall tile. The term has been adapted in internet forums to refer to verbal battles and debates. Each back and forth between forum users is called 'hitting a tile'.

@aiww The careful and cautious Obama has allegedly said he's coming to the Sky Dynasty. Hopefully, this kid will not be blurry on the question of human ****** for the temporary benefit of the United States. A leader without a firm belief in human rights and humanity would be a disaster, regardless of where he came from.
3.11.2009, 16:28:10

The Sky Dynasty refers to the Chinese Communist Party; it is a metaphor suggesting that the party has progressed little since the dynasty era.

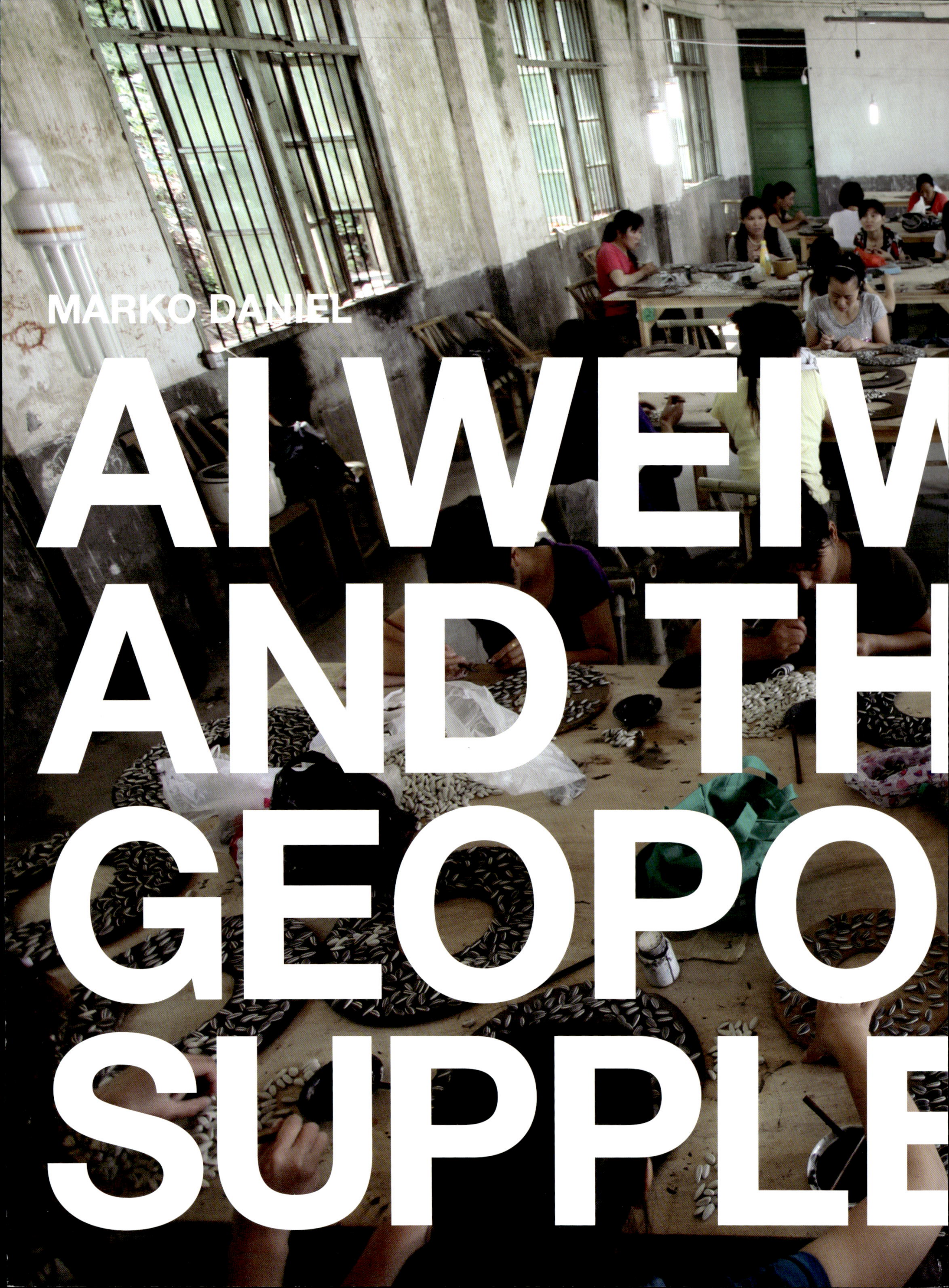
MARKO DANIEL
AI WEIW
AND TH
GEOPO
SUPPLE

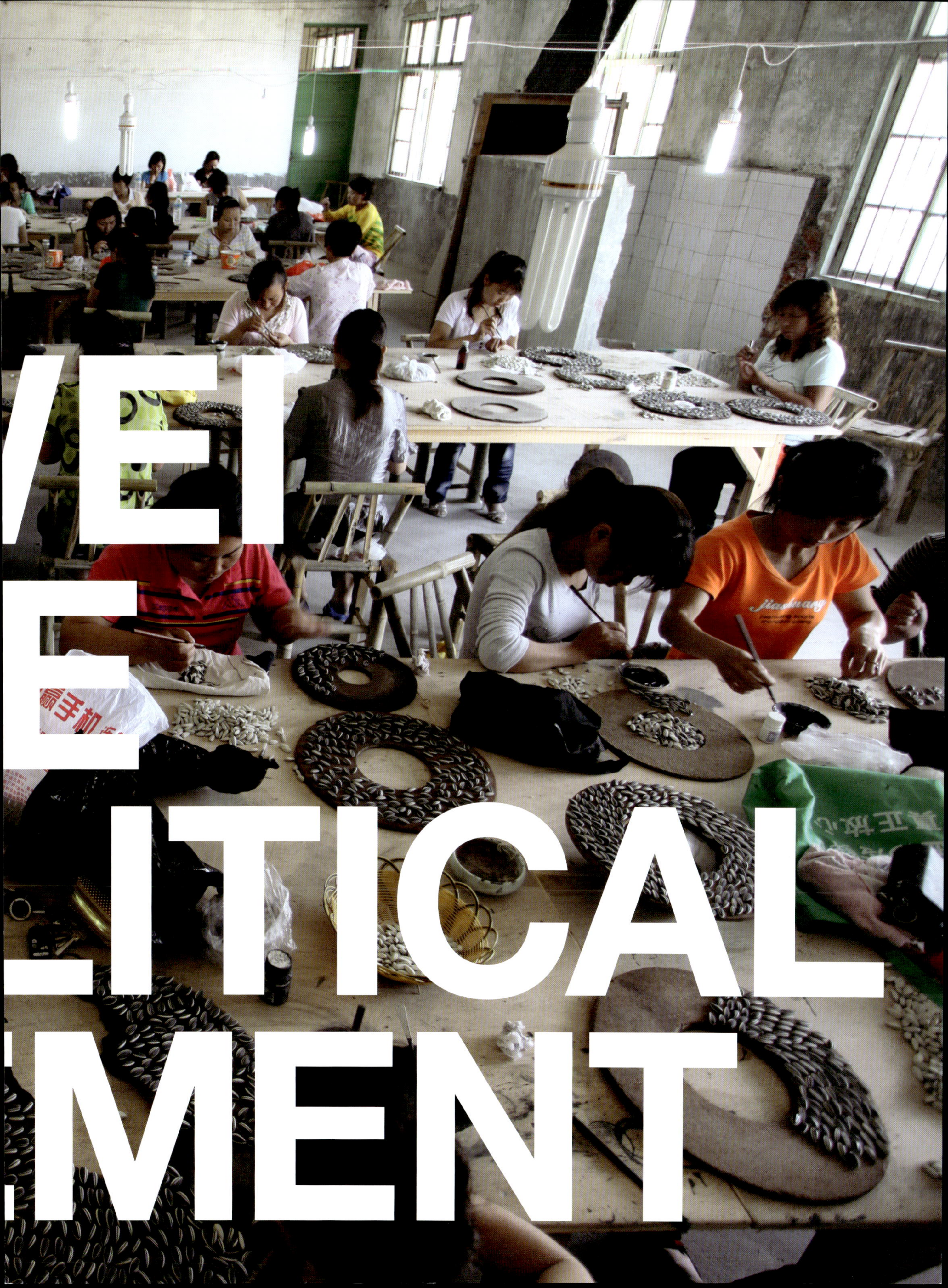

VEI
E
LITICAL
MENT

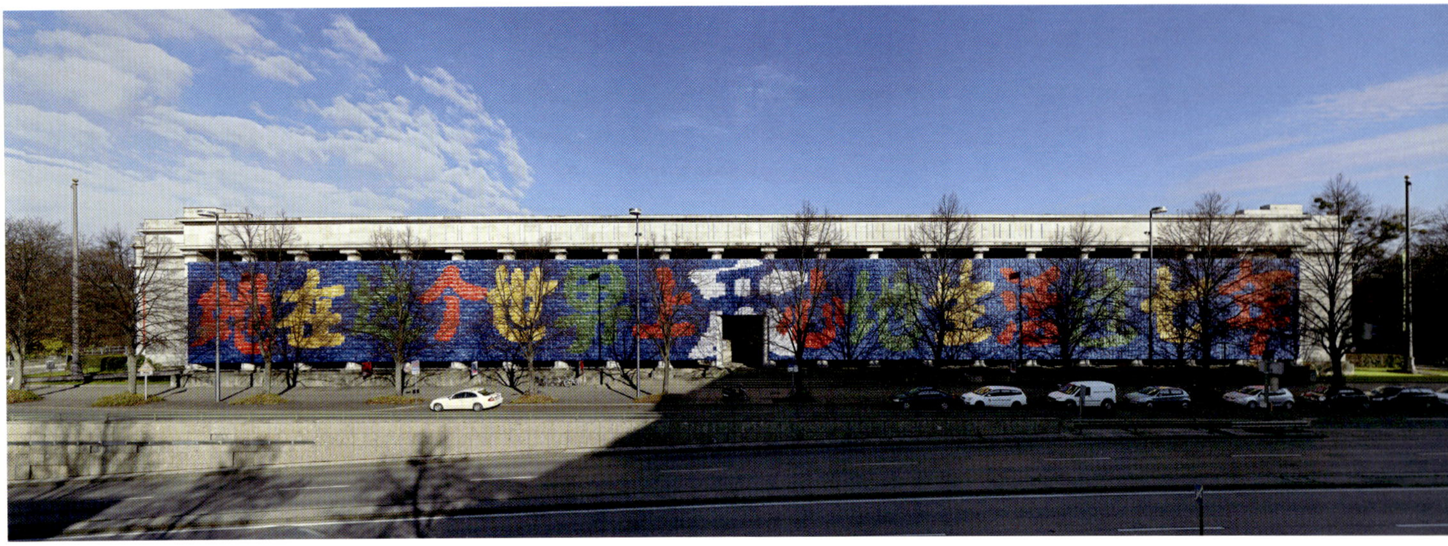

Over the last few years, Ai Weiwei has successfully carried out a number of spectacular projects that have cemented his unique position in the art world, both within China and internationally. Few visual artists can count among their works activities as diverse and ambitious as contributing to the design of the National Olympic Stadium in Beijing (the 'Bird's Nest') (fig.38) or *Fairytale* (fig.37) for which he took 1,001 Chinese people and the same number of antique chairs to Documenta 12 in Kassel, Germany. Then, in 2009, he covered the facade of the Haus der Kunst in Munich with 9,000 backpacks spelling out a pixelated lament for the schoolchildren who had died in the Sichuan earthquake a year earlier ('She lived happily for seven years in this world'; *Remembering*, fig.36). In the aftermath of that catastrophe, Ai was instrumental in a protest campaign to highlight the corruption that led to inadequately built schools collapsing while other buildings around them remained relatively undamaged.

36
Remembering 2009
Backpacks and metal structure
920 x 10605 cm
Installation on facade of Haus der Kunst, Munich 2009
(Photo: Jens Weber)

Gathering the names of these victims and publishing them on his blog gained Ai more recognition in China than any of his previous activities. More recognition, but also trouble: the blog, one of the most popular in China, was closed down on 28 May 2009 and Ai, who was beaten by police when he went to testify on behalf of an activist[1] in Chengdu, Sichuan, later needed emergency hospital treatment for a potentially fatal cerebral haemorrhage. At the time, Ai was in Munich, where he was preparing *So Sorry*, his exhibition at the Haus der Kunst. In his own Twitter coverage from hospital, the artist calmly looked at the camera while blood seeped from his cranium into a draining bag on his bed (fig.39). The international headlines following his hospitalisation contributed to the 'almost hysterical interest' in him as artist, but also, if not more so, as an intellectual and a social and political commentator.[2] And rarely has an artist been more willing to communicate. Ai spends hours every day online interacting with followers on Twitter and by email, in addition to the face-to-face interviews he ceaselessly gives to news media or specialist art publications for every project in which he is engaged.

Given Ai's remarkable range of approaches to art, one of the most striking aspects of the reception of his work in the West has been the emphasis on Chineseness in critical discussion, both of his more object-based artworks and his other interventions. This essay will briefly explore the persistence of this strategy or habit and its implications for our understanding of Ai's art.

Previous spread:
Production of sunflower seeds in Jingdezhen, southern China, 2010

In many ways, the critical approach to Ai's work mirrors the reception of contemporary art from China more widely. Precedents were set with the first wave of Chinese artists to make an international impact, in particular the painters of 'cynical realism' and 'political pop' in the early 1990s. Their ironic if politically ambiguous use of 'detourned' Mao memorabilia and Socialist Realist kitsch not only used the language of Pop art as an imported ingredient in their stylishly ambivalent mix, but also spoke directly to Western collectors and critics. In this, they were expertly capitalist, supplying a product that met or generated a keen demand in the West. Partly, this demand was due to the marketable qualities of the works (paintings, made just as the 1980s painting boom in America and Europe was petering out), and partly to the way in which they confirmed Western expectations. Here, it was felt, were artists who criticised the regime from the inside, mocking both the restrictive pressures of the Cultural Revolution and the newly introduced capitalist market reforms that led to a rampant commodity culture and increasing social inequality. What made this so

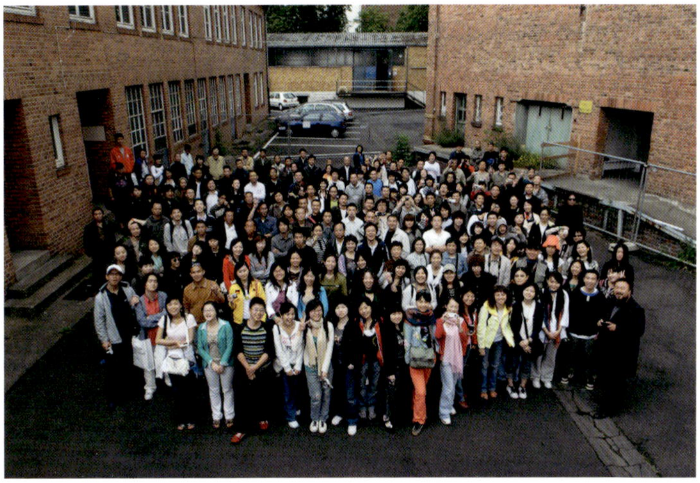

37
Fairytale 2007
1,001 Chinese visitors in Kassel
Project for Documenta 12, Kassel, Germany 2007

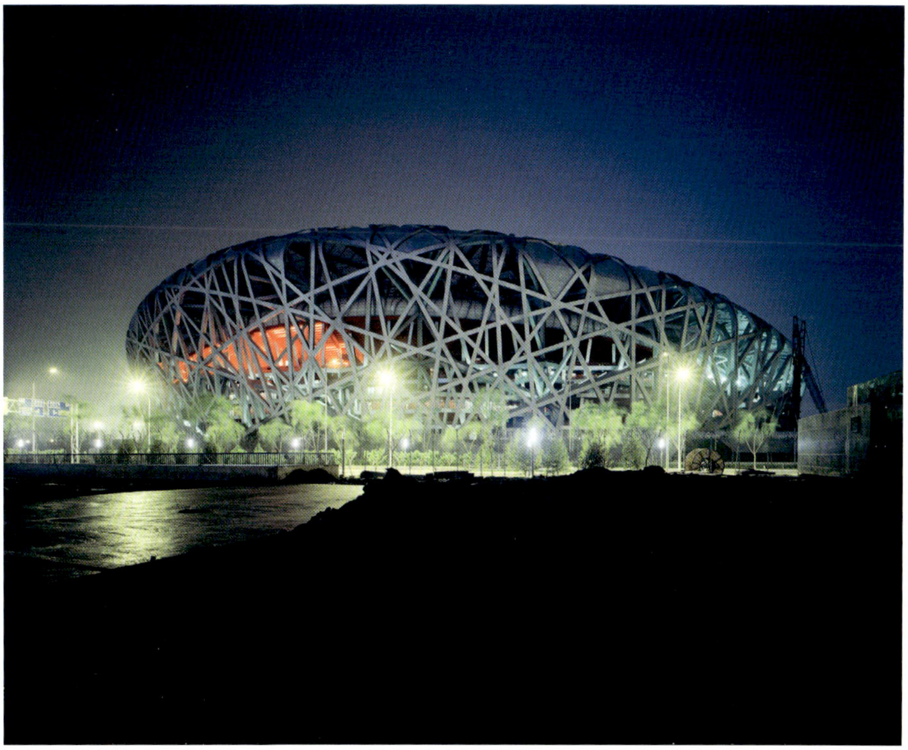

38
Beijing's 2008 Olympic Stadium ('Bird's Nest')

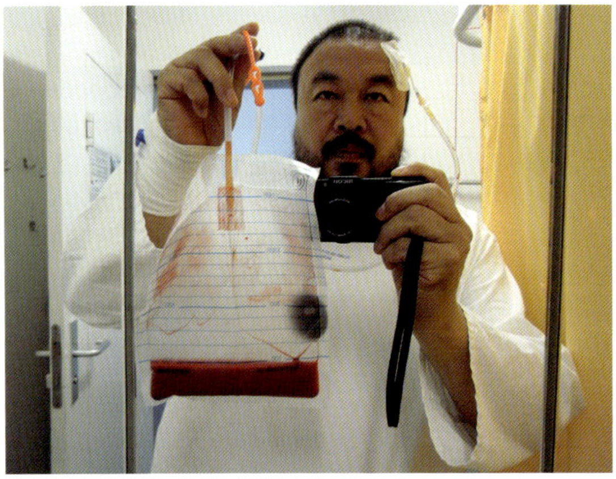

39
Portrait of Ai Weiwei in hospital, Munich, September 2009

problematic was the simplistic assumption that this was an endorsement of 'West is best' rather than the realisation that their stance was a manifestation of the implicit criticality of intellectuals taking issue with authority in all shapes and forms – while at the same time delivering goods for export. 'Pandering to the West', incidentally, is a criticism that has also been levied against these artists from traditionalists in China. Ultimately, then, they came to be seen not as representative of a particular art movement, but as helping to construct a particular vision of China as a whole: one that comfortingly suggested that despite the inexorable rise of its economy the country struggled to free itself from the yoke of old-fashioned Communist values, and remained socially and politically behind the times; but above all, that it remained ideologically packaged.

One can put a positive spin on this approach and acknowledge the fact that such readings provide a way into the art of China, particularly into what makes contemporary art in China distinctive. However, I am more concerned that the inherent essentialism of such a position functions as a screen: as if by identifying the Chineseness of a given work of art one has pointed to its true meaning, and this grander narrative then masks all else. A little sprinkling of references to Pop art or Coca-Cola among the massed ranks of young pioneers raise a chuckle precisely because of their perceived dissonance. Even ironically emphasising that this is now the real thing, present-day China in all its red capitalist glory, all too easily turns the entire work into a token of this vision of China.

If this was the fate of the painters of the 1990s, I argue that the reception of Ai's work, perhaps even of Ai as a person, in the West needs to be rescued from a fancier version of the same. All that has changed is that the artistic references are acknowledged to be more sophisticated. Ai tends to appeal to the phenomenal wealth of China's pre-communist art and craft (more on this later) while his references to Western art history focus only on the finest. Marcel Duchamp and Andy Warhol are his acknowledged masters and his works introduce touches of Minimalism's sparse elegance and repetition together with references to more socially engaged practice. Joseph Beuys springs to mind, not least because of the artist's explicit political discourse. But admiration for Ai's outspoken stance on social injustice, the thought that here at last is an artist and intellectual who actively criticises what is wrong in China, easily sits alongside deeply held, generalised assumptions about China. It contains an element of fear of global power shifts, fear of the much-noted extent and speed of modernisation, industrialisation and wealth creation in China. It becomes not just a critique of the undoubtedly negative local consequences that these changes have on social cohesion, freedom of expression and the environment over there but also a lament that, as China has become the second biggest economy in the world,[3] things will change in unpredictable ways over here.

This critique of the concept of Chineseness is indebted to Edward Said's thoughts on Orientalism. In his Afterword of 1995 he declared that he had 'no interest in, much less capacity for, showing what the true Orient or Islam really are'.[4] The same applies to Chineseness: it is not so much that the notions of Chineseness underpinning critical writing on Ai and contemporary Chinese art in general are insufficiently clear, but rather that they 'correspond to no stable reality that exists as a natural fact. Moreover, all such geographical designations are an odd combination of the empirical and imaginative ... The idea derives to a great extent from the impulse not simply to describe, but also to dominate and somehow defend against it.'[5] This emphasis on power structures and the relationships between them as they attempt to maintain or establish hegemony over one another is crucial, as is the mutuality inherent in the very construction of the concepts 'West' and 'China'. 'Each age and society recreates its "Others",' Said wrote,[6] and today for us this means China. Uli Sigg, a China expert and pioneering collector, acknowledged that with respect to contemporary Chinese art it was 'extraordinarily difficult to capture this dimension conceptually',[7] though I would argue that it is not so much a problem of the degree of difficulty as of the fundamental way in which one asks one's questions. Cultural critic Rey Chow identified this as the 'ethnic supplement': 'The collective habit of supplementing every major world trend with the notion of "Chinese" is the result of an overdetermining series of historical factors, the most crucial of which is the lingering, pervasive hegemony of Western culture.'[8]

The late Slovenian curator and writer Igor Zabel encapsulated this dilemma in clear and simple terms: 'In Russia … being a "contemporary artist" means to represent Western culture … In the West, on the other hand, a Russian artist must inevitably represent Russia.'[9] Tellingly, he also drew attention to the fact that this cultural traffic inevitably flows in both directions. Taken together, the above analysis sets out how the concepts of China and the West mutually reinforce each other's separateness and their own respective essentialism.

Ai, who left Beijing promising to turn into a Chinese Picasso, discovered Duchamp and Warhol in New York. *The Philosophy of Andy Warhol* was, by his own admission, the first book in English he read,[10] and among the many thousands of photos he took in New York, there is one of him carefully adopting Warhol's pose, as if testing out his role model's invariably cool attitude (fig.41). Ai's New York homage to Duchamp suitably took the form of an assisted readymade: a simple wire coat hanger bent into the outline of Duchamp's face (fig.40). With these two towering figures of twentieth-century art, Ai chose role models whose relevance is not restricted to any objects they produced or put forward as art, but at least as much due to their working practices and ways of thinking.

The twelve years he spent in New York were not easy. After outstaying his student visa, he only obtained his residency permit towards the end of his stay in an amnesty following the Tiananmen protests, and spent much of his time working in odd jobs and hanging out with friends and fellow Chinese artists and intellectuals. Thinking about life and art mattered most, particularly given how different the climate in New York at the time was from what he had experienced in China.

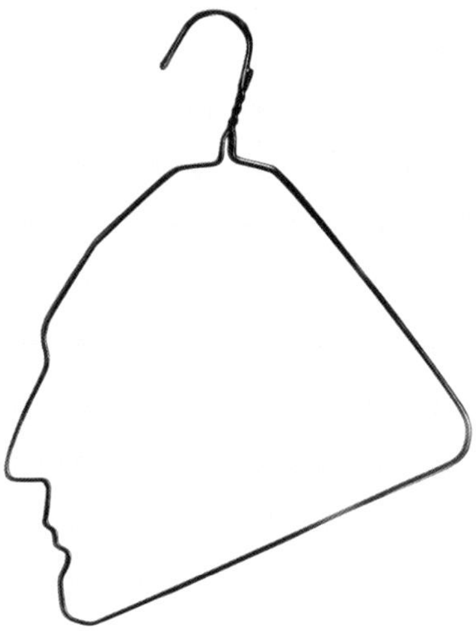

40
Hanging Man 1983
Clothes hanger 39 x 28 cm

41
Portrait of Ai Weiwei adopting pose by Andy Warhol at the Museum of Modern Art, New York 1987, from *New York Photographs, 1983–1993*

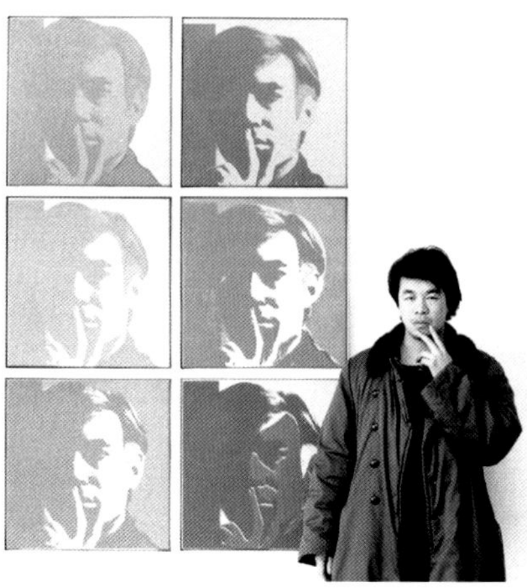

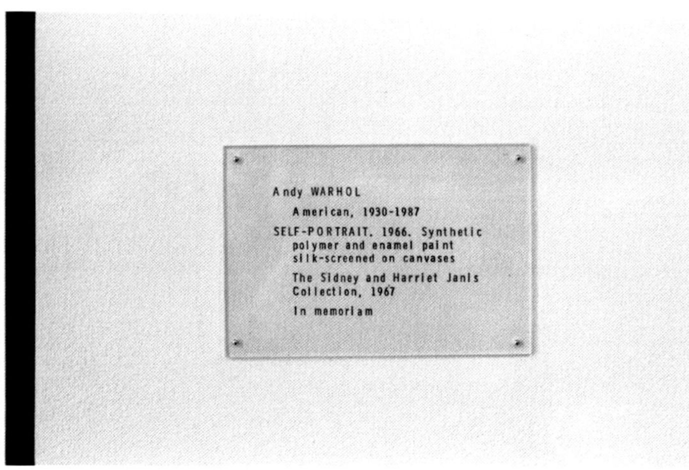

> Duchamp showed me a way not just out of my personal catastrophe but out of the cruel reality of New York with its materialism, its appalling art and culture business. Duchamp showed me another possibility, ie that art can be a way of life … Duchamp showed that art is engaging with the idea that in life there is always more than one way of doing things. He made it clear that the freedom of mind one develops through thinking is much more important than the form of expression.[11]

Ai thus found in Duchamp an alternative not just to the commercialism of American culture in general but specifically to the then virtually uncontested reign of the material object in the art world.

Without entirely dismissing the object, however, Ai shifted his attention to the 'potentiality of objects' and not only claimed Duchamp as the figure single-handedly responsible for all subsequent developments in art, but, in an intriguing reversal of the traditionally posited direction of traffic of ideas from the West to China, claimed Duchamp as being more at home in Daoism than in Western culture: 'Duchamp's success was the moment of enlightenment when he saw that art was a part of life. I see him as a kind of Daoist – although I don't know exactly what Daoism means – or a kind of mutation in Western contemporary art. Everything that came after him is ultimately caused by him.'[12] Ai is here playing an interesting game with his own biography and with the traditional conventions of cultural apprenticeship by, as it were, attempting to rescue Duchamp from Western discourse. Thus his frequent comments about choosing Warhol and Duchamp as his masters are balanced by counter-assertions to the effect that he did not leave Beijing for art's sake at all, but rather to escape political repression: 'Precisely because the

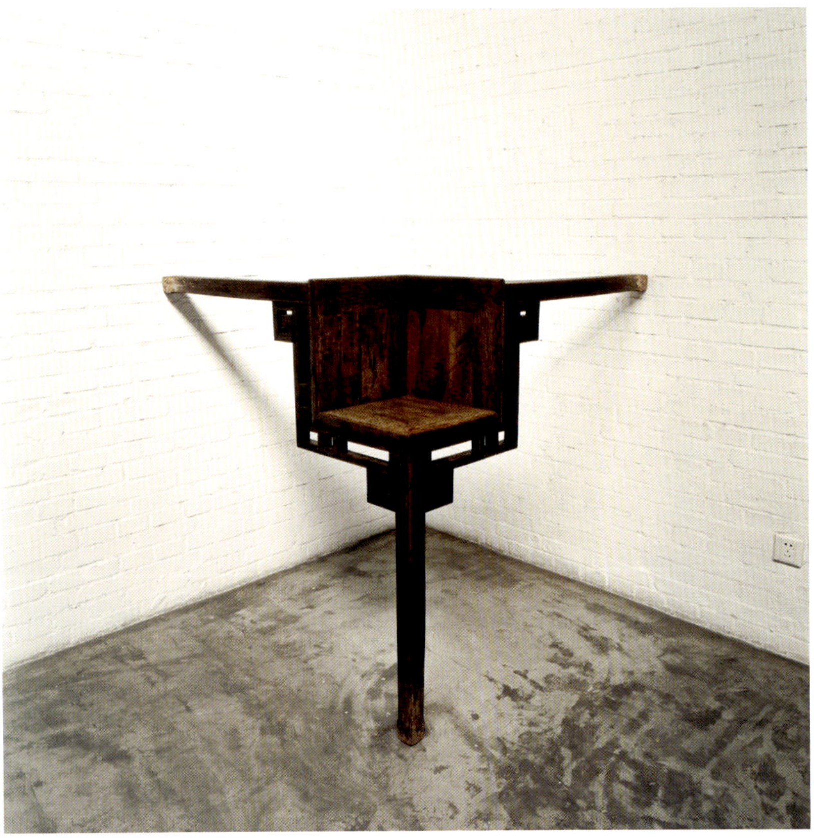

42
Table with Three Legs 2009
Table from the Qing dynasty (1644–1911) 120 x 120 x 120 cm

43
Two joined Square Tables 2005
Tables from the Qing dynasty (1644–1911) 136 x 168 x 92 cm

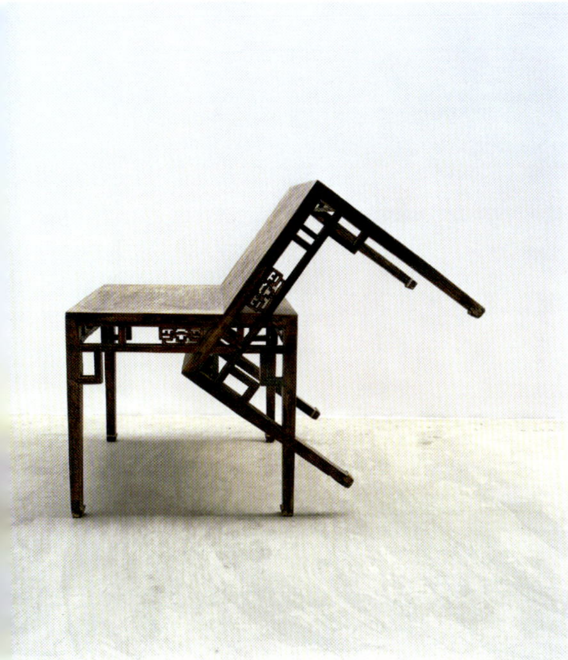

USA was called China's greatest enemy, it had the greatest attraction … My desire to go to New York had less to do with my interest in art than with my love of freedom.'[13] For 'greatest enemy' here one should also read 'greatest rival'. The USA not only promised individualism and freedom of expression but also the greatest provocation and challenge to a young artist.

Similarly, when talking about his views on European modernism, Ai has said that Dada and Surrealism were interesting 'because they placed culture in a larger perspective and so much related to what has happened in the world scientifically, culturally and politically. This also attracted me to Conceptual art which appeared clear-minded in its perspective as well as having a great deal of humour. Through this kind of work, I saw art in a very different perspective.'[14]

In all of these comments on what attracts him in Western art, Ai consistently remarks on non-aesthetic values, on the conceptual dimension and on the inseparability of art and life. Thus his assertion of being interested in the USA for political reasons rather than artistic puts forward a dichotomy that resolves itself in his very understanding of what art and politics are. Furthermore, despite readings that foreground the 'ethnic supplement' in his work, he himself gives short shrift to claims of a fundamental difference between East and West, pointedly denying the existence of geopolitically inflected art per se: 'There are no differences in art and thus Western and Chinese art are equal. Differences only come into play by virtue of the fact that all art is a way of seeing the world, a personal view, representing tradition and much more.'[15] Equally pointedly, he has said that while in New York he neither felt connected with the art scene there nor with the collections of traditional Chinese art in New York's major museums,[16] again emphasising his individualist stance.

So what is one to make of Ai's ongoing use of some of the most characteristically 'Chinese' forms of traditional art and craft? Once he started working with specialised craftsmen, there was one immediate clear consequence: by instructing these highly skilled workers to produce objects of the best quality and in accordance with their respective traditions, he relinquished a certain amount of control over the object, even though he invariably made the workers push beyond the norms and expectations of the established parameters of their respective crafts. Most crucially, the finished objects almost entirely lacked gesture. The perfection of expertly applied traditional skills means that the objects deny more romantic readings associated with the trace of the artist's hand. This coolness harks back to his discovery, through the art of Duchamp and Jasper Johns, of the value of appreciating emotional detachment or indifference in art, foregrounding rational thinking over the expression of emotion.[17] But while Warhol's Factory seems almost amateurishly artisanal compared with the operations overseen by Ai today, it would be wrong to see the furniture pieces, for example, as devoid of subtlety. Take a work like *Table with Three Legs* 2009 (fig.42). At first glance, it is the high polish of the re-crafted top that makes the piece look most authentic: a seamless joint between the distinct parts merged into one using perfect craftsmanship. Yet this rich, dark sheen of the polished surface is of course the most recent trace, furthest away from the grey, dry, worn and scuffed lower legs that initially attract less attention but bear witness to the previous, functional lives of the objects.

Ai's series *Map of China* 2003 (fig.21) perhaps shows most fully the complexity of the interplay between concept, process and object. The work is literally what the title suggests: a giant map of China. Lengths of ironwood timber reclaimed from Qing dynasty temples were joined together to form this carefully crafted assembly. Charles

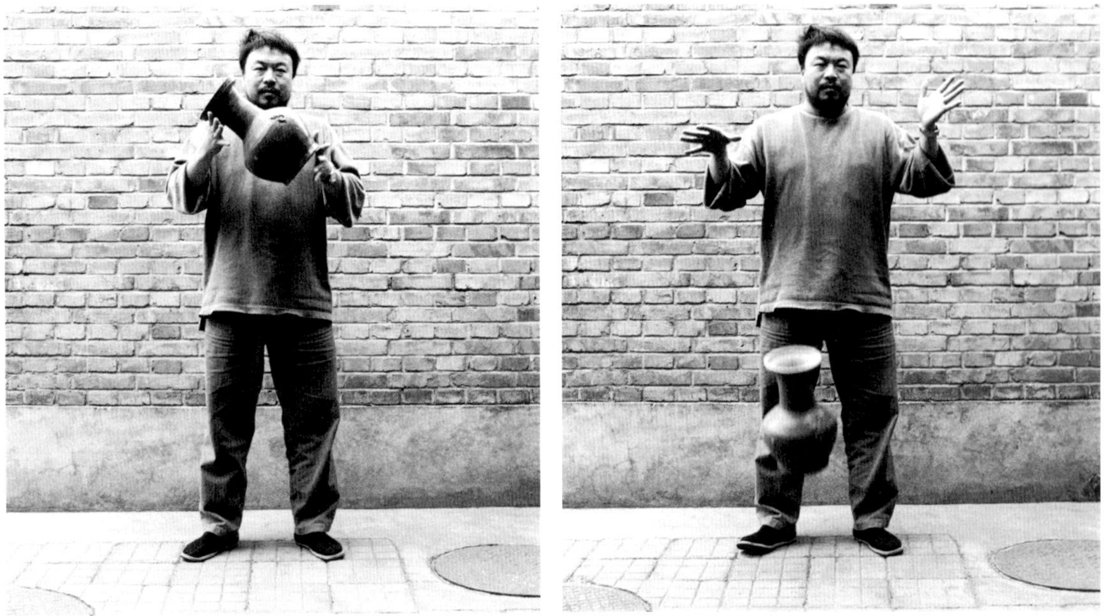

44
Dropping a Han Dynasty Urn 1995
Black and white photographs,
triptych, each 148 x 121 cm

Merewether argued that this slow process of binding together what looks like a single block of wood out of these many components could be construed as symbolic of the heterogeneity lurking beneath China's apparent monolithic cohesion. 'By making the map in this manner, the importance of the process of its construction – to make it appear a coherent whole – becomes apparent.'[18] A similar point was also put forward by Philip Tinari:

> *The Map of China* works announce and declare, but also limit and demarcate, the extent of China as a physical entity. In that way they represent an admission of the primacy of the state and its government in defining the more abstract notion of 'China', but also a sarcastic circumscription in which the nation is taken as nothing less, and nothing more, than its legal outline.[19]

The island of Taiwan, standing like an extruded dollop of timber next to the mass of the mainland, looks rather wobbly and unstable.

Ai has said the map itself was meaningless to him, but that he was intrigued to learn from the carpenter that would it take a year to make, and his comments also suggest that such a symbolically overdetermined shape leaks meaning even when it is claimed to be an empty gesture.

> This destroyed my original thinking about making the piece. The scale and process involved in making the object suddenly overwhelmed an otherwise meaningless gesture. The process itself is like putting together a puzzle. Not one piece is the same, they are all different so it's not simply a matter of putting together a square. All joints are made according to each specific shape. To make a few pieces join together has to be done individually. No one uses this process anymore because it goes against industrial processes of production. Yet, neither can it be duplicated because the piece and its components are so specific. The major problem was to resolve how to hold together a hundred pieces tightly and precisely. The map is just the shape of it.[20]

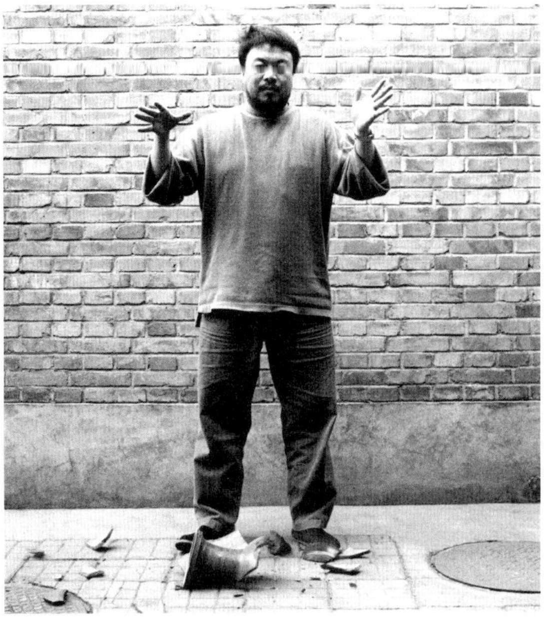

Clearly there is incontrovertible Chineseness right at the forefront of this work: the map itself, the solidity of its shape and the use of salvaged wood from – what could be more appropriate? – Chinese temples. Yet the special high-quality hardwood for these temples had itself originally been imported from South-East Asia, thus further confusing any simple sense of national identity in the map. And Ai's comments about the meaninglessness of the gesture, his emphasis on the process of construction and the fact that, as he put it, no one does this any more, lead one to see this object as a much more nuanced intervention rather than a bold assertion of 'sinochauvinism', as Rey Chow termed the mobilisation of a proudly nationalist trend among young intellectuals.[21]

Ai started working with explicitly Chinese artifacts, originally on a much smaller scale, involving less acrobatic production, but conceptually no less challenging. He said he found inspiration for these works in that period of cultural and social readjustment when he returned to Beijing in 1993. Scouring antiques markets, he was struck by the number of fakes and copies of famous artefacts.

> But it was very difficult to tell the difference between the copy and the original. My brother is an expert in this field and he told me many stories about the very precise expertise and skills needed to make copies. To have a combination of such expertise is a most difficult task and everything must meet a certain requirement to become a reality. It's very ironical – every decision: the color of the glaze, the curves, the way of painting, even each brushstroke – all of this reflects a high degree of decision-making … It takes an expert to recognize it. Yet, all those judgments are not based on scientific principles so much as personal feelings.[22]

The fact that the expertise of original maker, copyist and scholarly expert overlap to such an extent was itself a revelation, particularly when it came to inserting his own work within these conventions. 'Once I asked a classical furniture expert in China to look at my table. He responded by saying that now today he understands better the craftsmanship of the original object.'[23] And this change of perspective is one of which Ai is proud.

But these works also put into question the concept of authenticity itself, perhaps nowhere more so than in his signature work *Dropping a Han Dynasty Urn* 1995, a series of three photographs showing Ai standing before a brick wall (fig.44). The images make up a great sequence: in the first, he is gently holding the eponymous urn at chest height. In the second, he has opened his hands and let go of the pot. In the third, broken shards litter the ground. His facial expression remains coolly blank throughout. How could Ai be so unconcerned? Discussion of this work features in every account of Ai's 'iconoclasm', as it is generally described.[24] Pauline Yao argued against seeing such works as 'iconoclastic gestures in which the artist, utilising icons deemed representative of Chinese traditional art and culture, is seen to be negating or rebelling against China's past', pointing out how they also have 'to do with questioning the authority these objects hold and who assigns them such authority'.[25] I, too, consider it misguided to think of these works as a denial of or attack on China or her past, but neither is *Dropping a Han Dynasty Urn*, for me, an academic intervention in discussions of authenticity. After all, the conditions of production under imperial rule in antiquity and the destructions of that heritage in the Cultural Revolution make these artefacts far from ideologically straightforward.

Questions as to whether the urn was 'real' or not have always been met with very strategic answers, as have questions about his motive. Thus he has described his action as 'not powerful', since the vase was merely in the grip of gravity: 'It's powerful only because someone thinks it's powerful and invests value in the object.'[26] More recently, he explicitly drew attention to his role in the work: 'People just can't release their hands and let gravity do the work. I never hesitated.'[27] This decisiveness is what makes his action so remarkable. The work of art with which we are dealing is after all not the disembodied fact of the destruction of an urn but, on the contrary, a series of photographs that focus not just on the object but on the artist, too. His presence is essential, both executing the action and bearing witness to it, but solemnly and without display of emotion. The photographs represent a record of this action, a record that provides its own physical and temporal distance and whose matter-of-factness is perfectly in keeping with Ai's expression. And let us not forget the role played by the title of the work: 'urn' is both a technical term and one that confers specific values and associations, no matter how humble the pot to which it is applied. It speaks of antiquity, of ritualistic uses in 'former times' irrespective of whether the pot is authentic. These connotations and the viewer's speculations about authenticity shatter at Ai's feet.

Clearly, though, Ai is toying with notions of identity and fully aware of the fact that most of the object-based work he has produced so far has ended up abroad, in exhibitions and collections, where questions of Chineseness are invariably asked about his work. While he has been credited with being one of the first artists to 'transcend the China pigeonhole',[28] the nature of his work means that ethnicity is a measure that keeps being applied. *Fairytale* was a perfect example. On the one hand, Ai himself played the intercultural exchange card, calling it a 'human readymade, a symbol for the relationship between East and West' and argued that 'because one does not speak the same language, communication is quite different. Difficult, yes, but possible.'[29] On the other hand, he consistently stated that the most important dimension of the work was how the 1,001 Chinese nationals, whose travel he arranged individually, experienced their stay in Kassel at Documenta 12. Most critics, though, loved to focus on that other dimension. 'A tremendous transcultural image-machine that shows us our own reflection in the eyes of the other' was the somewhat pompous but unerringly post-colonial angle of the *Frankfurter Allgemeine Zeitung*.[30] But *Fairytale* also received the almost comically ethnocentric complaint that it lacked visibility, since Ai's guests 'were indistinguishable from local residents, or the numerous curators and critics from China, Hong Kong, Singapore, and Taiwan visiting the exhibition. The exotic Other was neither different nor identifiable.'[31]

Without such spectacularly ambitious projects and the heated debates surrounding them, Ai would not have the status he enjoys now. Nor would he reach the same diverse audiences that follow him on Twitter and in the art world, which allow him to use his clout for the social and political engagement to which he is so committed. Art, he insists:

> can serve a social and political function in that it is independent and self-critical … This is the most important political attitude to have today, because governments, nations, political and economic institutions, as well as education, fashion all have powerful political goals and economic interests which normally dominate the major part of everyone's life. This applies whether you're Asian, American or European.'[32]

NOTES

1 Tan Zuoren, environmentalist and writer, who coined the expression 'tofu pulp' to refer to the shoddily built schools in Sichuan and set up the database of victims' names that Ai first published on his blog and then on Twitter.

2 'Man könnte meinen, Ai Weiwei habe Glück, dass China so böse zu ihm ist, denn hierzulande erregt er geradezu hysterisches Interesse', Alex Rühle, 'Ai Weiwei im Haus der Kunst – Der Pandabär der Kunstszene', *Süddeutsche Zeitung*, available at http://www.sueddeutsche.de/kultur/2.220/ai-weiwei-im-haus-der-kunst-der-pandabaer-der-kunstszene-1.36856. Accessed 4 August 2010. Google Trends, the ultimate measure of global celebrity, shows a rapid increase in search and news volume relating to Ai, beginning in early 2009 and continuing unabated, with the sharpest spike in autumn 2009 (http://www.google.com/trends?q=ai+weiwe).

3 Liu Li and Aaron Beck, 'China FDI Growth Drops; Sharp Slowdown Seen Temporary', *Wallstreet Journal* (http://online.wsj.com/article/SB100014240527487045541045754346820740 61318.html?mod=googlenews_wsj). Accessed 18 August 2010.

4 Edward W. Said, *Orientalism: Western Conceptions of the Orient*, London 2003.

5 Ibid., p.331.

6 Ibid., p.332.

7 Julia M. White, *Mahjong: Art, Film, and Change in China*, Berkeley, California 2008, p.19.

8 Rey Chow, 'On Chineseness as a Theoretical Problem', *boundary 2*, vol.25, no.3, Autumn 1998, pp.1–24.

9 Igor Zabel, 'We and the Others', in David Elliott and Bojana Pejic (eds.), *After the Wall: Art and Culture in Post-communist Europe*, exh.cat., Moderna Museet, Stockholm 1999, pp.110–13.

10 Jonathan Napack, 'Ai Weiwei', in Charles Merewether (ed.), *Ai Weiwei: Works: Beijing 1993–2003*, Beijing 2004, p.204.

11 Heinz-Norbert Jocks, 'Ai Weiwei: Was heißt Leben?', *Kunstforum International*, no.194, November–December 2008, p.233.

12 Ibid.

13 Ibid., p.237.

14 Charles Merewether and Ai Weiwei, 'Changing Perspective', in Merewether 2004, pp.19–35.

15 Jocks 2008, p.239.

16 Ibid., p.26.

17 Ibid., p.24.

18 Charles Merewether, 'At the Time', in Urs Meile (ed.), *Ai Weiwei: Works 2004–2007*, exh. cat., Galerie Urs Meile, Lucerne 2007, p.175.

19 Philip Tinari, 'Chairs and Visitors', ibid., p.9.

20 Merewether and Ai 2004, p.34.

21 Chow 1998, p.6.

22 Merewether and Ai 2004, p.29.

23 Ibid., p.30.

24 Charles Merewether, in particular, has given a detailed analysis of this work, as have Yao, Pakesch, Napack and many others.

25 Pauline J. Yao, 'Between Truth and Fiction: Notes on Fakes, Copies, and Authenticity in Contemporary Chinese Art', *Yishu: Journal of Contemporary Chinese Art*, vol.4, no.2, Summer/June 2005, p.20.

26 Merewether 2004, p.31.

27 David Piling, 'Lunch with the Financial Times: Ai Weiwei', *Financial Times*, 23 April 2010.

28 Karen Smith, 'Portrait of the Revolutionary as an Artist', in Karen Smith and Sue-An Van der Zijpp, *Ai Weiwei*, Rotterdam 2008, pp.12–17.

29 Ulrike Knöfel, 'Mit Gießkannen zur Kunst', *Der Spiegel*, no.25, 18 June 2007, p.187.

30 Niklas Maak, 'So wird die documenta 12-Ein Kurzführer', *Frankfurter Allgemeine Zeitung*, 16 June 2007.

31 Jo-Anne Birnie Danzker, 'documenta 12', *Yishu: Journal of Contemporary Chinese Art*, vol.6, no.3, Fall/September 2007, p.34.

32 Chin-Chin Yap and Ai Weiwei, 2004, 'Conversations', in Merewether 2004, pp.52–3.

@AIWW

@aiww In which sense can it be called a country? It established a strong army but despised and trampled the law that is open and fair; gathered thousands and thousands of ***ciples [disciples] but abandoned the common faith and wish of mankind; indulged in quick changes but suppressed the voices of freedom; owned the largest population but supported evil education and health-care systems; promoted extreme power and despotism but practised the organisation and behaviour of a mafia.
2009-11-09, 06:21:19

@aiww An awakening without action is just a way of being sly. Action is self-rescue; it is the most powerful meaning of life. – Ai Fart
9.11.2009, 16:24:23

@aiww Expressing its attitude towards a despotic totalitarian rule should be the responsibility of a large civilised country. Since all civilisations were to a certain extent built on other people's misfortune, Obama shouldn't play the role of a philanthropist; otherwise, I have to ask you, have you ever heard of the word 'pretentious'?
13.11.2009, 08:04:14

@aiww The Public Security Division was very serious in its investigation; [it lasted for] over three hours. This behaviour has proved that, for them, there is no moral or ethical bottom line. I'm not surprised. Allegedly, I was involved in a 'fraud'. I was overjoyed. At least they were sharing their honour with me.
19.11.2009, 05:07:14

The Twitter post refers to an investigation that the Public Security Bureau carried out on the financial standing of Ai Weiwei. Officers were sent to the Bank of China to check the transactions in and out of Ai Weiwei's bank account, and his family members also received phone calls. (Source in Chinese only: www.rfi.fr/actucn/articles/119/article_17578.asp)

@aiww What can they do to me? None other than exile, kidnap, imprisonment or fabricating a disappearance. They don't have any imagination or creativity, and they lack happiness and the ability to fly. Such a political group is a pity.
19.11.2009, 05:41:06

@aiww If you take up a burden, this world won't change; if you don't take up the burden, the world still won't change, but you will have changed.
2.12.2009, 04:01:4

@aiww Ask questions, because darkness cannot survive questioning. One day, you'll discover that the sky becomes bright because of questions.
2.12.2009, 04:19:16

In China, the sky is commonly used as a metaphor for righteousness, since it was believed that the gods lived in the skies.

@aiww In the end, answers belong to those who ask questions; power belongs to those who use power. Crimes need us to point out their hurtfulness and evil. The lack of choice on moral grounds is a mind-boggling aspect of living nowadays.
2.12.2009, 04:28:10

@aiww If everyone was concerned about AIDS, then Dr Gao Yaojie wouldn't need to drift about overseas at over 80 years of age. Anyone who thinks that the government's transparency, openness and fairness, as well as that the people's right to know and to supervise is absolutely necessary, should apply for the publication of information on 512. Don't give up the rights that belong to you.
2.12.2009, 19:32:06

Gao Yaojie was an AIDS activist who campaigned against selling blood contaminated with AIDS and was active in AIDS prevention. Because of her work, she spent time under house arrest for subversion of state power. 512 refers to the earthquake that began in Sichuan on 12 May 2008.

@aiww I will return; this is my place. Because of that, I have nothing to fear or worry about. Fear is not a part of me that I'd like to keep. My biggest concern is connected to those who are not concerned about me.
11.12.2009, 09:03:24

@aiww The disinterest, obliviousness, indifference and insensitivity of all the people is the societal ethical basis that provided the opportunity for the crime of 'subversion of state power' to be implemented.
11.12.2009, 16:03:06

@aiww Everything here came very easily; it must be because my compromise produced arrogance for the despotic totalitarian power.
11.12.2009, 16:33:58

Here, 'everything' refers to the general oppression that the Chinese people experience in their lives.

@aiww Sichuan: after the earthquake you refused to give out the names of the children who perished. From then on, my grief was inexpressible. Today, you refuse to say that dirty name of yours. My anger will inevitably turn into flames.
15.12.2009, 04:41:54

@aiww Today, Chinese people must be crazily uncooperative, so as to wash away the humiliation of several generations who have tolerated a violent despotic rule.
17.12.2009, 07:45:55

@aiww Violence on its own is not enough to build up fear. Fear comes from the common approval of heavy-handed power and the lack of sympathy for other people's pain. This is enough to suffocate anyone.
23.12.2009, 13:41:49

@aiww The rule of totalitarian power is a story about one's death. And this one happens to be yours.
25.12.2009, 17:25:00

@aiww My motherland, if I have to have one, would be the internet. She is enough to satisfy my imaginings about spaces and boundaries. All the other so-called countries – you can take them all.
29.12.2009, 14:44:39

@aiww The meaning of education is to make those who receive it become independent people.. Independence refers to a condition in which one has the capacity to have one's own feelings and self-expression. Civic education is about guiding people to participate in the maintenance and the burden of universal human values.
30.12.2009, 13:14:21

@aiww Twitter has made this world, one with the least hope, begin to have a temperature, hubbub, light and shadow, and the possibility to watch and listen.
1.1.2010, 10:25:01

@aiww Yardstick, oh yardstick, what kind of yardstick should I use to make you happy? This has always been a problem that bothers Han Han.
9.1.2010, 18:18:53

Han Han is a writer and rally driver whose controversial writings often become triggers for debate and censorship.

@aiww What I can see from the reality of Google's exit is a mix of tragedy and happiness. The winner knows about his win, but the loser doesn't know his loss. The glorious one knows his glory, but the shameful one doesn't know his shame. #GoogleCN
13.1.2010, 02:17:10

The post was written when Google announced its intended exit from the Chinese market, in reaction to censorship, by April 2010, a move that reportedly angered the Chinese government (nytimes.com/2010/01/13/world/asia/13beijing.html). Google has now successfully renewed its licence in China and has returned to the market (www.businessweek.com/news/2010-07-11/google-wins-renewal-of-its-china-license-xinhua-says.html).

@aiww Carbon dioxide and unknown gases spreading from the Chinese self-immolation campaign caused by the government's forced demolition have created an incalculable impact on the air quality and temperature change of the earth's surface.
14.1.2010, 15:55:26

@aiww Short-sighted people can only see the shortcomings of demolition and relocation, but are oblivious to the enormous profits and survival ethics produced by heavy-handed powers. The government's forced demolition is the most open, largest-scale and longest-lasting mafia crime in human history.
14.1.2010, 16:22:38

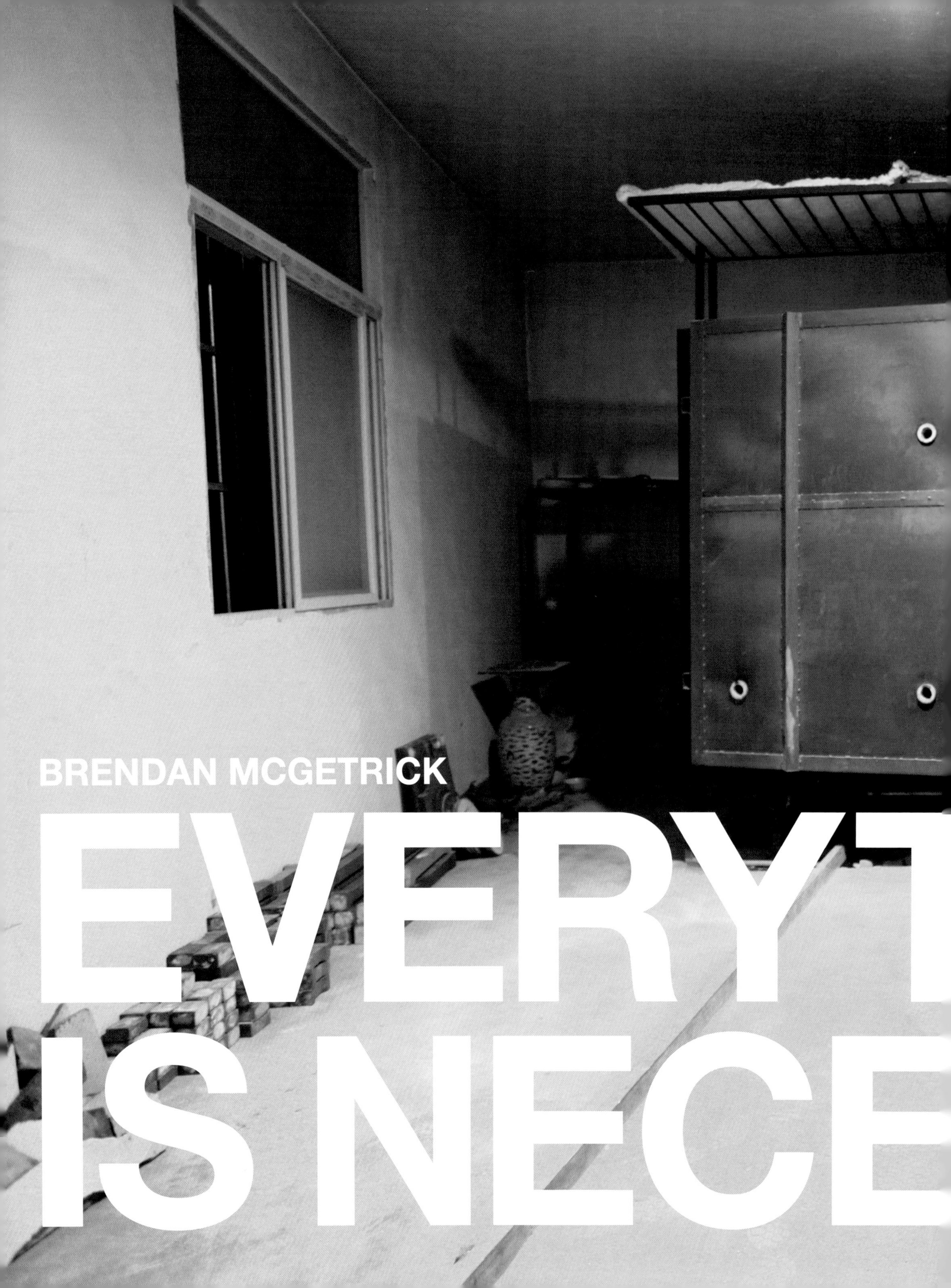

BRENDAN MCGETRICK

EVERYT
IS NECE

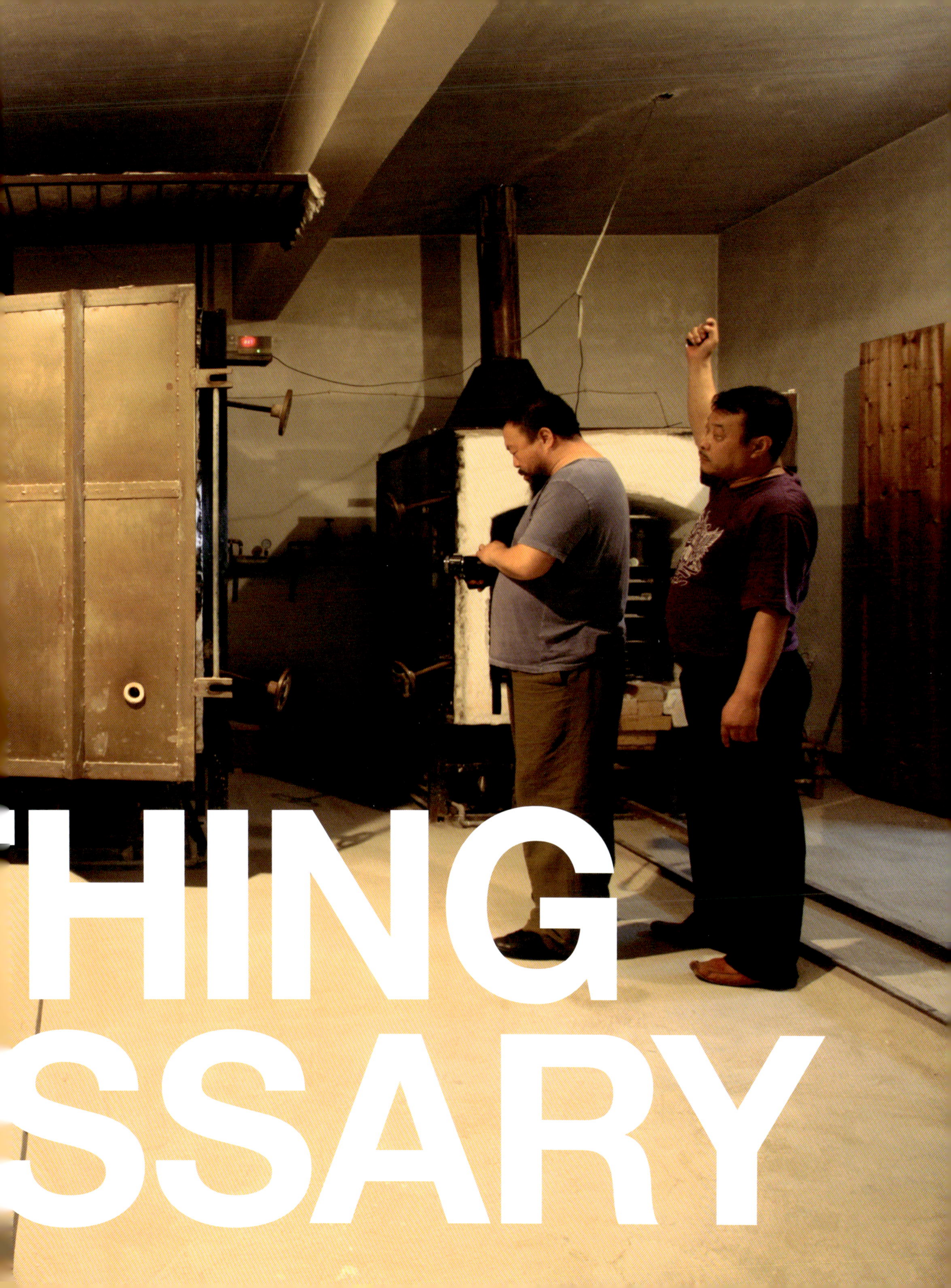
'HING
SSARY

I arrive at Ai Weiwei's studio on a weekday in June. It's a warm, uncharacteristically clear morning in Beijing and I find Ai sitting outside, in a T-shirt and shorts, with three young assistants. We exchange pleasantries and then the talk turns to business. I've been invited to write about a new work that Ai is developing. I know where it will show and when the show opens, but very little else.

What little I do know is based on a chance conversation I had weeks earlier with Inserk Yang, one of Ai's collaborators. He'd spoken about the work in impressive, unclear terms. It was a very, very big production, he'd said. That didn't surprise me. Ai has done some big projects in the past, and the venue seemed to demand a tribute of scale. When I asked what the content was, Inserk was cagey, but he gave a clue. 'It's not something,' he said, 'it's many things'.

Ai is more direct. Ceramic sunflower seeds, he says, 100 million of them, each handcrafted and spread across the floor of Tate's Turbine Hall like stones in a Zen garden. I'm not sure how to respond. Sunflower seeds. I search my thoughts for some personal associations and come up empty. But I know enough about Ai's work to see where they fit in. For years, he's been rendering commonplace objects in precious materials – coal hives in bronze, junk doors in marble, and watermelons, backscratchers and even urine in porcelain (figs.45–8). The sunflower seed is next in line. There must be a connection.

'I think it's interesting that you're not an art writer,' the artist says, 'you can talk about other things.' Like a commissioning editor, Ai begins offering possible angles: 'The social involvement is important', he comments. 'I like that the project involves so many people.' Then, 'It's made in a very traditional location.' Finally, 'Each piece seems identical, but they're all different.'

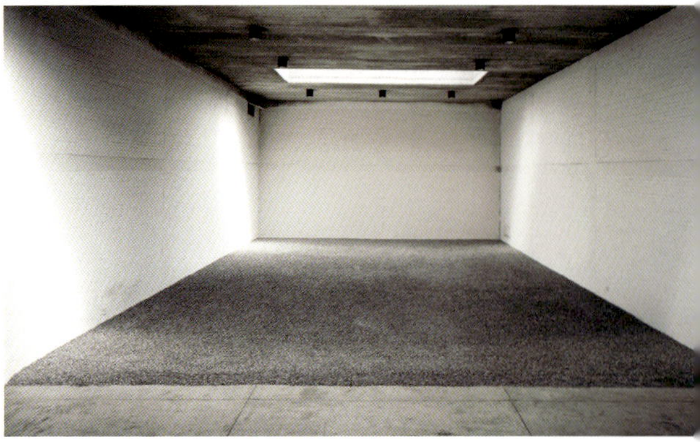

Sunflower seeds at Ai Weiwei's studio, 2009

Previous spread:
Ai Weiwei in Jingdezhen, southern China

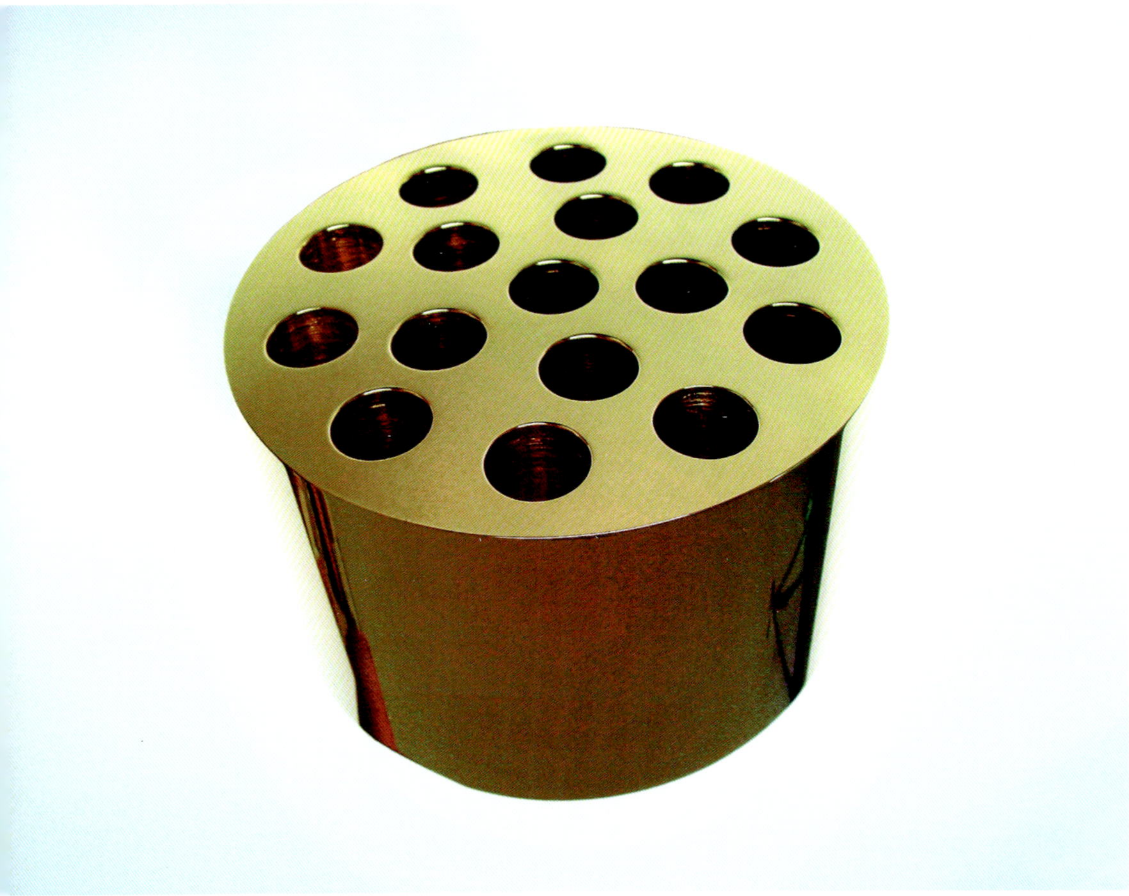

45
Coal Hives 2000 (detail)
Bronze, steel, and gold
8 x 12 cm (diameter)

We head inside to see a mock-up of the installation. I'm not sure what to expect. What I find is hard to describe. The floor is covered in an unidentifiable, granulated grey matter, about ten centimeters thick. I try to place its look, but again draw a blank. It doesn't look like seeds to me. From a distance, it appears totally generic, a kind of placeholder substance, something you might use to pave a driveway or line a coat.

We don't spend much time in the studio. After briefly stomping on the seeds, I accept the assignment and say goodbye.

I return to the studio a couple of days later. It's early morning and the place is mostly deserted, but Ai has been up for hours already. I find him at his computer, enthusiastically composing a Tweet. Beside him is a plastic bag with a few steamed dumplings inside. He hands it to me, and I watch him type.

I'm better informed this time. In the forty-eight hours since our last meeting, Inserk has sent me a PDF entitled '1 – 125,000,000'. It's an illuminating read – part proposal, part polemic, part memoir – penned by Ai in passionate, imperfect English and intended to explain the installation to its commissioners, envisaging a total of 125 million seeds.

'The times I grew up', it begins, '[the sunflower] was a common place symbol for the People, sunflower faces the trajectory of the red sun, so must the masses' feeling toward the communist party.' Beside the text are the lyrics to a children's song of the time:

When the Chairman goes past waving
Brilliant sunshine fills our breast ...

When the Chairman goes past waving
Countless sunflowers bloom towards the sun ...

Chairman Mao, Chairman Mao
You are the reddest red sun in our hearts!

I have a weakness for Cultural Revolution stories, so I decide to start our sunflower-seed discussion there. Ai obliges.

'When we grew up,' he says, 'the Communist society had a very limited vocabulary. We didn't have many images, besides the hammer and sickle, Chairman Mao's book ... probably ten images or less defined that time. Everywhere – in children's books, on posters and in newspapers – we saw the same images, and one of the most important was the idea that Chairman Mao is the sun and we're all sunflowers. The idea was to represent how loyal people should be during the Cultural Revolution. It's a very, very nice image.' I ask for more.

'Even in the remote part of Xinjiang Province where I grew up, if Chairman Mao uttered a new instruction from Beijing in the afternoon, by the next day we'd all wake up to the sounds of drums and cymbals, and people would march in the streets, shouting this new sentence. "We have to insist on class struggle!" or something like that. Then we'd dance and shout this slogan. It was very brutal.' Ai takes a bite of dumpling and offers the bag to me again. It's early still, and the office is empty, just us and an orange cat who is enthusiastically ripping up a sheet of newspaper by the door. Outside, several conversations are taking place and beyond that the clanging sound of construction. I ask how it felt to be a part of these events. 'As children we felt a kind of release of our pressure and anger,' he says. 'Because you could really yell out, even though you didn't know what it meant. It was a strange way of surviving.'

'After this slogan was announced, the commune would organise its own gathering, and everybody had to attend, from old to young.

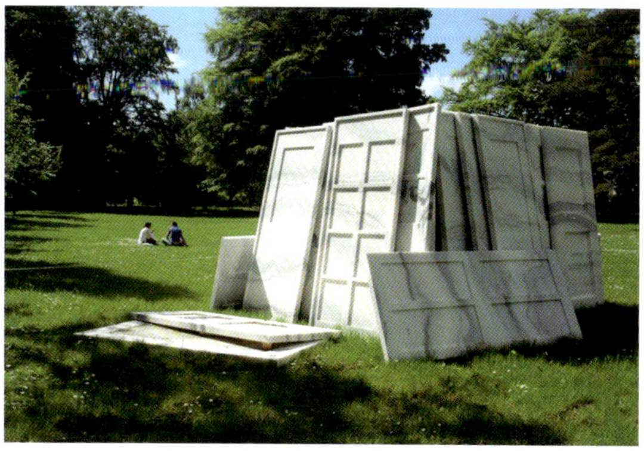

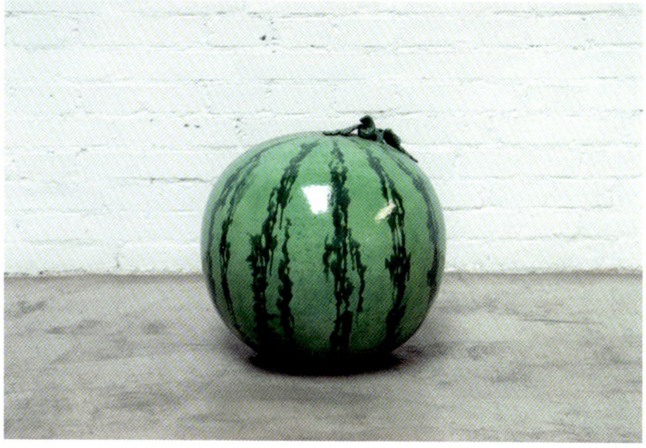

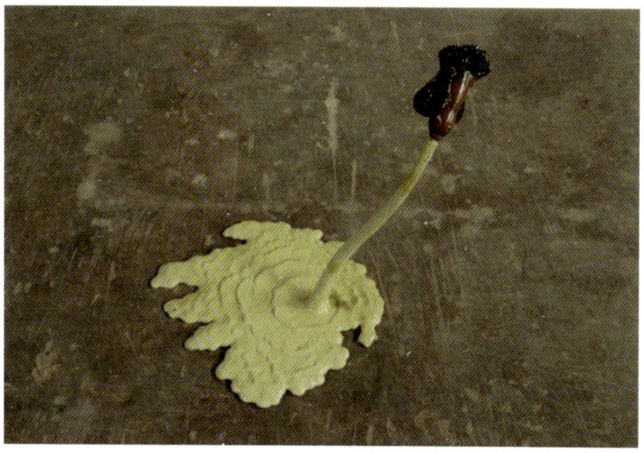

46
Monumental Junkyard 2006
Marble 40 pieces,
each 213 x 91 x 6 cm;
20 pieces, each 210 x 80 x 6 cm

47
Watermelons 2006 (detail)
Porcelain, each 44.5 x 38 cm (diameter)
(Photo: Glucksman Gallery)

48
Pee 2007
Porcelain 60 x 39 x 44.5 cm

Every commune had a big hall for this. Ours was empty, like a gallery, but huge and rough, made from red bricks. The floor was dirt, and there were no chairs, so everyone brought a stool from home. Then they'd sit down and start to eat sunflower seeds from their pockets.' He finishes his dumpling. 'Because they had to do something. Normally those meetings made everybody very nervous, because nobody knew what would happen. So people ate sunflower seeds and everybody would have a pile of shells in front of them and you could see immediately who was the most skilled, because their pile would be much bigger. My mother can eat them very quick. And her shells would be very clean, never cracked – like a bird.'

What were you doing during these meetings? 'The children would sit there watching the adults' activities. I normally felt very sleepy – sleepy mixed with scared. Because my father would always be singled out. They'd say, "OK, let's bring all the counterrevolutionaries onstage!" and some people would have to stand up and be insulted. There were ten to twelve people in the village like this. They were from the five bad categories: former landlords, rich peasants, counterrevolutionaries, bad elements and rightists. My father was a rightist. Those people are the enemies of the state and the people. And their children are also bad.'

All this he says with the detached, deadpan expression with which he often describes his work. But, as in his work, there seems to me so much smoldering beneath the flat surface of this anecdote. Within a single childhood memory, so much insight into the spirit of a time: the radical reduction of symbolism, the atmosphere of uncertainty, the threat of violence and frequency of celebration, the fervour and sanctimony, the deliberate opaqueness of the directives, providing their author plausible deniability and their enforcers maximum creative licence, the pseudo-statistical identification of five 'bad categories' and transfer of guilt to children. And somewhere within all this, the humble sunflower seed – snack, symbol and sedative.

'That's all they had', he says, and I'm not quite sure what he means. 'The seeds were the only little treasure they had.' He is speaking with objectivity but his tone has softened. 'Sunflower seeds were a part of conversation; it was a very natural act. On the train, on the bus, waiting for the bus, everywhere. Of course, at weddings and any celebration, you'd see them. You'd feel a natural connection eating them with someone.' One of Ai's assistants comes in with news of an upcoming appointment. I think I'm beginning to get it: during the Cultural Revolution, the sunflower seed was a kind of peace offering. In an atmosphere of pitched ideological struggle, it soothed and built intimacy. I begin to wonder if, despite its revolutionary symbolism, the sunflower didn't subvert Mao's fundamentalist programme, and whether the sharing of seeds wasn't a form of passive resistance – a way for would-be adversaries to acknowledge their common humanity, a subtle means for even the most zealous Maoist witchhunter to show compassion for a bad element like Ai Weiwei. 'But of course,' Ai continues, 'it was all unconscious. You wouldn't think about who'd passed them to you.' And there the conversation cuts off, overtaken by the artist's obligations. I pledge to return the next day to spend some time testing his mock-up.

When I arrive the next morning, the compound is already active. An antique dealer has laid out several pieces of Neolithic pottery in a column along the wall. A brown dog is inspecting a mound of bubble wrap by the front gate. Ai is conversing with a middle-aged man who is holding a life-sized replica of a surveillance camera carved out of marble. The artist orders a few adjustments, then leads me into his studio and onto his latest work.

I ignore the visual this time and focus on hearing. Each step produces a satisfying crunch. It's a familiar sound, disarming and rural, evocative of country lanes and gravel driveways, and the more I walk, the richer the accent becomes. Different motions produce different effects. A sweep of the leg brings a thin, shimmering sound; less natural, almost digital. A kick scatters seeds in all directions, each landing with its own trebly tone depending on the distance. I grab a handful and shake. They clack like dice. I drop them back. They sputter and snap like a Geiger Counter.

I pick one up and take a look. Almond shape, slightly thicker than the sunflower seeds I've encountered in nature. Clearly ceramic – smooth, hard and off-white – with a pointed oval painted in charcoal-coloured ink on each side. It is coated in a light powder that stays with me after I've dropped the seed. I begin to wonder about the social involvement that Ai mentioned.

The production of the seeds is taking place in Jingdezhen, a small city in the south famous for its porcelain. All of Ai's ceramic works are produced there and from what I've heard there's a small army racing to complete this one. To understand this work, I think I need to see the process. I find Ai and he offers to set up a visit. Coincidentally, Liu Weiwei, his long-time collaborator and the man responsible for the seeds, is at the house. 'He's leaving tonight', Ai says. 'Can you go tomorrow?'

Jingdezhen is the pottery centre of China and the original home of the world's porcelain industry. It has held this position for hundreds of years and changed remarkably little even amid the turmoil of imperial transition, foreign invasion, Communist revolution and post-communist reform. It owes its preeminence partly to geology: Jingdezhen has a natural advantage over China's other ceramic-producing cities due to

Production of sunflower seeds in Jingdezhen, southern China, 2010

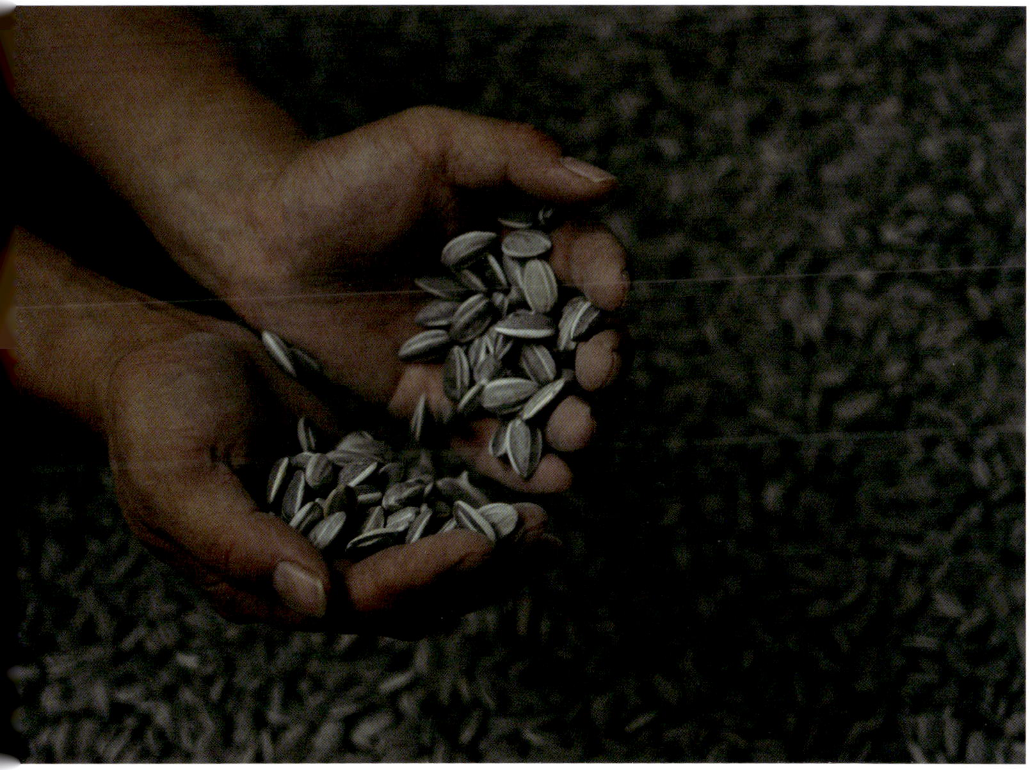

its ample, easily accessible supplies of clay and feldspar, the essential ingredients of porcelain. The low, rocky hills surrounding the city have been mined continuously for generations and yet these raw materials are almost never in short supply. The miners have to dig deeper now, their work is more dangerous, but it continues to yield the precious minerals on which the city's reputation and livelihood depend.

To reach one of these mines, Liu Weiwei drives an hour or so outside of the city. In Jingdezhen, the line between urban and country is sharp, and crossing it feels like time travel. The high rises and sooty buses and busy people disappear and you suddenly find yourself in a medieval world of rice and tea, lethargic oxen and stooped labour. The air feels cleaner; the stink of the city – exhaust, spilled fuel and sulphur – is replaced by the earthy smell of wet roots and peels. The buildings are made of wood and roughly mortared brick, and even those that are undergoing expansion have an air of decay. As you drive further, the road gradually decomposes until you find yourself on a narrow dirt lane that stops abruptly before a heap of broken rock.

The mine itself is fairly unremarkable. The entrance is inconspicuous: just a small arched opening on the side of a hill, below a sign that reads 'Safe Production'. The grou\nd is tracked to allow for mine carts, and the roof drips water. According to Liu, the shaft extends for two kilometers, but we don't take more than a few steps in. I had hoped to speak to someone, but the place seems deserted. The only indication that the site is still active is a small shrine built by the miners. A slight scent of incense still hangs around it, so I assume it's been in recent use. A small sign above it reads 有求必应 (Ask and ye shall receive). I ask Liu what the miners wish for. He says, 'Safety', and we leave.

On the train from Beijing I'd read an account of the porcelain manufacturing process written by a missionary stationed in Jingdezhen in the early eighteenth century. It is a fascinating text, a mixture of ethnography and industrial espionage in which the author describes in detail the arduous process through which hunks of raw rock were turned into the milky chinaware coveted by his European readers. It describes Jingdezhen as a marvel of mass production – a city given over to a single industry, operating at an enormous scale through entirely pre-industrial means. I'd read the piece mostly for entertainment, assuming that the procedures it described were long since outdated. This is not the case.

Not far from the mine is a small plant where the excavated rock is processed. I suppose you would call this place a refinery, although that term evokes heavy industry and air pollution. This place is not like that; it's all natural. Its heaviest piece of equipment is a wooden, water-powered machine that pounds porcelain stone into powder. Liu's assistant says that this device has been in use for over a thousand years, and it looks that way. He explains how it works. The pieces of stone are first broken with iron hammers, then the fragments are collected in mortars where trip hammers pulverise them. The hammers rise and fall based on a system of levers connected to a small water wheel. A stream feeds the wheel and provides perpetual motion. It is a clean, efficient operation that apparently requires very little human supervision, because the plant is empty.

Making powder constitutes step one of the refinement process, and there are several others, the products of which are visible in piles and stacks along the walls and on the floor. To understand these, I rely on the missionary account, which, despite its three hundred years, I now assume is still relevant:

> The powder is then put into a great vessel filled with water, and stirred vigorously with an iron shovel. When it has been allowed to

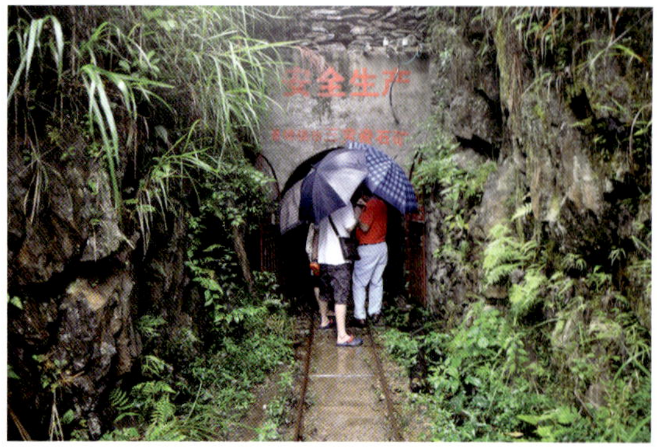

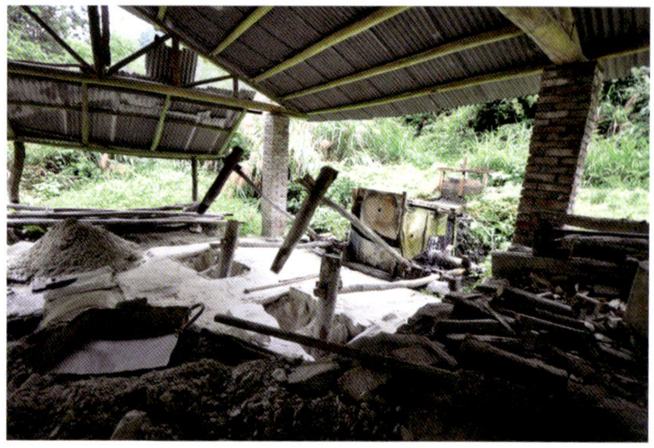

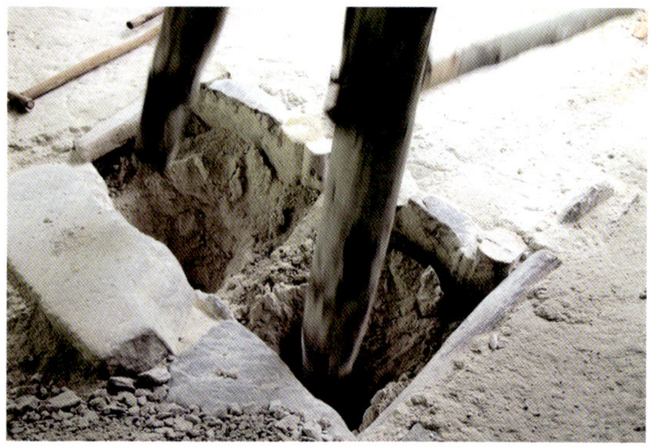

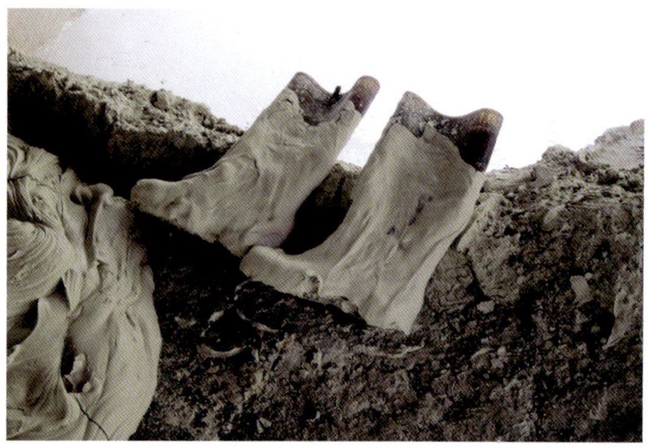

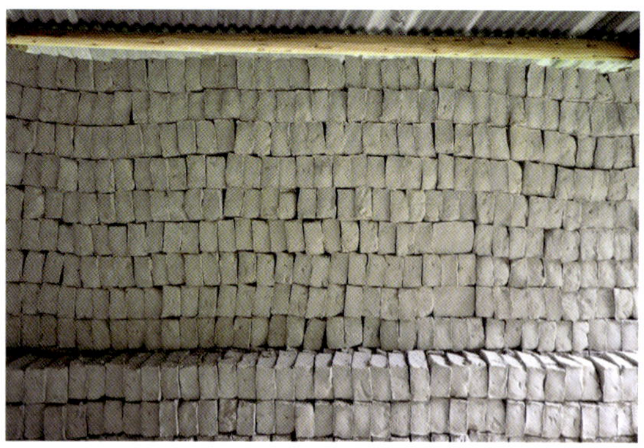

Production of sunflower seeds in Jingdezhen, southern China, 2010 (Photos: Brendan McGetrick)

> stand several minutes, a kind of cream forms at the top four or five fingers thick; this they take off and put into another vessel full of water. The mixture in the first vessel is stirred up several times, and each time they remove the scum that gathers on the top, until nothing is left but the larger particles, the weight of which makes them sink to the bottom; these are finally taken out and again pounded.

This skimming process produces a thick paste, which resembles meringue. Enormous gobs of it are laid out on tarps in the centre of the plant.

> This paste is then thrown into moulds, which are a kind of large and wide wooden box, the bottom of which is a bed of bricks with an even surface. Over this brick bed a coarse cloth is stretched, up to the sides of the case; this cloth is filled with the paste, and soon afterwards they cover it with another cloth on the top of which they put a layer of bricks laid evenly, one by the side of the other. This helps to squeeze out the water more quickly without losing any of the porcelain material which, as it hardens readily, takes the shape of the bricks. Before it has become quite hard the paste is divided into little bricks, which are sold by the hundred.

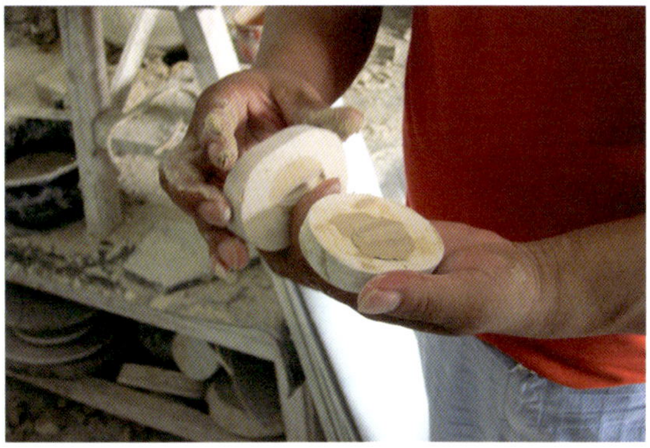

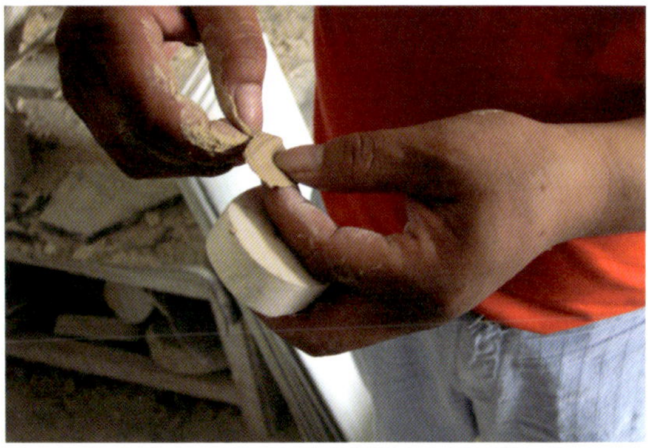

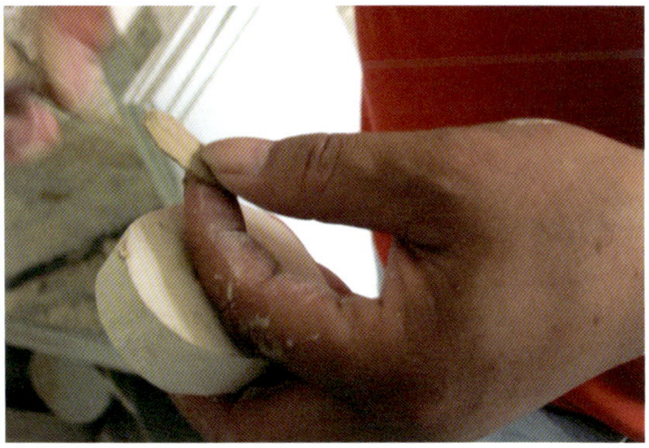

These soft, off-white bricks are stored on racks and lined up on the floor. From here they are shipped to porcelain factories, where the powder is further refined, then mixed with clay to form a cohesive, camel-coloured material that I will watch Liu hand-press into a sunflower-shaped mould later that day.

Liu is forty-nine. He has a plump face and a low, gravelly voice with a slight lisp. He speaks in short declarative sentences and dresses in casual luxury brands. He was once a dealer of Chinese antiques, but now spends most of his time creating porcelain artworks for Ai Weiwei. The courtyard of his home is filled with fruits of their collaboration: a cobalt blue orb ('Ai showed me beautiful photos of these on a beach in Miami'), an oil droplet ('It was supposed to be bigger, but it always cracked, so the size had to be reduced'), human organs ('The most difficult piece we've ever done'), a grid of interlocking tubes ('These are in an exhibition in Basel right now').

He doesn't speculate on the significance of the work, and says that he and Ai don't discuss it. He considers himself a producer and he does his work with care. He's happy to work with Ai. They've been friends for sixteen years and the collaboration is a natural extension of that friendship. It started small and gradually built up, each successful realisation leading to another. 'You could say he's my boss,' Liu says that night over tea in his courtyard, 'but he's never bossy to me. We're friends first.'

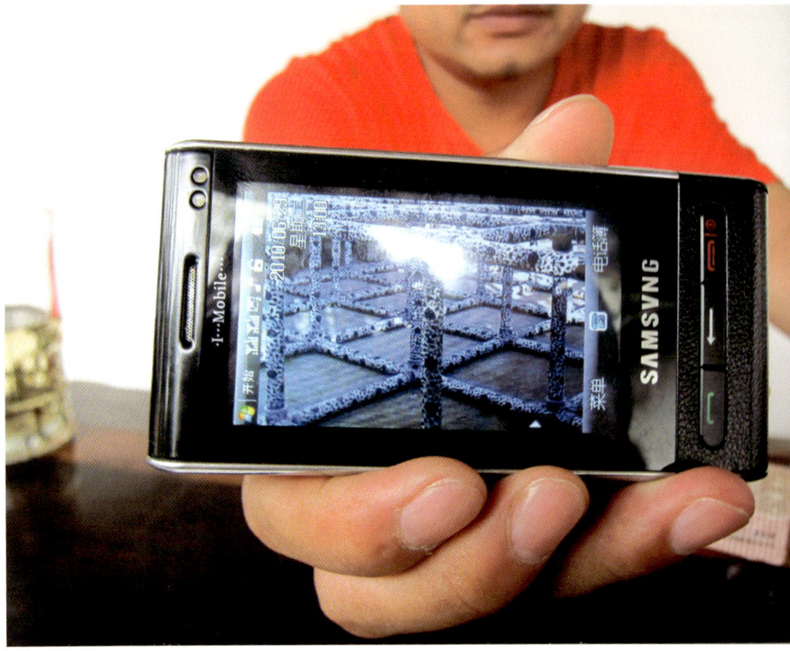

Liu Weiwei's mobile phone showing an image of Ai Weiwei's work, 2010 (Photo: Brendan McGetrick)

It's my final day in Jingdezhen and we've been through all the major production steps, except one. Why this was left till last I don't know, since it's the step I'm most curious to see. Back in Beijing, Ai had spoken passionately about the painters. 'Each one is different', he said. 'You show it through your own control of the brush and your breath and your own body gestures. You pick a seed up and you put on ink, more ink or less ink, lightly or thickly painted. Then you have to turn it over and place it down. It's such a beautiful act.'

The painting takes place in an unfurnished two-storey house on a leafy street somewhere in Jingdezhen. We pull up in Liu Weiwei's van and one of his assistants immediately starts unloading sacks of unpainted seeds from the back. Through the windows we can see groups of women – only women – hunched over plywood tables. The air outside is filled with the smell of alcohol-based ink and the soft sound of female chatting. We enter without introduction. When the women notice the visitors, they become quiet, diligent.

Before each of them is a pile of blank ceramic seeds, like the ones we've just brought over. I'm not sure where to look, so I watch the woman closest to me. She's wearing black jeans and a slim-fitting polo shirt with bright stripes. Like most of the painters, her hair is black and tied back. To her right is a shallow bowl of black ink and beside that an identical bowl filled with water. To her left is a flat wooden ring half covered with painted seeds.

She places a finished seed on the ring and immediately picks up a blank one. She holds it in her left hand, between the thumb and index finger. Her right holds the brush, which she grips like a pen. As she paints, both hands work in tandem, the left gently gliding the seed beneath the brush while the right holds it steady. She ends each stroke with a slight upward flick of the wrist. Four strokes and one side is done.

Liu Weiwei is no longer in the house. He is outside discussing the work with a woman whom I presume to be a supervisor of some kind. They're bent over a sack of painted seeds. Some are OK, he says, but some are not. The bad ones can't be used.

Across the street is another house where more painters are

working. It's dingier than the first one and not as well ventilated. The women inside range in age from late teens to early forties. They're sloppier than the other group, and chattier. I start asking questions.

Q: Do you know what these seeds are for?
A: Adornment.

One word, then back to painting. I've started off on the wrong foot. I try another approach.

Q: Is it hard work?
A: It's OK, the time is flexible. We can also work at home.

Maybe this more sympathetic question has warmed the atmosphere, because all five women now look up from their seeds.

Q: Are you all painters?
A: Not all.

Q: What did you do before this?
A: Some of us used to paint porcelain.

Q: So this is much simpler than that?
A: Yeah, it's easy once you know how to do it.

Q: How many do you paint in a day?
A: Two to two and a half kilos. On average, each one of us has painted over 500 kilos.

500 kilos. At about 700 seeds per kilo that's 350,000 seeds. 2.8 million brush strokes. It's hard to fathom in this tiny, ink-scented room. I take another shot at discussing the significance of their work.

Q: Do you know where these are going and what they'll be used for?

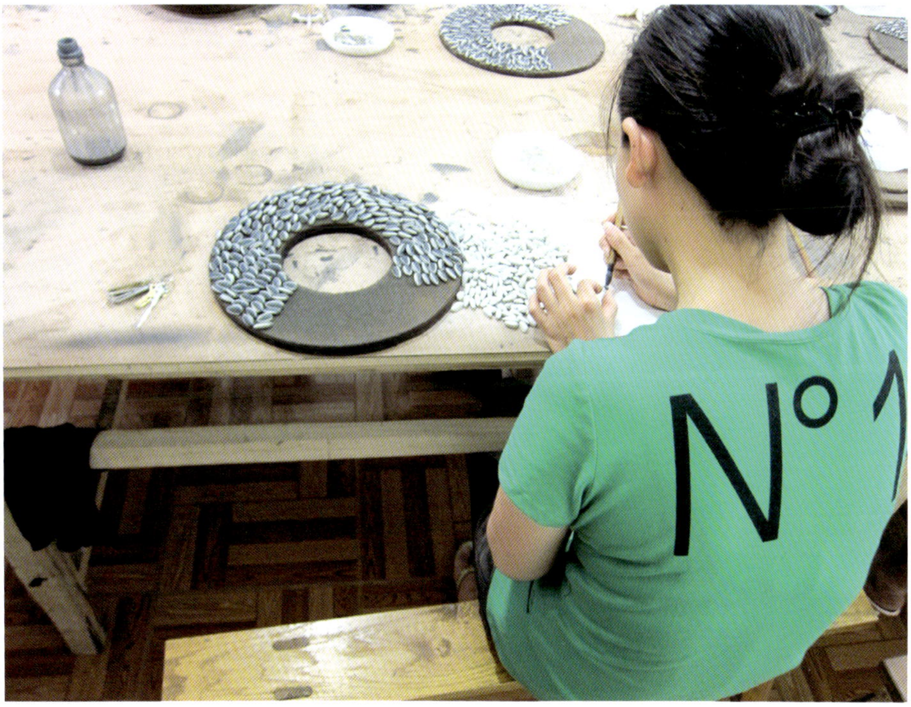

Production of sunflower seeds in Jingdezhen, southern China, 2010 (Photo: Brendan McGetrick)

A: No, we don't know, but we know they'll be used to make money. Another brief, withering response. And, again, my impulse is to retreat to tame personal queries.

Q: After all this, do you still like sunflower seeds?
A: Yes. These are more beautiful than real ones. Hahaha …

An icebreaker! I try to probe deeper.

Q: How do you feel about doing this work?
A: To me, if people understand art, they might enjoy it.

As we head back to his house, Liu Weiwei begins to speak about himself. He doesn't have creative aspirations of his own, he says. Although he's one of Ai's co-creators, Liu is foremost a businessman and he describes his creations not as works of art but feats of production. From this perspective, the sunflower seeds are his masterpiece: never has a single project required this much investment, organisation and overseeing. 'I had to buy five vans to transport the seeds', he says as we pull up to his front gate. Then, with less emphasis, 'More than a thousand people have worked on this.'

A *thousand*? And this for a production that, from what I've seen, barely uses electricity. I ask how he maintains quality with such a large team. He says, 'We have many people taking care of the quality. We're all very strict. If we see bad ones, we just throw them away. That's a loss for me, but we have to be tough on this, otherwise it would be hard to control.' I'm finding my emotions somewhat hard to control. Despite its superhuman scale, nothing in this production is automated. The seeds are handcrafted: the porcelain stone is excavated by hand, pulverised, and mixed by hand. The clay is hand-pressed into millions of pieces that are baked and dumped into large sacks that, despite being made of woven Polypropylene, appear to be hand stitched. These are placed in vans and hand-delivered to studios, where each piece is painted by hand, then sent back for another firing, after which it's hand polished and dried. For someone like me, a digital labourer whose work is based on remote communications and impossible-to-understand search algorithms, the directness, intimacy and raw human power of this production is overwhelming.

When I get back to Beijing, I go to visit Ai again. I tell him I've seen the manufacturing process and am amazed that it's so productive and so low-tech. That's what makes Jingdezhen special, he says; it hasn't lost its primitive ways. 'In the culture you see in Jingdezhen, there's really no deficiency.' As before, he's speaking objectively, but not without feeling. 'You can be handicapped or weak, but still there's something to do and, by doing it, something beautiful can come.' He pauses, as if to make certain that he possesses all the correct words to say what he wants to say. 'Value isn't just measured by competition – that creates too much waste. The tradition you see there was the same a thousand years ago, during the Song Dynasty. It survives because it's so efficient. It doesn't need electricity. Everything that's done is necessary. You cannot beat it.'

It's an unusual argument: an ancient social philosophy expressed through the concerns of the modern business leader – reducing waste, increasing efficiency, saving energy, adding value … But this apparent mismatch is to be expected; it's simply one of the dozens of incongruities that spring to mind when considering his sunflower seeds – millions of pieces of ceramic, mass-produced but handmade, inspired by Communist symbolism but sponsored by a capitalist conglomerate, produced through pre-modern methods and displayed in a post-industrial space. The overlap between supposed opposites is fertile ground for Ai. He is continuously exploring it, intervening in it, inviting others in. It's an area strewn with preconceptions and misunderstandings, and its impurity is what attracts the artist. As Ai speaks, it dawns on me that his installation is essentially an elaborate device for producing this condition inside the Turbine Hall; all of it – the mining, the moulding, the painting, the five vans, the thousand workers, the 100 million seeds – all of it amounts to a single attempt at creating an environment in which incompatibilities meet and multiply.

In the hope of developing the thought, I ask Ai a final question. He's taking a photo of my T-shirt. I say, 'How do you think the visitors are going to react?' He replies, 'I don't know.' Silence. I remember the painter's response when I asked her to speculate on the work, and in that instant of reverie Ai has posted his picture of my shirt on Twitter. Then, as if fulfilling a terms of use agreement, he responds some more. 'I think people will be charmed … when they first enter the hall they'll think it's real, then realise it's not real, then they'll wonder if it's machine-made or hand-made or painted.' He looks blankly at a group of students fidgeting in the doorway. 'Those things all affect perception. We only remember a piece by the way it made us question our original concept. I feel very charmed by that.'

Production of sunflower seeds in Jingdezhen, southern China, 2010

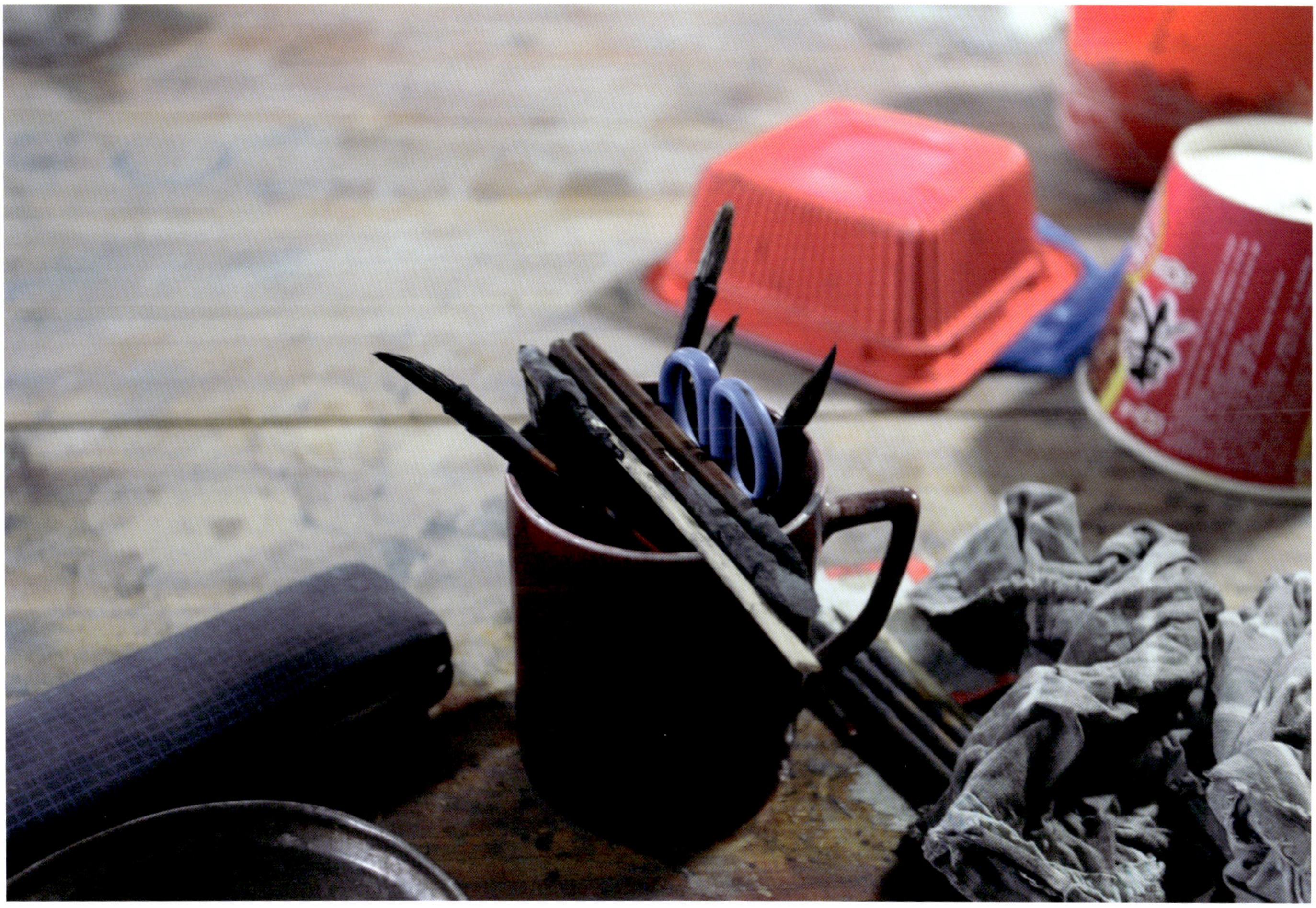

@AIWW

@aiww From the judicial murder of Yang Jia to today's direct gun execution on the streets, the efficiency of suppression has increased, and the costs have decreased. If the awakening of the people is further elevated to self-immolation, then it will be perfect.
16.1.2010, 18:06:38

@aiww The ethical basis of abolishing the death penalty is to see the value of life as higher than all other ethical values of mankind. It's not a matter of will or no will.
26.1.2010, 08:33:50

@aiww What the Sichuan government does not understand is that Tan Zuoren is a part of us. The best part is going stay with us. We will not hand him out. #tanzuoren
9.2.2010, 08:42:46

@aiww In this world, there's no outdoor exercise that's more elegant than throwing stones at despotism. Similarly, there's no mass assault that's more exciting than the exchange happening in a numerical virtual space.
3.10.2010, 08:03:08

@aiww One can put it this way: liberty within the so-called definition of a society is gained after defending the independent position of the law.
17.3.2010, 23:47:41

@aiww The country sees the people who speak the truth, the people who have an opinion, the people who think independently, the people who are willing to express themselves and the people with no fear, as its enemies. #tanzuoren
28.3.2010, 08:05:06

@aiww The vile dictator always delivers the whip into your hands. #tanzuoren
28.3.2010, 08:08:14

@aiww No one pays attention to me anymore, nor cares about what I'm saying or the difficulty that I'm having. My difficulty, unfortunately, is also the difficulty of China.
29.3.2010, 15:52:39

@aiww If you hope to understand your motherland, you're already on the path to crime. #zhaolianha
30.3.2010, 09:49:02

#zhaolianha probably refers to Zhao Lianhai, the parent of a child who developed kidney stones as a result of melanmine-tainted milk. Along with other parents, he initiated an investigation into the cause of the kidney stones and announced the scandal to the public. He was subsequently arrested for provoking social disorder (www.guardian.co.uk/world/2010/feb/03/china-contaminated-milk-campaign-social-disorder).

@aiww If you're hopeless, desensitised, giving up, and no longer care, you've turned into what your opponent hoped you'd become.
2.4.2010, 12:05:47

@aiww Lies and violence are the two main pillars of totalitarian power. One can also say that lies are alternative forms of violence.
8.4.2010, 06:40:59

@aiww Half of this country's energy is spent on cutting off possibilities for people to gain information and exchange. The other half is spent on sending people who have the correct answers and who are willing to share them, to jail.
16.4.2010, 22:07:51

@aiww If you say that you have nothing to do with politics, why don't you say you have nothing to do with primates? It would be more realistic.
16.4.2010, 22:18:12

@aiww You ride above the country and the law. Your power and status cannot be touched and you have no room for doubt. You put those who differ from you to death or make them disappear. You rely on creating, terror and lies to maintain yourself. You cover up, falsify, dishonour, cheat and rob. And still you dare not to admit that you are the mafia?
16.4.2010, 22:30:48

@aiww I only defend one kind of system – that is, the kind that allows subversion.
20.4.2010, 06:53:51

@aiww The nature of the deaths in the Chinese earthquake was murder. What was done afterwards was just destroying the evidence.
20.4.2010, 23:54:29

@aiww The world only has two kinds of governments. One seeks to be scolded, called a democratic government; one seeks death, called a totalitarian government. 2.5.2010, 11:35:15

@aiww Not every house will collapse, not every life will be forgotten, not every bridge will certainly be cut off, not every wish will certainly be lied about. 'Nian'
12.5.2010, 07:24:51

@aiww Totalitarian power won't make you disappear; totalitarian power only makes your emotions and morale completely disappear.
13.5.2010, 02:12:41

@aiww There were two 'land revolutions'. The first, 'Attack local tyrants, divide the land', used the name of the people to rob others' wealth and to gain political power. The other is happening today: lying and robbing from farmers, forcibly taking over land that belongs to all people in exchange for political power stability and an obscene profit for a minority.
21.5.2010, 08:11:32

'Attack local tyrants, divide the land' was a propaganda slogan used by the Chinese Red Army as early as 1927, reflecting Mao Zedong's political position and encouraging farmers to begin a revolution against the ruling class. The second land revolution mentioned here probably refers to the widespread forced demolition taking place in China.

@aiww If you've never been extreme, then you've come to this world in vain. If in China you're not a grass mud horse, you haven't even arrived.
21.5.2010, 08:34:43

@aiww Not one inch of land belongs to you, yet every inch of land can imprison you.
21.5.2010, 09:10:19

@aiww Foxconn's death miracle has been collectively, accumulatively accomplished by every user of products made in China, but you have no idea, or pretend to have no idea.
28.5.2010, 11:14:47

Foxconn is a manufacturer of electronics and computer components, including products for Apple, HP, Dell and Sony. It has been alleged that poor working conditions at its factories triggered a spate of suicides by workers who jumped off the factory building (www.bbc.co.uk/news/world-asia-pacific-10702689).

@aiww If you're passionate about life, you're already a potential enemy of the country.
9.6.2010, 08:35:47

@aiww Anonymity is a show of weakness to those in power.
13.6.2010, 07:42:50

This Twitter post was published when Ai Weiwei began the 'Say Your Name' campaign, where he asked his Twitter followers to announce their real names on the micro-blogging platform. Whilst this may seem a neutral act to the Western world, the campaign addresses Chinese Twitterers' fear of being identified online, since using Twitter, as well as many other forms of social media, is banned in China.

@aiww Not one bit of arrogance from despotism is not built on the cowardice of those who remain anonymous.
13.6.2010, 09:06:57

@aiww I can also love this country. However, the precondition is that I can convince myself to love eating shit, to love being whipped, to love being stepped on, to love being forgotten and falsified, to love violence and cheating, to love lies and theft, to love laziness and stupidity, to betray my grass mud horses, then I can say shamelessly, 'Oh I love the country.'
15.6.2010, 20:35:28

@aiww If I were persecuted by government officials, I would use silence as a way to abstain from defence, to abstain from appeals, to abstain from any means of cooperation as a form of protest, and to express my contempt for the existing judicial system. 28.6.2010, 09:26:21

@aiww If you enjoy privileges, then you must be tolerant; if you have emotions, naturally the heart has compassion.
6.7.2010, 08:05:47

This Twitter post was published around the time that Ai Weiwei released 'Sanhua', a documentary about his investigation of cat-eating and cat-meat vendors. 'Privileges', refers to the privileged existence of humans over cats: we need to be tolerant and let cats live their own lives. The second phrase points directly to the cruelty of the cat-eating practice: anyone with compassion would not do such a thing.

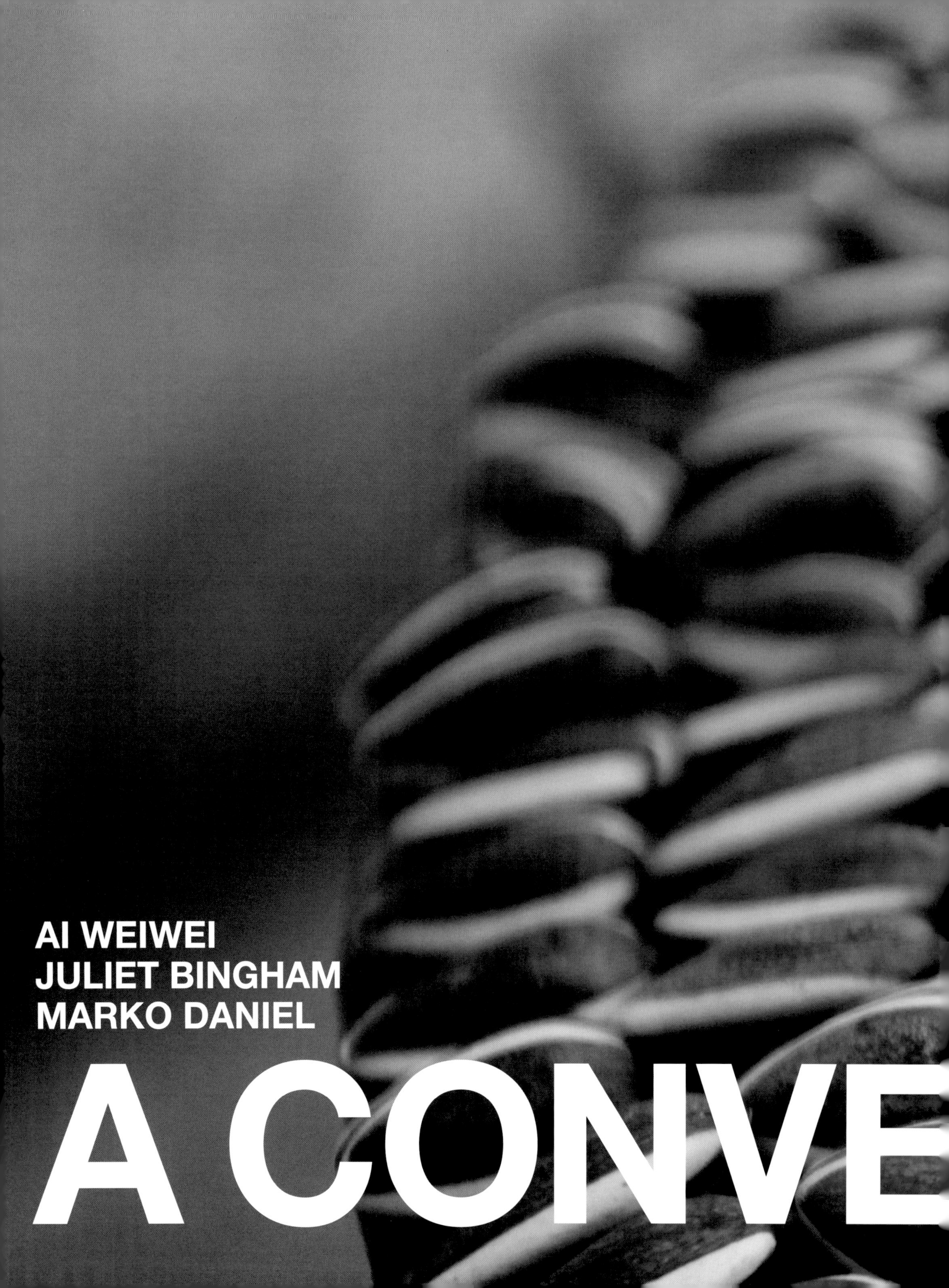

AI WEIWEI
JULIET BINGHAM
MARKO DANIEL

A CONVE

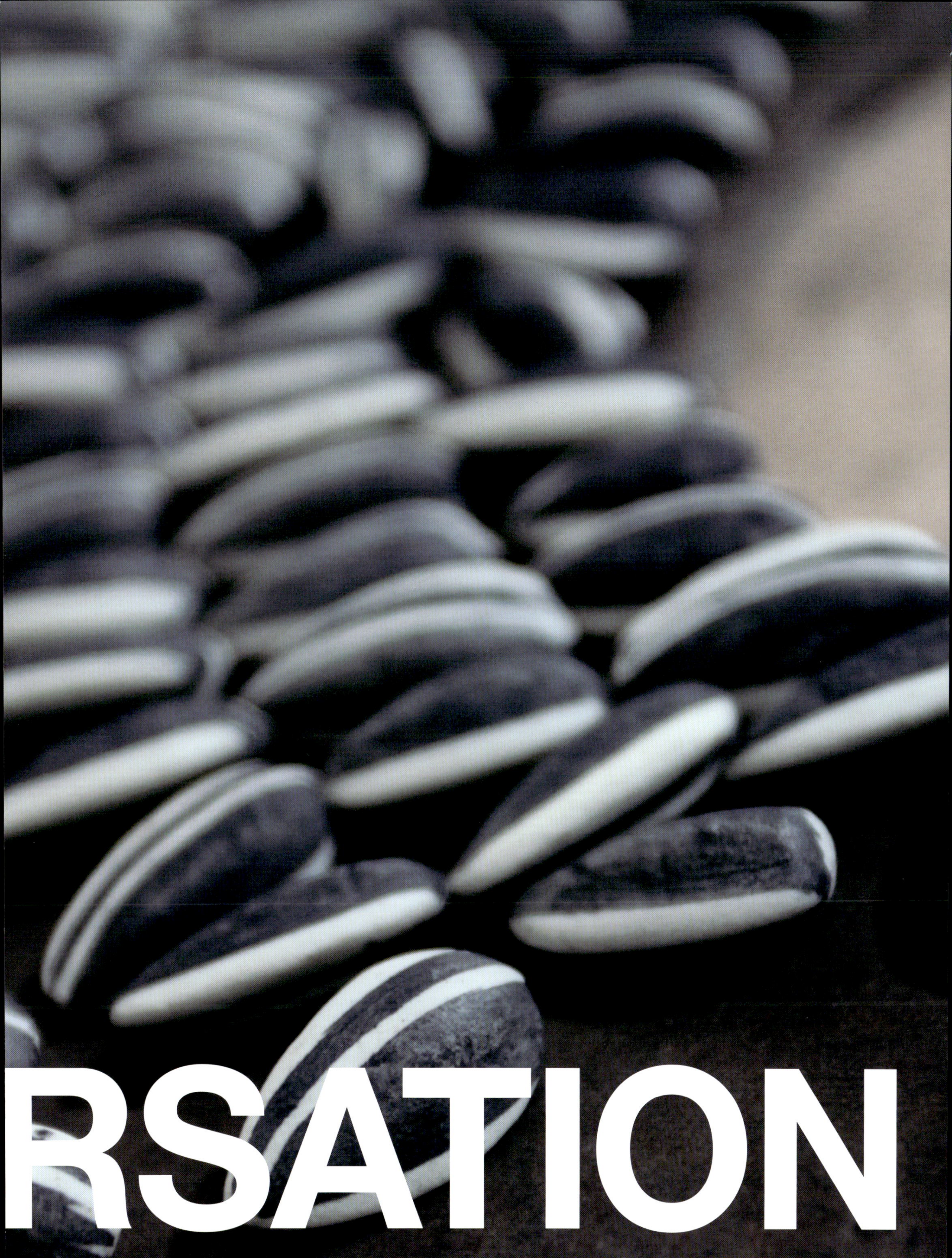

RSATION

A Conversation between Ai Weiwei, Juliet Bingham and Marko Daniel, 31 May and 1 June 2010, Beijing

Previous spread: Production of sunflower seeds in Jingdezhen, southern China, 2010

Detail of single sunflower seed, 2010
Porcelain, dimensions variable
(Photo: Tate Photography)

JB The work that you've created for the Turbine Hall consists of millions and millions of porcelain objects individually hand-crafted and painted to look like real sunflower seeds. In terms of creating this landscape of seeds for Tate, how were you thinking about the building and the Turbine Hall space itself?

AW Well, anybody would first think about this space because it's so unique and so overwhelming, larger than most artists can fill. For the Unilever Series, artists have taken very different positions with very different intentions. It's always a challenge for the next artist to express his own understanding through a work that at the same time can make sense within this space. We went through a lot of thinking and different perspectives, but finally we came down to this. We're very lucky that we started the research and production much earlier. Of course, I never imagined then that it would reach these kinds of quantities. We focused on this idea not only because it challenges the space through the number of objects but also because it offers a more psychological and social meaning. So much of it relates to what I've been doing on the internet, Twitter activities, mobilising the social masses and seeing the potential of individuality. I have to present a work that I really believe in: it's not just to please others, but is deeply rooted in my own practice and concerns. So I'm very happy and convinced by it.

JB It's a visually subtle work, but also incredibly powerful and thought-provoking.

AW It has a kind of psychic power because it's so quiet, it looks so minimal and the space remains otherwise untouched. Firstly, people will recognise that these are sunflower seeds. Then they'll start to understand that these are sunflower seeds but nothing can grow from them: they're all hand-painted by individuals. That will come as a shock. It's a kind of mental game, like in Duchamp's work. It reminds me of *Why Not Sneeze Rose Sélavy?*, the birdcage containing what look like sugar cubes, but are in fact marble cubes, which you discover when you try to lift the cage: it's too heavy [fig.49]. It's a tricky act: you see something that's not what you think – it's much more. With the sunflower seeds, there are many layers of meaning. People will try to understand how it's been made and then what's behind all those numbers. I like that part very much.

The work reflects on the fact that each seed is individual yet at the same time looks identical to the others. And when they're accumulated in this large number, they become something else. You see it and you don't see it because it disappears through this massiveness.

MD When we saw the sunflower piece in the studio it did look very beautiful. What's the relationship between the beauty of the piece and its political dimension?

AW Each seed appears as this kind of beautiful grey, with the details of the white lines and the evenly shaded grey colour, which are often considered very nice minimal tones, and which capture light and shadow. But the meaning of the work has nothing at all to do with its appearance. It's very divided. And the

49
Marcel Duchamp
Why Not Sneeze Rose Sélavy?
1921, replica 1964
Mixed media 11.4 x 22 x 16 cm
Tate. Purchased 1999
© Succession Marcel Duchamp / ADAGP, Paris and DACS, London 2010
(Photo: Tate Photography)

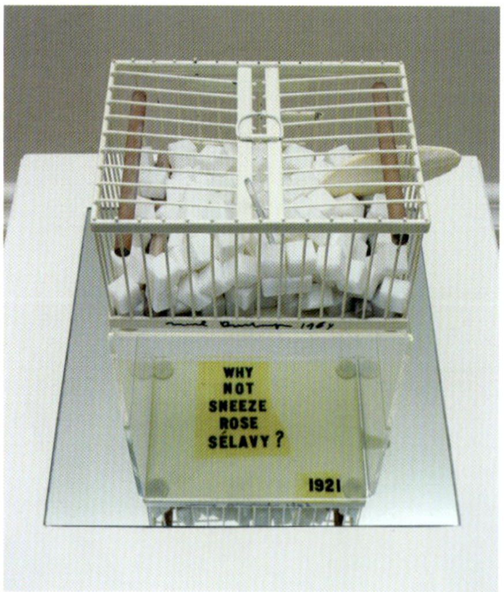

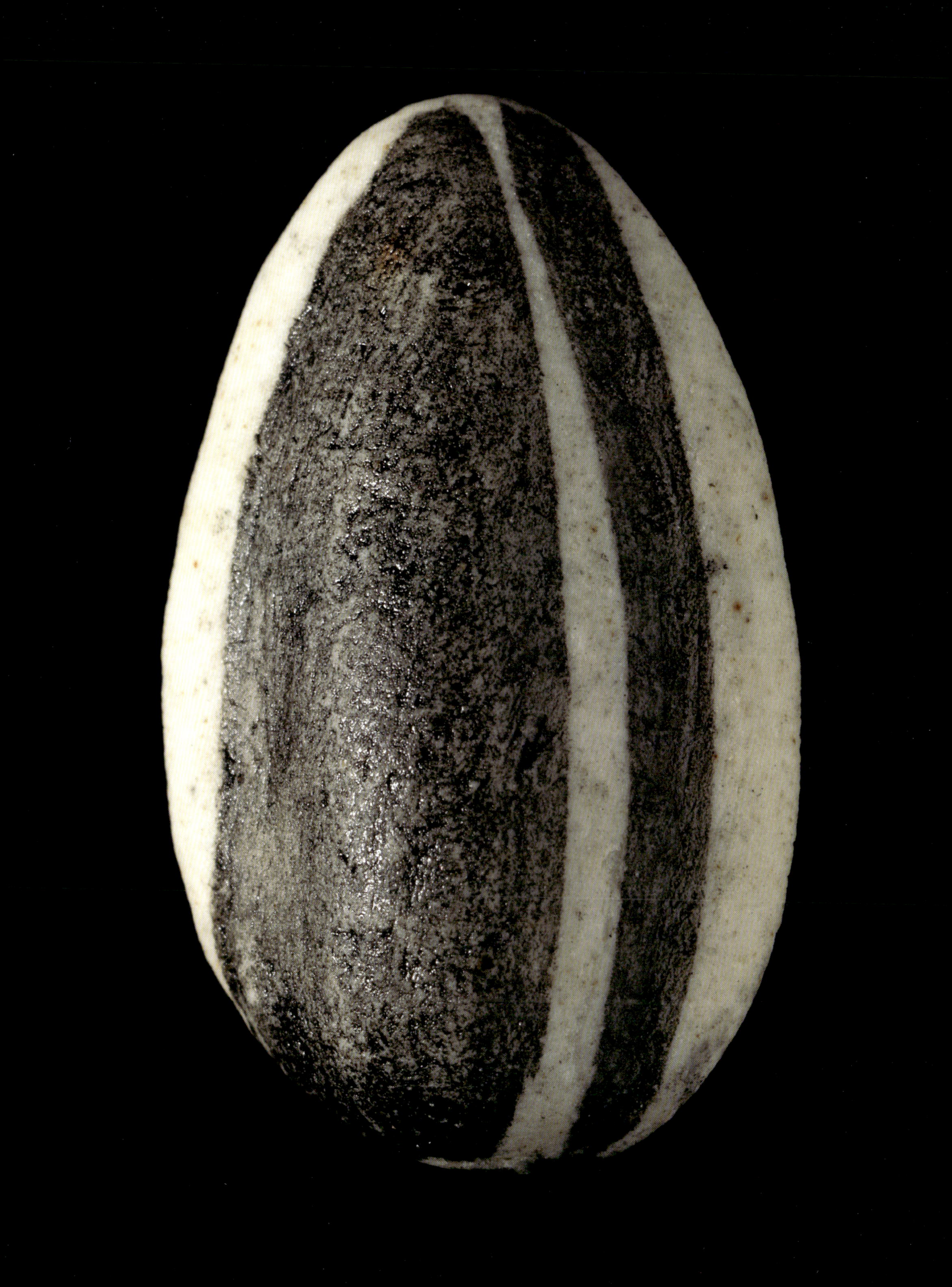

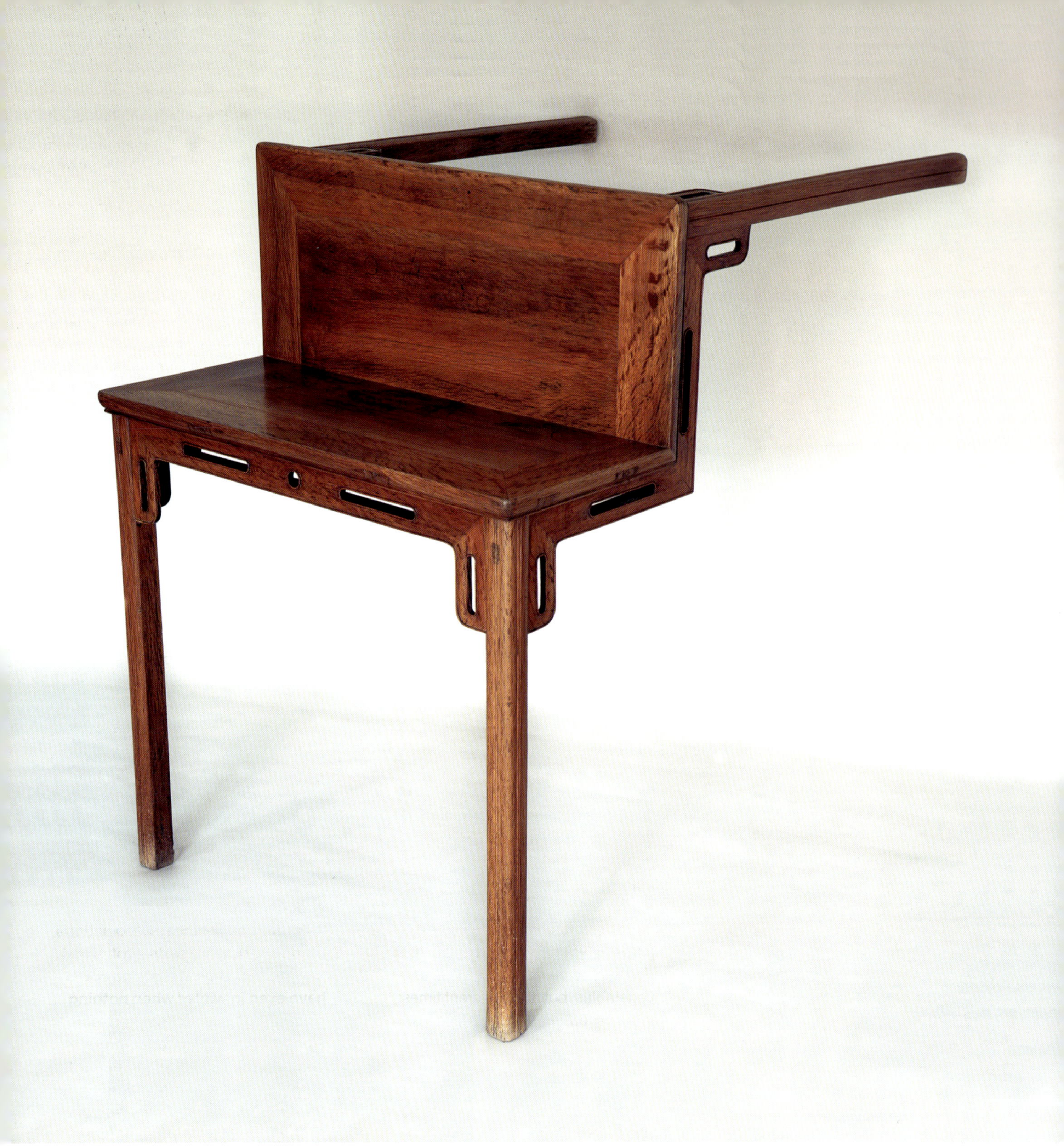

50
Table with Two Legs on the Wall
1997
Table, Qing dynasty (1644–1911),
91 x 118 x 122 cm

understanding of the process also goes against its appearance. So what you see is not what it means. And if what you see is not what it means, then there's a struggle there.

JB That contradiction is often embodied in your works.

AW Yes, it's a bit misleading and a contradiction, a self-contradiction even, that the work can destroy itself. It can ask questions, have a certain content and a message, but at the same time destroy the meaning. For example, in the 'Furniture Series' [1997–ongoing], the making, the materials and the aesthetics all relate to classic Qing-style furniture. But at the same time, I completely 'destroy' it or present it under another condition. All the patinas and the joints are so perfectly made that nobody can tell if it's the original or not, or what has happened to it, not only in terms of function but also in the making. So you have a struggle in your mind. But we're convinced because of this misleading element.

JB I was wondering about the significance of the sunflower seed itself and your memories of sunflower seeds when growing up in China. When we last met, you talked about a sharing experience or a social dimension to the sunflower seed.

AW In China, when we grew up, we had nothing, except maybe a bed, a stove, a stool or a chair. Whatever you see today, we didn't have. We didn't even have light-bulbs or electricity; it was very primitive. Every year we had maybe five different kinds of vegetables, but all at different times: in winter onions and potatoes, in summer watermelon and some green vegetables – squash and cabbage. It was always just a few, very limited things. But for even the poorest people, the treat or the treasure we'd have would be the sunflower seeds in everybody's pockets. We'd have sunflower seeds because these lasted the; whole year (they don't need a refrigerator, which we didn't have). So during a marriage ceremony or important meetings or before the movie came on – everybody went to see these same five movies that had been circulating for maybe twenty years – we always had this secret friend and we could always eat it. If you went to somebody's home, they would – at that time we didn't have tea – just serve sunflower seeds. So we'd all talk and eat them. It was partying. [laughs] This is a really strong memory of Socialist society. It was so common and everybody accepted them. With many Chinese people, you'll see they have a crack in their front teeth from eating sunflower seeds. You wouldn't think that this soft thing could really make such a crack there, but after you eat thousands and thousands of them, they make a mark.

MD It reminds me of soft water hollowing out a stone.

AW A Sinologist [Nikos Kazantzakis], published a book in 1938 about his travels in China and Japan. He saw these Chinese people in the northwest who were all cracking sunflower seeds with their teeth and he said something like, 'This takes patient and skilful work.' Many Westerners can't do it. My mother can do it very fast. She just uses the tip of her tongue; then the kernel comes out and is perfect, not ruined. I think Westerners sometimes just chew the skin. All Chinese know how to do it: like a bird. So the Sinologist says that he thinks if there was no such thing, maybe there'd be some kind of revolution or social change, because this takes so much patience and effort and skill. I think it's very interesting because it's such a popular behaviour.

MD If we think about these associations of the sunflower seeds – with food, with a special treat that you could have even in winter when nothing was growing – such a mass of seeds is quite a powerful image.

AW It's true. In China, even in the poorest, most remote area, everybody would always have a few sunflower seeds in their pockets. So it's a kind of confidence you have. It grows and you can eat it.

MD I've seen a sample of the sunflower seeds and they look to me like they're slightly bigger than real ones.

AW Actually, there are bigger real ones than these. We chose the smaller ones. In the place where I grew up,the sunflower seeds are quite big.

JB The seeds are being made in the city of Jingdezhen in southern China. How has the production been going?

AW This is the most complicated type of manual work to do, which could only happen today in China. This work could never be made in any other place. It's very difficult because of the time limit and the nature of this project. We now have 1,600 people involved on the production, with six units. People are joking about it, saying that the entire city is involved in this production, which is very exciting because it's a work about mass production and repeatedly accumulating the small effort of individuals to become a massive, useless piece of work. But it's doing well. Everything is manageable and under control.

JB Can you talk a little bit more about this idea of mass production?

AW What China is doing today isn't really sustainable. They sacrifice almost everything for a quick profit – environment, education, social standards, morals – all those things are being sacrificed just to get rich quick. China is blindly producing for the demands of the market. We're seeing the lowering of standards and basic values in general in both China – of course, in China it's a dream – and in the West. But because of the political and economic situation, people are shy to insist on those values, which are, I think, the foundation of society. Sooner or later the problem of this neglect will

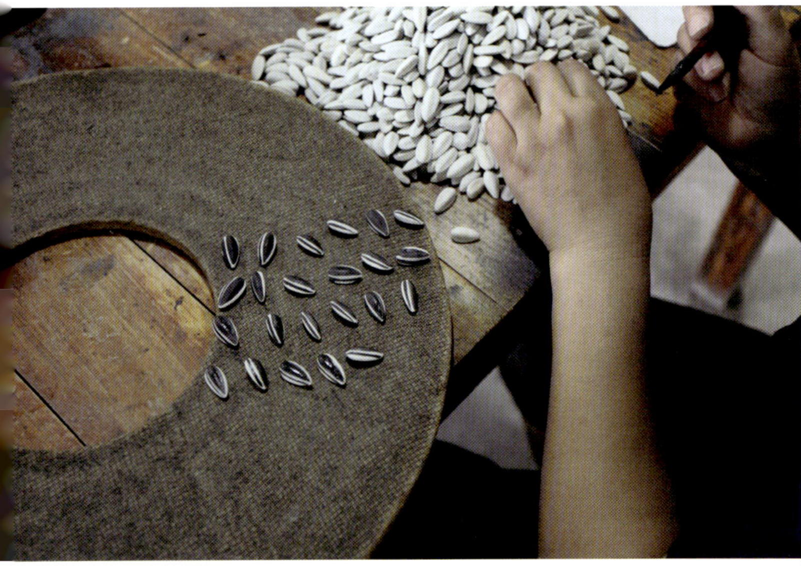

Production of sunflower seeds in Jingdezhen, southern China, 2010

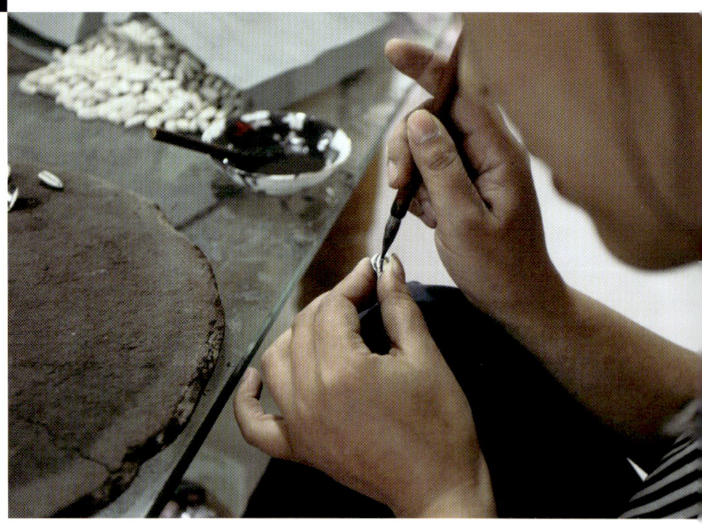

show. There's a general blindness and ignorance about these things.

JB And there's more of an extreme gap between people in society.

AW Yes, society quickly develops into two levels: a higher level who just want to maintain stability and make a bigger profit and be stronger, and the general public who don't feel capable of being involved. My work very much relates to this blind production of things. I'm part of it, which is a bit of a nonsense. The sunflower seeds can never be planted and can never grow, but the process of continuously doing something that's not really useful in such a massive way and takes such a long time and with so many people involved reflects those conditions.

MD What's so interesting for me about this work is the fact that it's on an industrial scale but it's a manual process.

AW This kind of porcelain-making is one of the earliest human activities that relates to artefacts or art. It started thousands of years ago. China is famous for porcelain because the Imperial Court always sought the best quality and was so in love with this art. So the process has been highly polished and defined throughout history. Jingdezhen was the base of production of the Imperial Court pieces, so it has a very strong tradition and skilful craftsmanship that involves modelling, sculpting, firing and hand-painting. The process of making the sunflower seeds is no different from making any other porcelain pieces: it takes twenty to thirty different kinds of processes.

MD Is there a division of labour in the processes? Are there specialists carrying out the individual steps?

AW Yes, it's always been done like that.

MD In the West, we often think of this kind of process as Fordism, as an invention by the car manufacturer Henry Ford, but in fact it's a much older invention.

AW Oh, much, much older. The profession is so sophisticated and mature. When we talk about culture or civilised society, we're really talking about how clearly all those processes are defined – you know, this kind of language, those vocabularies, how rich and how refined those divisions are. They have very clear rules. It's fascinating to look at how Chinese culture developed in older times through these rich vocabularies in all different kinds of making, through carpentry, porcelain, paper-making and printing.

MD How do our contemporary conceptions of distinctions between art, craft and design relate to the production at the Imperial Court? It seems to me that those concepts were understood quite differently, more fluidly, perhaps?

AW In ancient times everything was designed for one person to appreciate, which was the Emperor. Everything had just one standard and everybody was trying to reach that level: to perfect the product, which is of very high quality and definition. If we go to museums to see objects from that time, we'll still be very surprised by the quality. Today, of course, we still use the same technology and the same kind of skills. Jingdezhen has this tradition, but we're using that perfection to meet a contemporary understanding and definition of life so that it can apply to the general public. This is why we're making things on such a massive scale and with such effort and for such an institution, while at the same time the object itself – which we call art – is of no use. We can't use it or apply it to our struggle of surviving. In ancient times in China there were very few cases when objects were purely for aesthetic appreciation or to make some kind of statement. But today, this phenomenon will be experienced by millions and in the most publicised location. People will realise that these are really individual pieces, even though it looks as if it's one piece. Each one is identical with the other 100 million. And those numbers relate to the individual under this massive condition. They're all sunflower seeds, but there's no real connection there: they're just accumulated together for the event.

MD So the work refers to the relationship between the individual and the mass. Is there any specific meaning to the number of seeds that make up the work, which are estimated to be 100 million seeds?

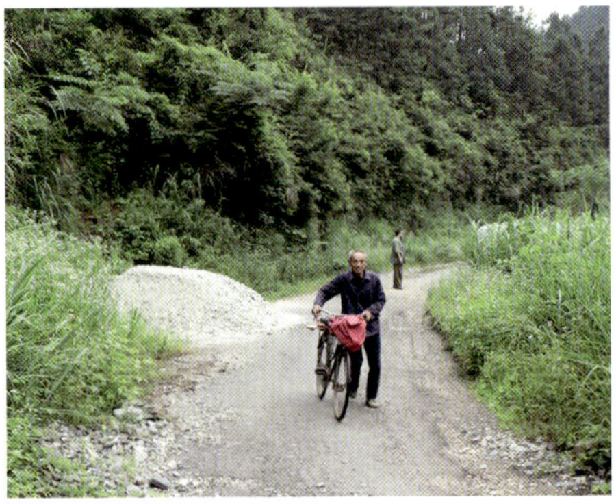
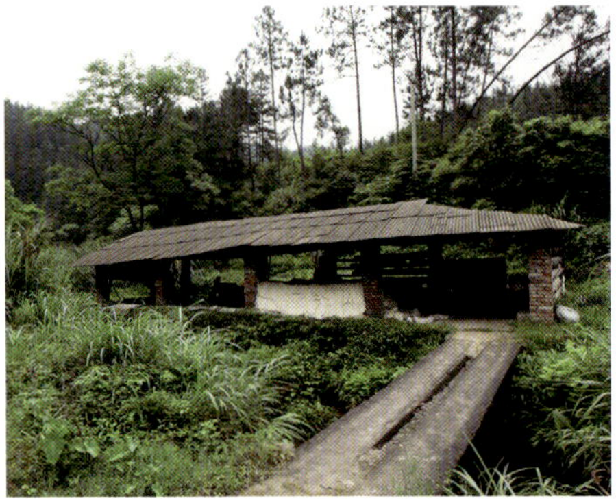
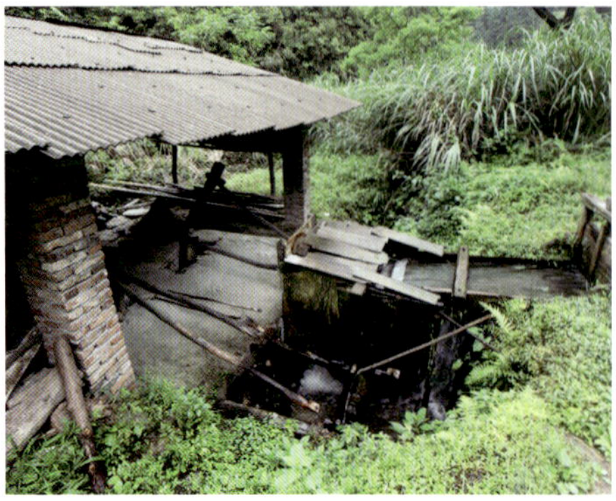
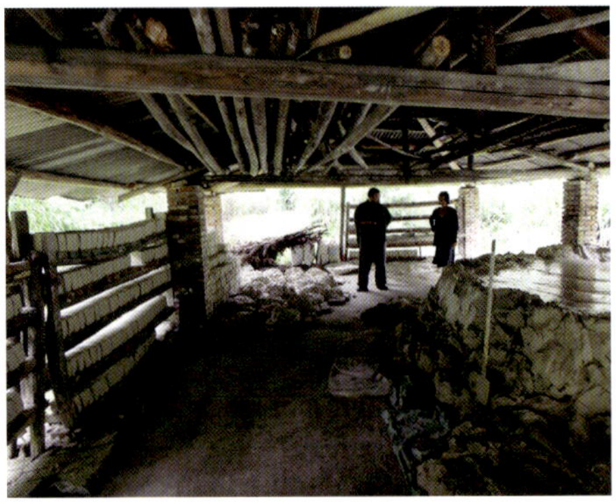
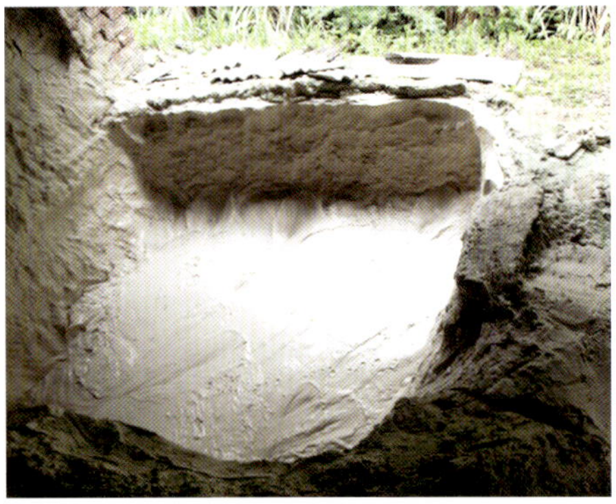
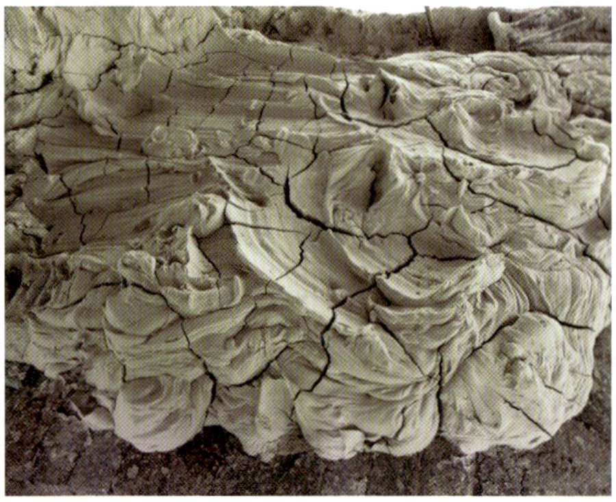
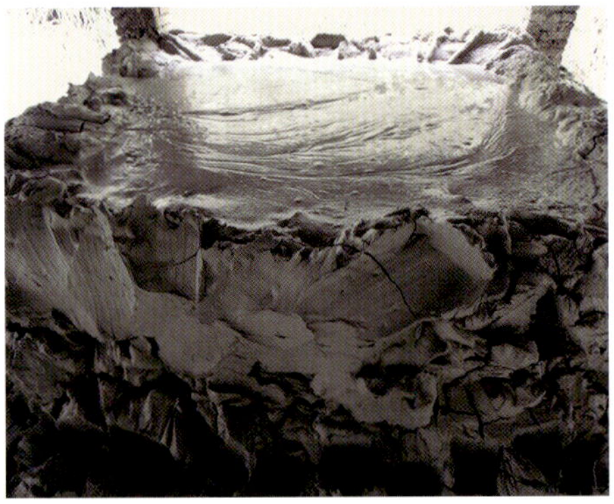
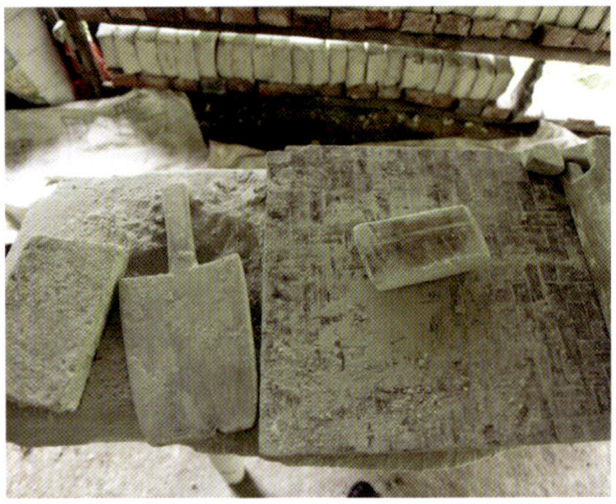
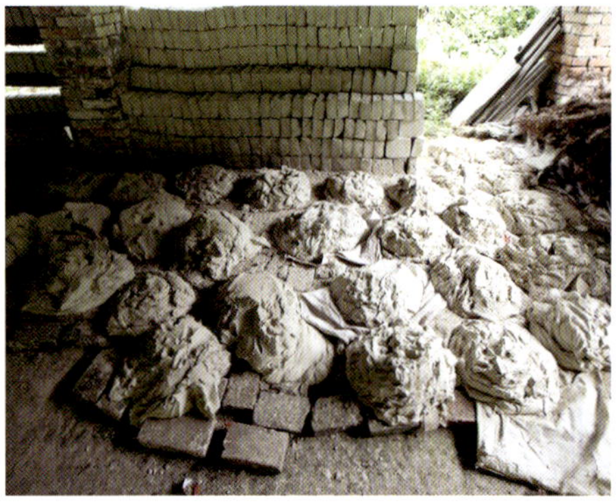
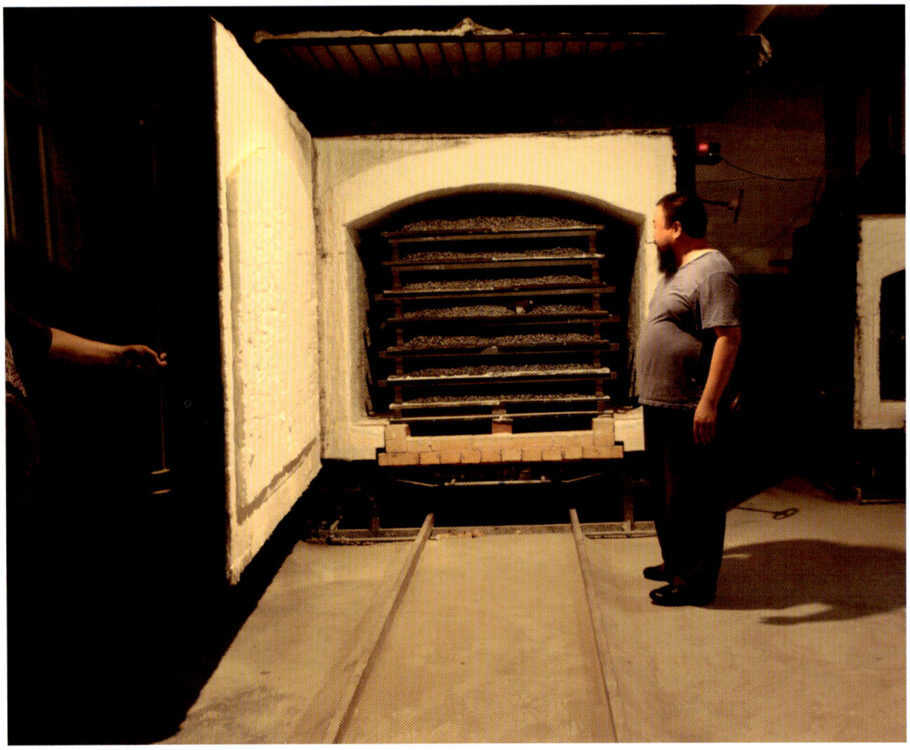
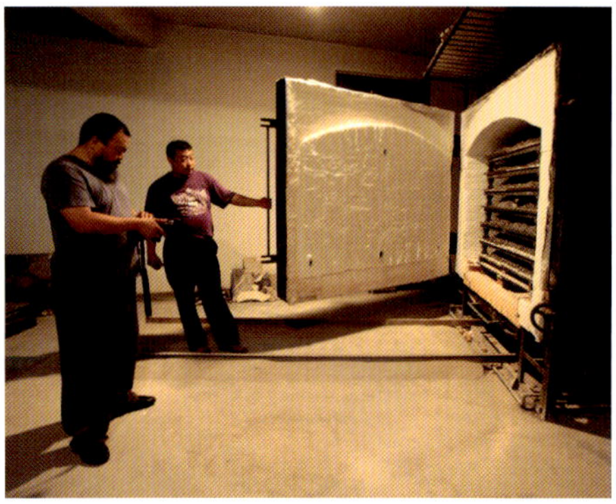
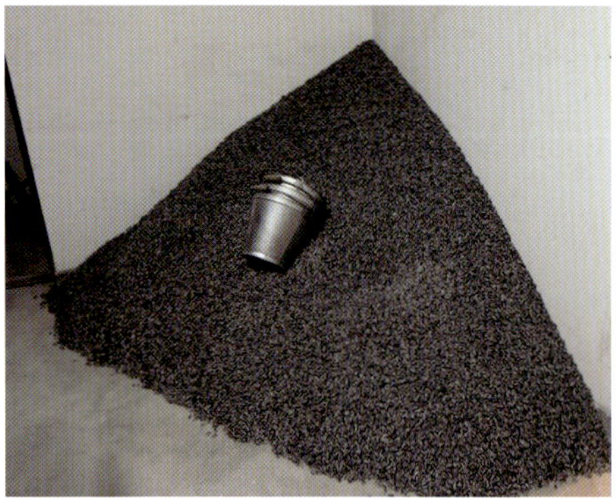

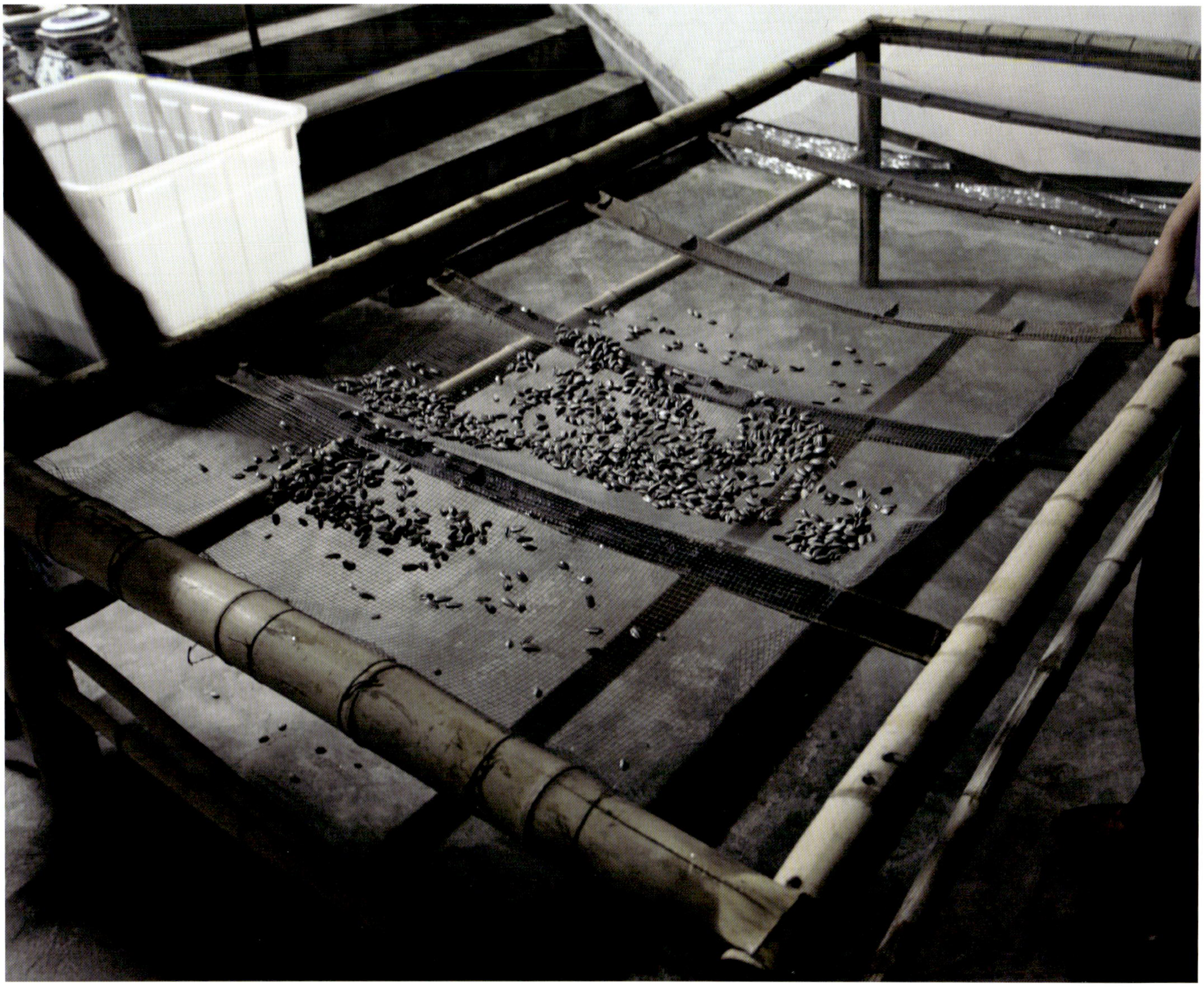
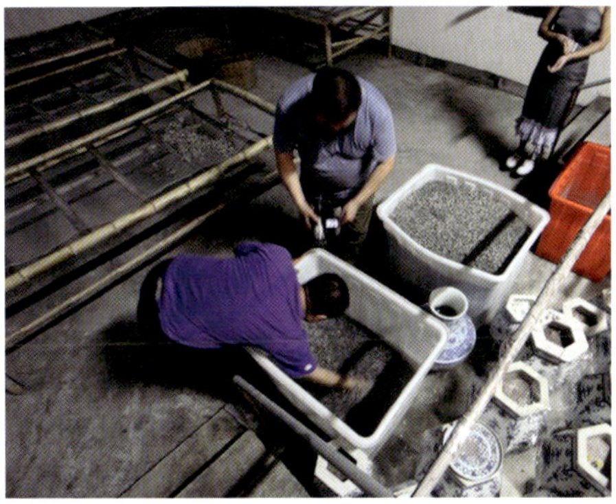
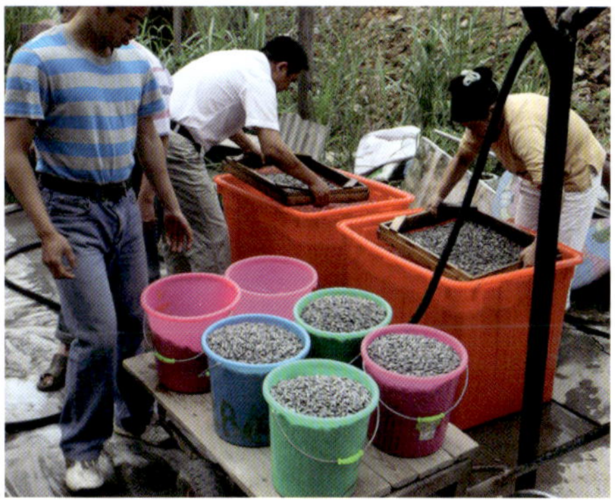
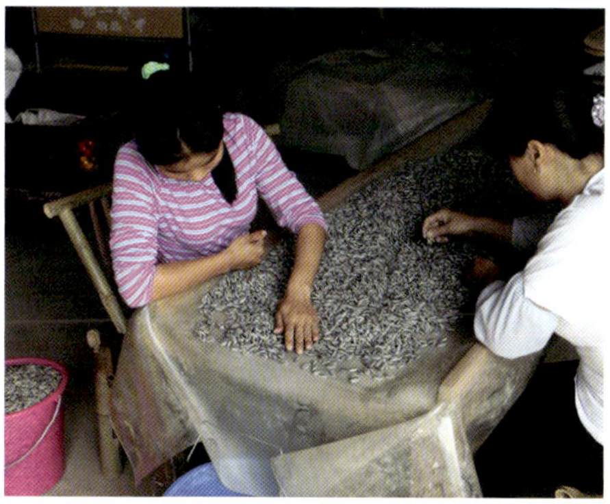
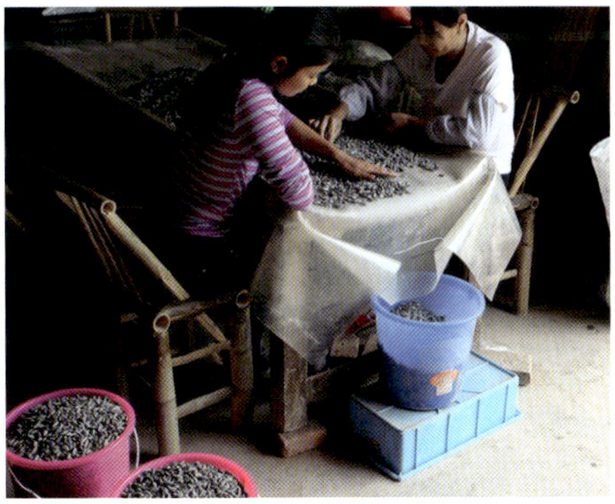
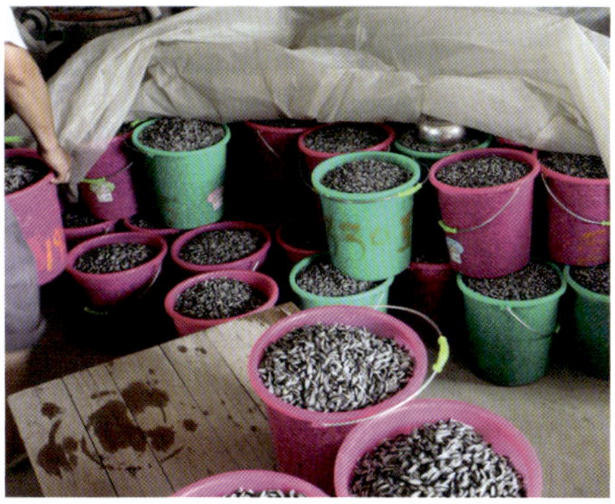
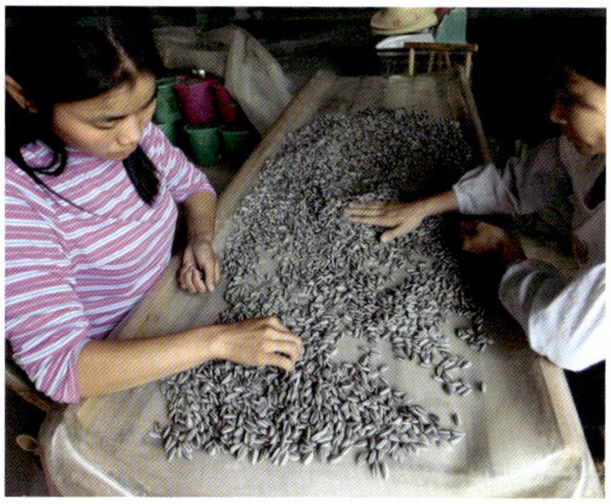

AW The number can relate to everybody's experience. If there's a single object that can express my understanding of numbers in China, or has meaning that everybody can share, then it's the sunflower seed. The Chinese have been called sunflowers because Chairman Mao was referred to as the sun and the sunflower always faces the sun. That was perhaps the most published image during the Cultural Revolution. We were all sunflowers. There was a lot of music, literature and writing about this. It was very funny. [figs.51–2]

When we made the first pile of three million seeds, I realised that this was the number of vehicles in Beijing. Then I said: 'Oh, my God, this isn't possible, it looks so massive!' Then we made twelve million seeds. We realised that this was still less than Beijing's population. Even when we've produced the whole work, it will still be only one tenth of China's population. For over two and a half years, so many people have worked on this product. Even if we kept up this speed, it would take us ten years to reach the number of the entire population. So it's almost impossible. You realise the reality is often bigger than we can imagine. And then you think about the issues that relate to this: how everybody needs to eat, how everybody has their own desires, their consumption, and then you think about nature and resources. You can easily drive yourself mad just by thinking about those things. Often we think, did we calculate this right?

JB I'd like to return to a comment that you made earlier, when you mentioned a connection between the concept behind the sunflower seeds and your activities on the internet. In recent projects you used your blog, until it was shut down in 2009, and now you use the social networking site Twitter to create a social dimension in your work, inviting individuals to participate directly.

AW Yes, in the past three or four years I've been working very passionately on the internet. Many people have said this work is like Twitter: Twitter is ocean-like; it can spread very fast amongst millions of people; each Tweet looks identical, but every one is different. The organisation for *Fairytale* 2007, the work I made for Documenta, which involved bringing 1,001 Chinese to Germany, was carried out through the internet. It was very efficient. It was a miracle that we can't repeat; handling all those people. It was a unique experience for them – either that or people suffered and were damaged by the experience! [laughs] Every day I talk on the internet for over eight hours. Last night, I stayed up till two o'clock. I only had five hours sleep. For me, the internet is about how to act as an individual and at the same time to reach massive numbers of unknown people who you can identify with mentally or in discussion. It's so fascinating. I think this changes the structure of society all the time – this kind of massiveness made up of individuals. It reflects today's condition much better than the old society and the old structures. Of course, we're still trying to adjust to the new condition every day.

JB It seems as if communicating through the internet is extremely popular in China, more so perhaps than in Europe, and you appear to have a huge following and presence.

AW China now has an internet-user population of 450 million – so that's amazing. But the internet is heavily censored. You can't freely access the four biggest international sites – YouTube, Twitter, Facebook, Google – they're all censored or blocked. Because education abandoned them, the younger generation from the 1980s and 90s are all immersed in the internet, so that's why I act on it. I'm learning too; it's like university. And I can talk to people about my opinions or my interests and everybody can see it. It's so transparent. You can easily understand a person through just one sentence. I can't think of a better means of communication than that for the masses.

MD When the internet was invented, the people behind it were convinced of its revolutionary potential as a democratising tool. They thought that it would change the way in which human beings interact with each other, but also with authority and systems of power. It was often

Previous spread: Production of sunflower seeds in Jingdezhen, southern China, 2010

51
Below and right:
Item and badges from the Cultural Revolution (1966–76)

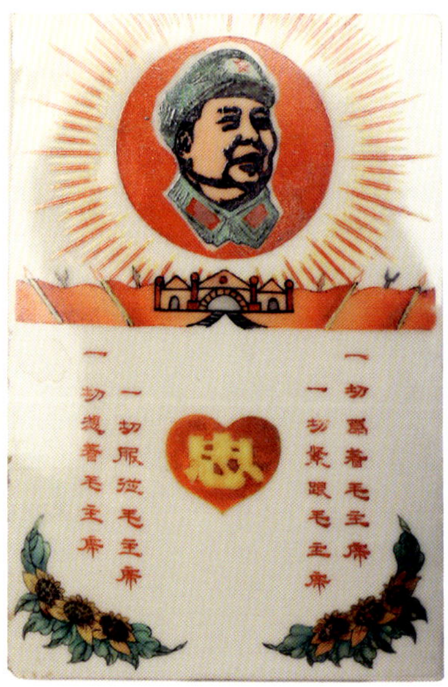

contrasted with broadcast systems, which only go in one direction, because it allowed people to talk to each other. Over the last ten years, many sociologists in Europe and America have become more sceptical because it's been adopted very successfully by organisations that repeat a kind of one-directional broadcasting. But at the same time, there are always new tools that surface, like Twitter, that return power to individuals. So we think of the internet as a very complex tool that has great potential, but also has the potential for control. That's also something that we see in China, isn't it?

AW It's true. Look at the recent economic collapse: we probably thought, with today's scientific developments, that things couldn't go so badly wrong. But people just manipulated all the numbers on the computers and suddenly they realised they'd created this big problem. All tools are designed and used by people, and people, of course, have all kinds of intentions as to how to use the internet. The government in China is trying to control information and to control human minds. This is how they maintain power. The new technology has made it more difficult. Twitter and blogs have become a channel for people to exercise their own voices, even if it's very limited, and to find the right information and the right path to associate with. The real potential is not yet clear. If we look at what's happening in Iran, or what's happening in China today, we can see that the internet has played a great role. Walking along the street in China today is so different from even two years ago. If I walk for perhaps two hours, I'll be recognised by a few people. I don't know them, but they've even memorised my words. So you can see how influential it can be, because I'm not a social person; I don't go out; I don't go to parties or openings; I only socialise though the media. So this is a truly miraculous situation. People can select information, build their own knowledge structures and express themselves. That makes us individual. In the history of human development, it's never been like that.

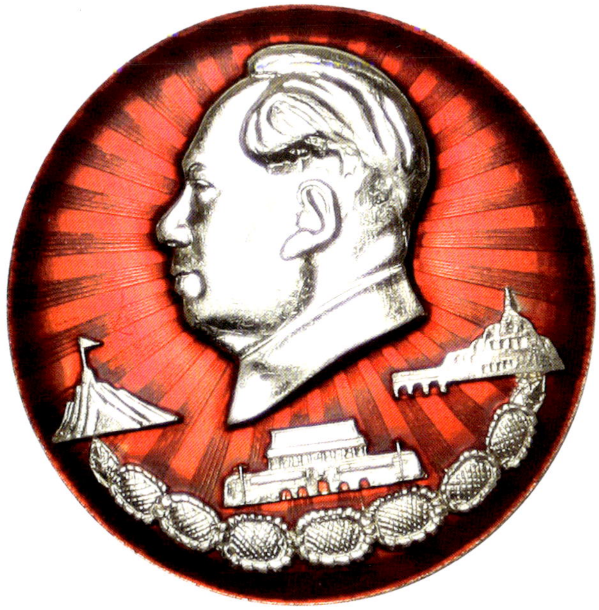

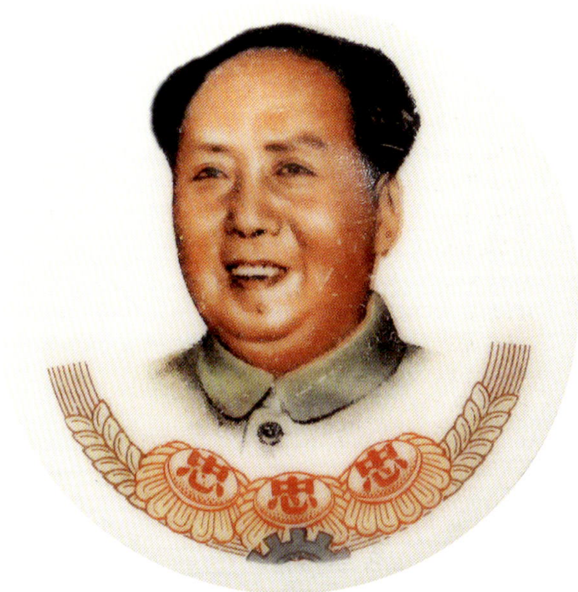

MD It changes the way in which individuals become individuals.

AW It puts everybody in the same condition, because it's a tool that everybody can freely use.

MD I wonder about the relationship between China's economic growth and the internet in China. Over the last ten or twenty years, China has become the place where computers are made and so perhaps access to computers is easier even for poor people compared with other parts of the world. So to some extent the democratic potential of these tools is related to capitalist production systems.

AW Yes, in many cases you see undeveloped countries speedily catching up. And this is happening so fast, even we can't believe it. Everything has to be made here in China. It reminds me of what Lenin said: when capitalists want to be more prosperous they try to exploit poor nations but at the same time they equip them with the higher skills and management and that could kill the capitalist society.

People in China have come from a history in which there was no individualism; everybody was just a piece that identified with another, more like a military type of unified society. Now, gradually the society is becoming a mass of independent minds with independent behaviours – nobody knows what's going to happen. It's too big and the phenomenon is too new for us to cope with. What about the natural resources, the skills for surviving and the struggle when all those people become more efficient and they all have stronger demands? What's going to happen?

MD The Italian philosopher Giorgio Agamben has written about what he calls the condition of 'bare life' – the condition of people in parts of the developing world who live on a subsistence level. We saw some of that this morning when we drove through the areas that are being completely pulled down and saw people who live in the destroyed buildings, cleaning bricks to recycle them. How do you feel about this condition of 'bare life' in a country like China, which is developing so fast and generating so much wealth that it seems as if the differential between the very poor and the very rich is getting bigger and bigger?

AW China is a special case because it's become a world power in such a short time through a few unique conditions. It's like it took a hundred years to dig this big hole, then suddenly they let the water start to flow in, and it created this tremendous volume and pressure. So it's a phenomenon that nowhere else has. Chairman Mao used to say: 'Under the Communist leadership, when we have the men we can create the miracles.' But the Communist party is very skilfully profiting from capitalism. It's become even more powerful because money is coming in – they're taking property that belongs to the nation for their own profit. You know, small privileged circles. So that makes social injustice and unfairness become much worse than historically. At the beginning, Communism was fighting for social justice, then suddenly it becomes national Capitalism, which is the most powerful because all the rules and laws are designed for its own interests. It's basically a ruthless mafia-type power. But of course, this may cause a revolution. So China is at a very uncertain stage. There are a lot of social problems.

MD The early Marxists talked about the way in which the bourgeoisie in Capitalist countries worked to avoid revolution by making minimal concessions to the working classes, to keep people at a level just below revolution. Do you feel that the Chinese government is trying to play that game as well – trying to avoid revolution and social change?

AW I think at the very beginning they just thought of becoming rich. It's like when you're hungry, you think: let's have a banquet. But then once you've had the banquet, you realise that there are a lot of problems associated with it – your health, how much it costs, and all those things. The Chinese government is trying to manage China as a vehicle on the fast track. Now it's on the fast track, they realise there are tremendous problems with the engine and the system. But they

Pot from the Cultural Revolution
(1966–76)

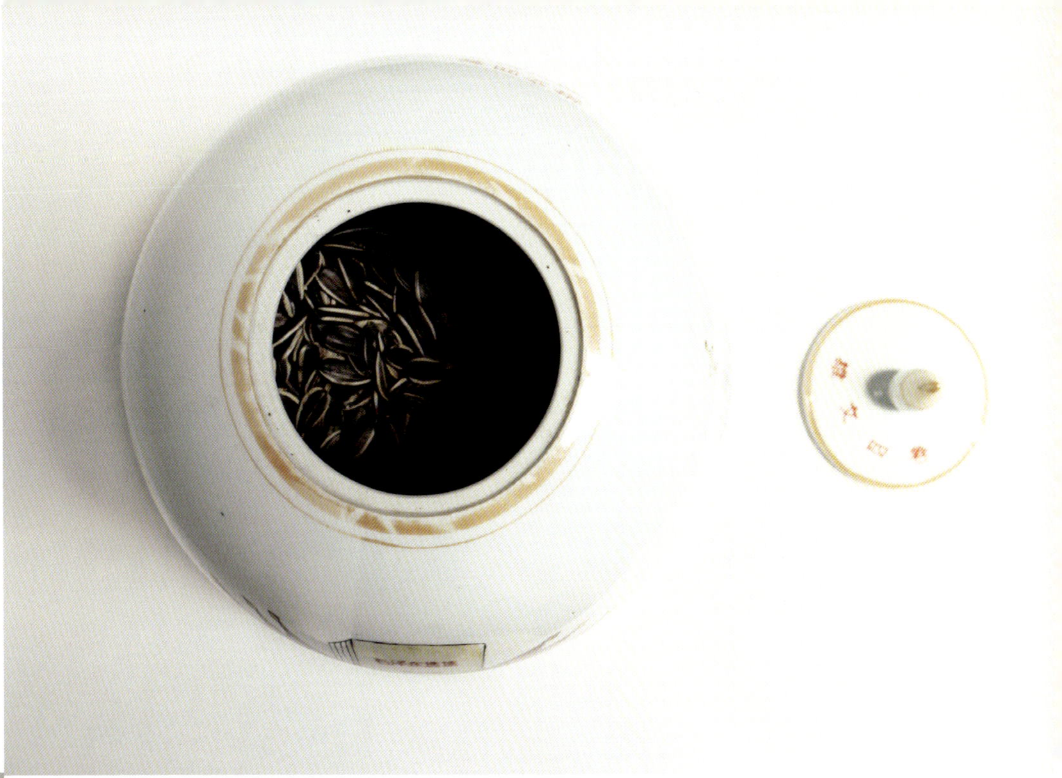

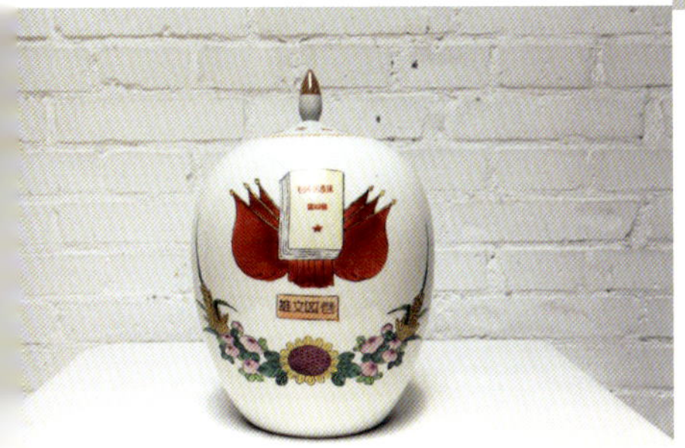

can't get off the fast track. And all the people driving on this highway are very cautious because it could cause big problems. I think it's very dangerous, but it seems there's no way out. Of course, society has become much richer. But the problem is, when people become richer they become more conscious about fairness. They have more demands. So people start to question the government's capability: why is the structure so old? Why do they have to be there? And then the government becomes ridiculous. Everybody starts to laugh at them. That's something the government still can't resolve, because they refuse to have multi-parties or elections or an independent judicial system or an open forum to discuss matters. There are no different levels of society; it's simple: it's the government and the mass, which is very problematic.

MD There have recently been particular problems in factories in China, for example in the Taiwanese-run computer factory Foxconn.

AW Yes, that's a very interesting case. Within quite a short space of time, thirteen people jumped out of the window there. As a factory they have some 300,000 people in one base. Actually, it's a modern jail. Of course, the conditions there are probably better than the previous conditions, which is why people joined. They can play ping-pong or use the library, but still it's a jail. There's almost no other life beyond the factory. How can humans be treated that way? The difference when they paint the sunflower seeds is that those people can go home; they can come or not come; they act more like farmers. But in the factory, it's not like that. It's like the military. That drove those people crazy. They thought their lives could never be better than that. They became part of the equipment. But who's the real killer? The real killer is anybody who uses computers and who appreciates how 'cheap' modern technology can be. It's so wonderful, huh? We all push for a better, more efficient society, but somebody has to pay for it. It's not 'not' paying. But nobody cares in the West. People just want to have cheaper products and those manufacturers make a lot of money – crazy money. And it seems everybody's happy, but really not everybody's happy.

JB In this situation, what's the role of the artist? What's the responsibility of the artist?

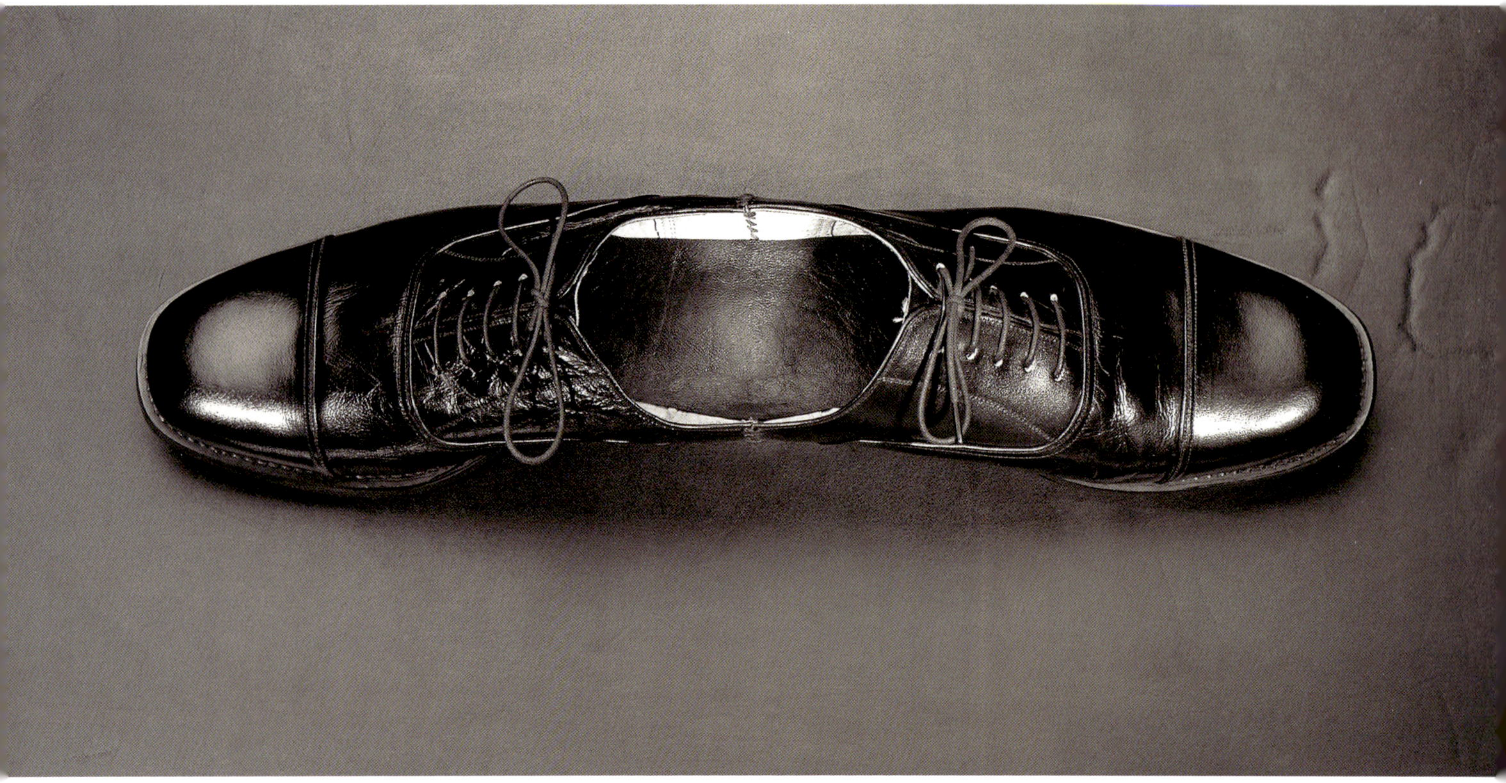

53
One-Man-Shoe 1987
Shoes and wood
58 x 29 x 15cm

AW The artist doesn't produce food and doesn't make clothes, so I think the role of the artist is somehow apart from the real struggle. The artist can ask questions or express opinions that are more independent, to raise a kind of consciousness. Actually, I don't think there's much an artist can do. Most artists are corrupt. But good writers or good philosophers or people who really care about human behaviour and society are always needed.

MD Do you think the fact that an artist makes things that are useless in some way means that he or she has a perspective on what's going on in society, a detachment, a distance from this struggle?

AW Useless or useful: it all relates to value judgement and aesthetic judgement. It also relates to morals and philosophy, which always need to be announced, whether as a human or as a society. We need this kind of practice that can be disassociated or detached from daily struggles.

MD So in that sense, there's a continuity between the work that you do as an artist and the other activities that you carry out – as an architect, on-line, in other media.

AW From a very young age I started to sense that an individual has to set an example in society. Your own acts or behaviour tell the world who you are and what kind of society you think it should be. You do this by making something or acting on it – it has to be visible. I don't believe a society would have a conscience without those acts. So to make art is to give a clear definition, which people can argue about. It doesn't have to be a loud announcement, it can be very small, almost invisible, but it has to be a fragment of the truth. As individuals, we're always conditioned. We have our own mental conditions, and those conditions have to be clearly defined.

MD I'd like to go back to when you were talking about the conditions in a factory compared with the working conditions of the people painting the sunflower seeds. Both of them are large industrialised processes, but you were very clear that there was a difference between the two for you: that the people making the sunflower seeds are less alienated in their work than those who work in the factories.

AW The people who are making the sunflower seeds work more in a tradition of craftsmanship, like the condition of workshops, which is the condition they're used to. They can work at home with their children playing nearby, they can do it now or later, or not do it at all. But the difference from what they were doing before – a very big difference – is that previously they understood what the object they were making was for. They made pottery – a bowl, or objects that they've made for thousands of years – and they knew exactly what it was for, why this pottery was good or not good. But with the sunflower seeds, they'd never understand what they're for. They have to make so many, in such quantities, the whole town is doing them now – the elderly, the young, they're all participating. But they wouldn't understand that it's for an exhibition. That's a very big problem.

I remember another case that's strangely connected: I made a pair of shoes (*One-Man Shoe* 1987; fig.53) and I wanted to polish them when I was in New York. So I went to the neighbourhood shoe-maker, a Polish couple who always polished my shoes; they have a machine so it's easier. I gave the shoes to the man. He looked at the shoes and his face became very serious. He went back behind this small booth to call his wife out and they both looked at them. Then they looked at my feet, and then they said to me, 'We don't have this black polish.' I said, 'No, don't worry, brown polish is fine.' Then they said 'Our machine's broken.' And then I realised that they were very angry because their lifetime's work had been doing something that's meaningful, that helps society and these were shoes you couldn't wear. They didn't like that. They appreciate a better quality shoe. To perfect a craft means you're really helping society – you have some kind of pride. It's rewarding besides the money. But then you realise, something that's meaningless – that can drive you crazy! That's why those people killed themselves when they jumped out of the factory, because that situation reduces the meaning of life.

JB You've worked with other craftspeople, for example in your 'Furniture Series' [1997–ongoing; fig.54]. How did the carpenters, who'd previously been producing objects for use, relate to the objects they were making?

AW It's the same situation. You know, when you have to 'destroy' a nice piece of Ming furniture – I don't think that I did destroy it – but to deconstruct or re-construct it into other forms really damages our understanding of its meaning. The whole establishment is to do with value and usage. Wittgenstein said: 'Meaning is use.' So when we're making something so precise and so perfect but with no use, then it completely destroys the meaning. I don't think you could destroy the meaning any more effectively than by doing that. That's a characteristic of my work: to ask this question about those simple meanings. For the carpenters, at the very beginning it was very difficult; later, they saw some exhibitions and I think they've become more used to it. I wouldn't say people understand it. Actually, I don't really understand it! [laughs] But I'm fascinated by the act.

JB If we think about the materials that you've used in your work – for example Neolithic vases [5000–3000BC] and dismantled temple wood [Qing Dynasty, 1644–1911] – it's interesting the way that you look at history and the past with a kind of archaeological approach. Looking at artefacts and what their value and meaning is seems to be something that runs through your practice.

AW People think that I'm interested in Chinese traditions, which isn't true. I'm more interested in our past human behaviour and our understanding of values, and I explore this by dealing with some existing readymade concept that everybody accepts as

Below:
Ai Weiwei in his studio, March 2010
with pile of seeds

54
Grapes 2008
17 stools from the Qing dynasty (1644–1911)
167 x 180 x 157 cm

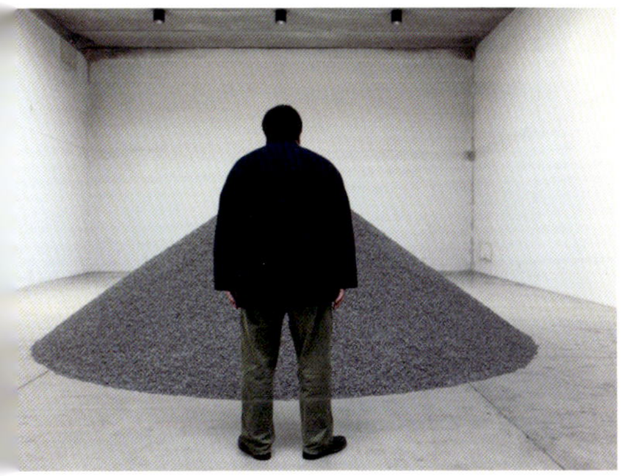

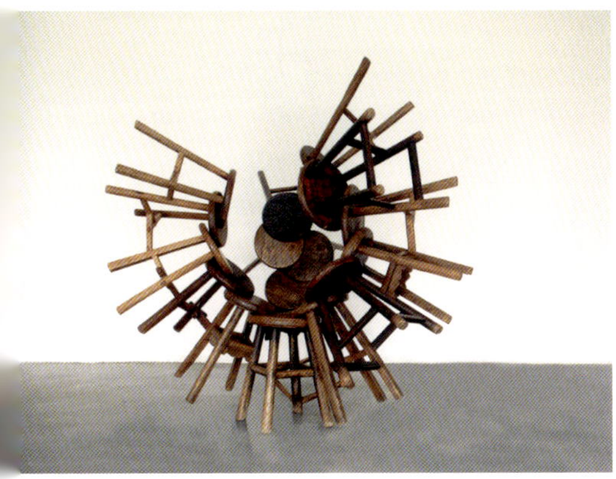

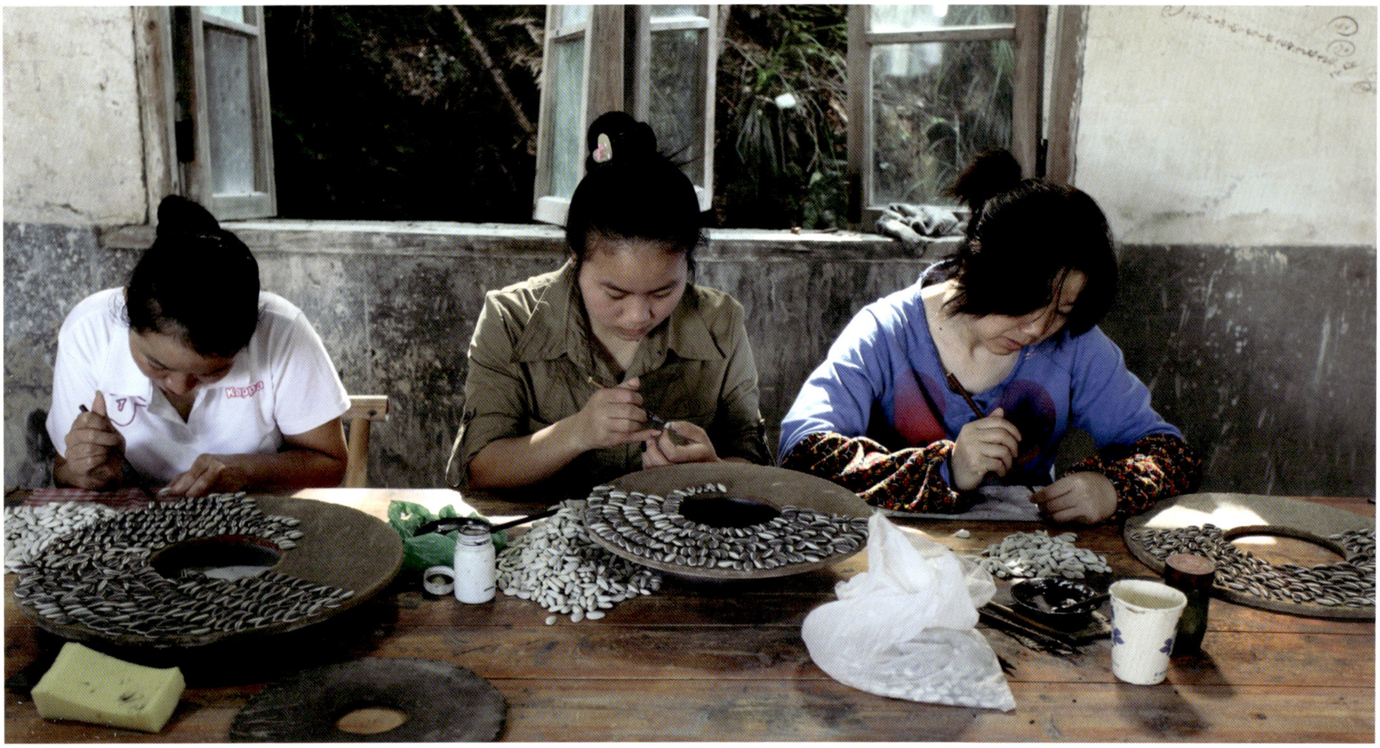

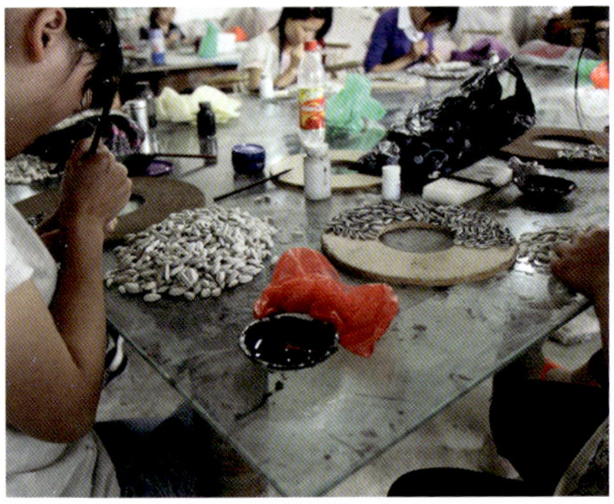

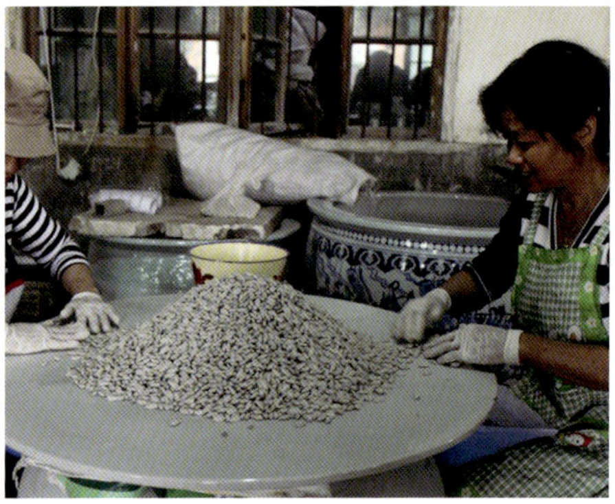

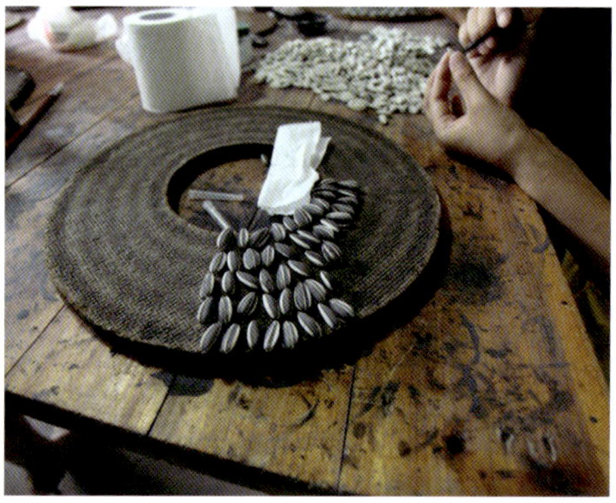

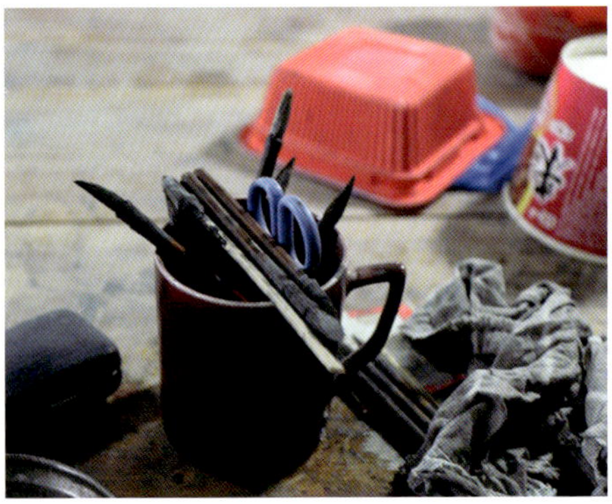

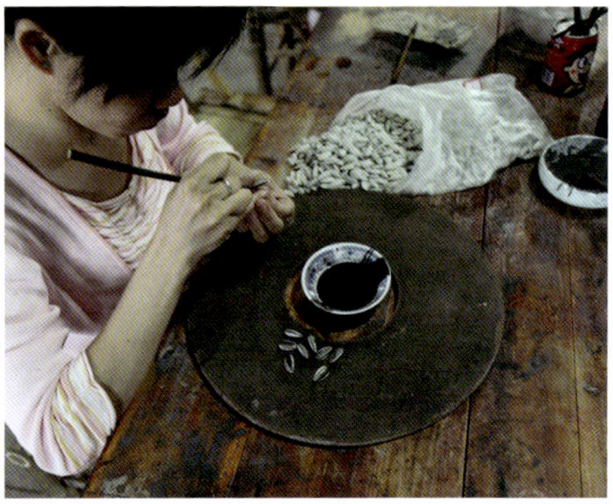

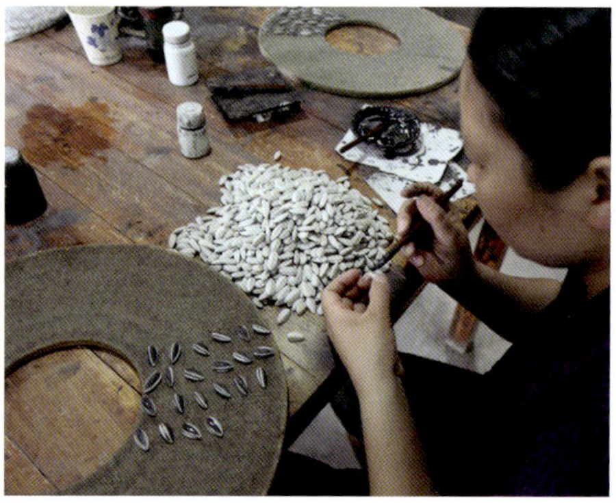

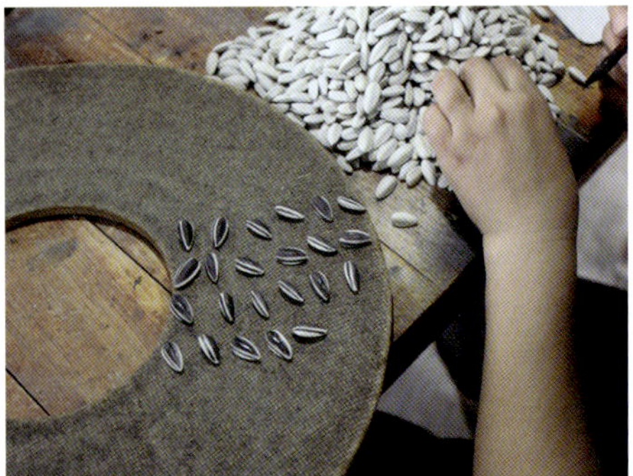

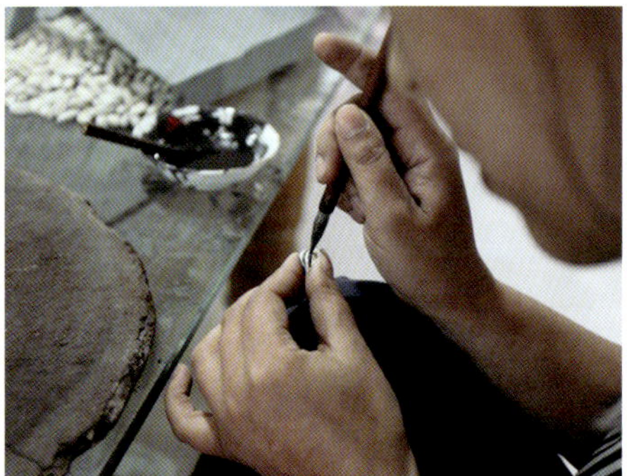

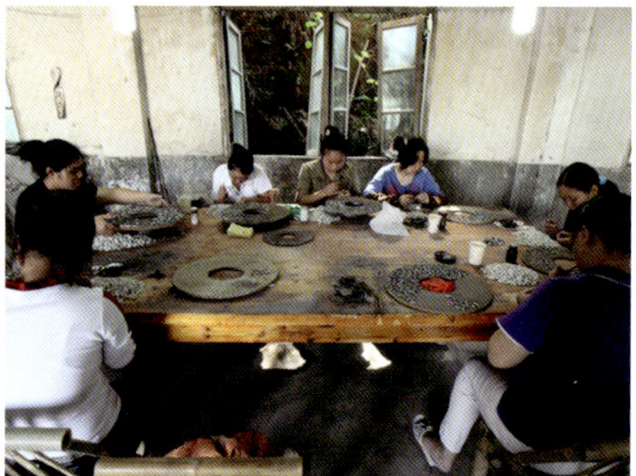

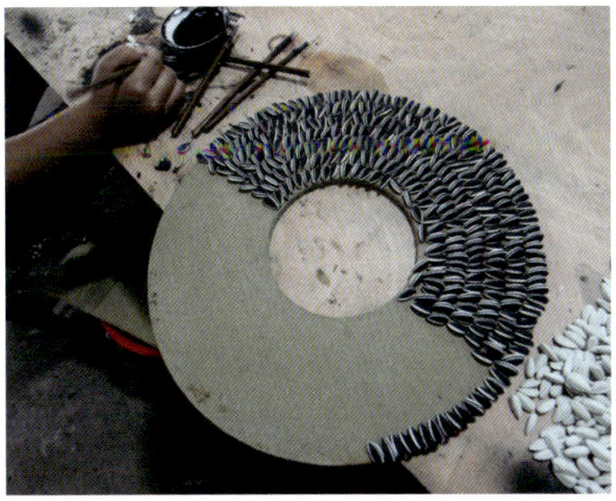
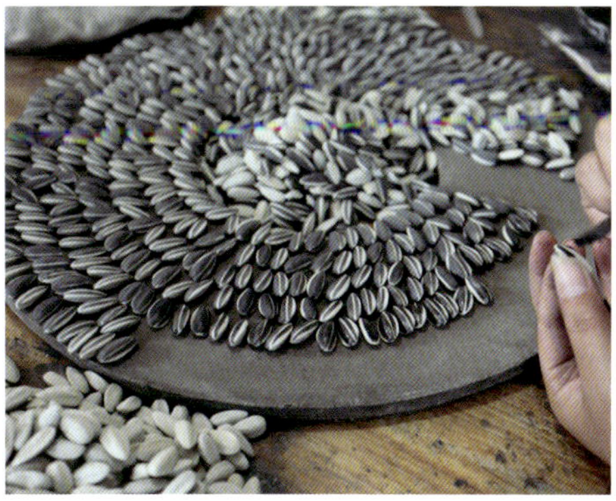
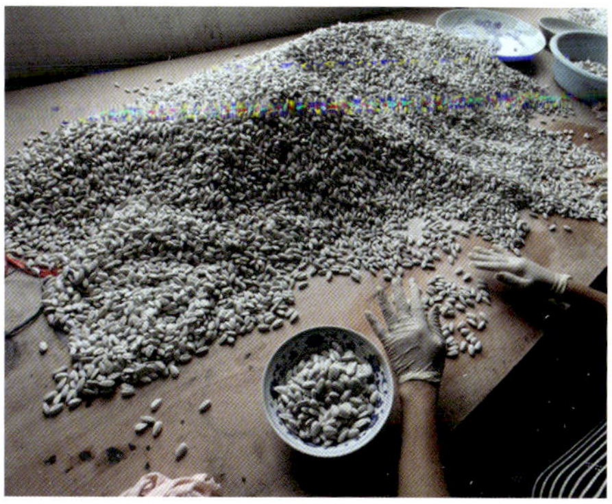
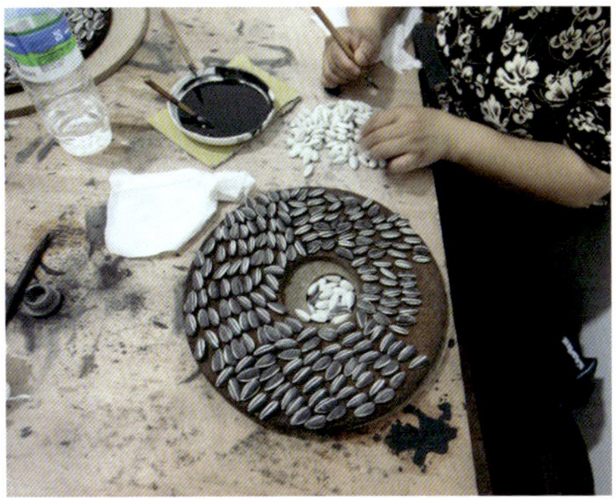
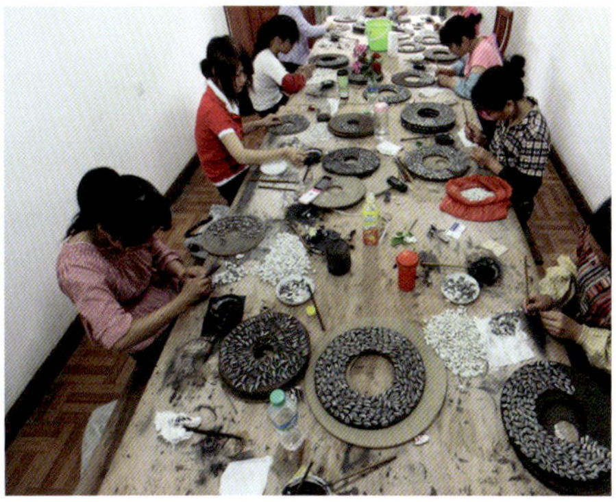
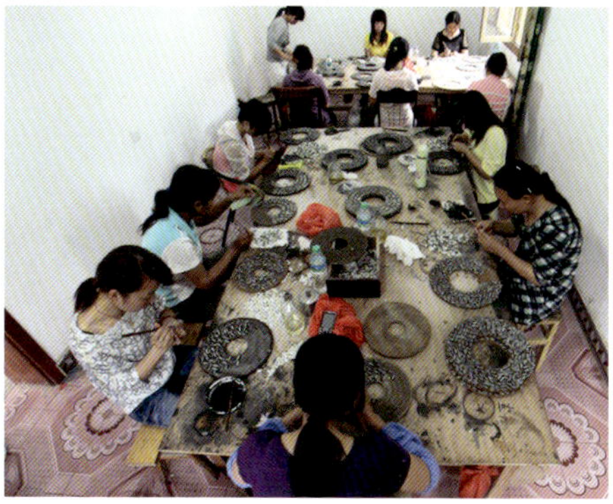
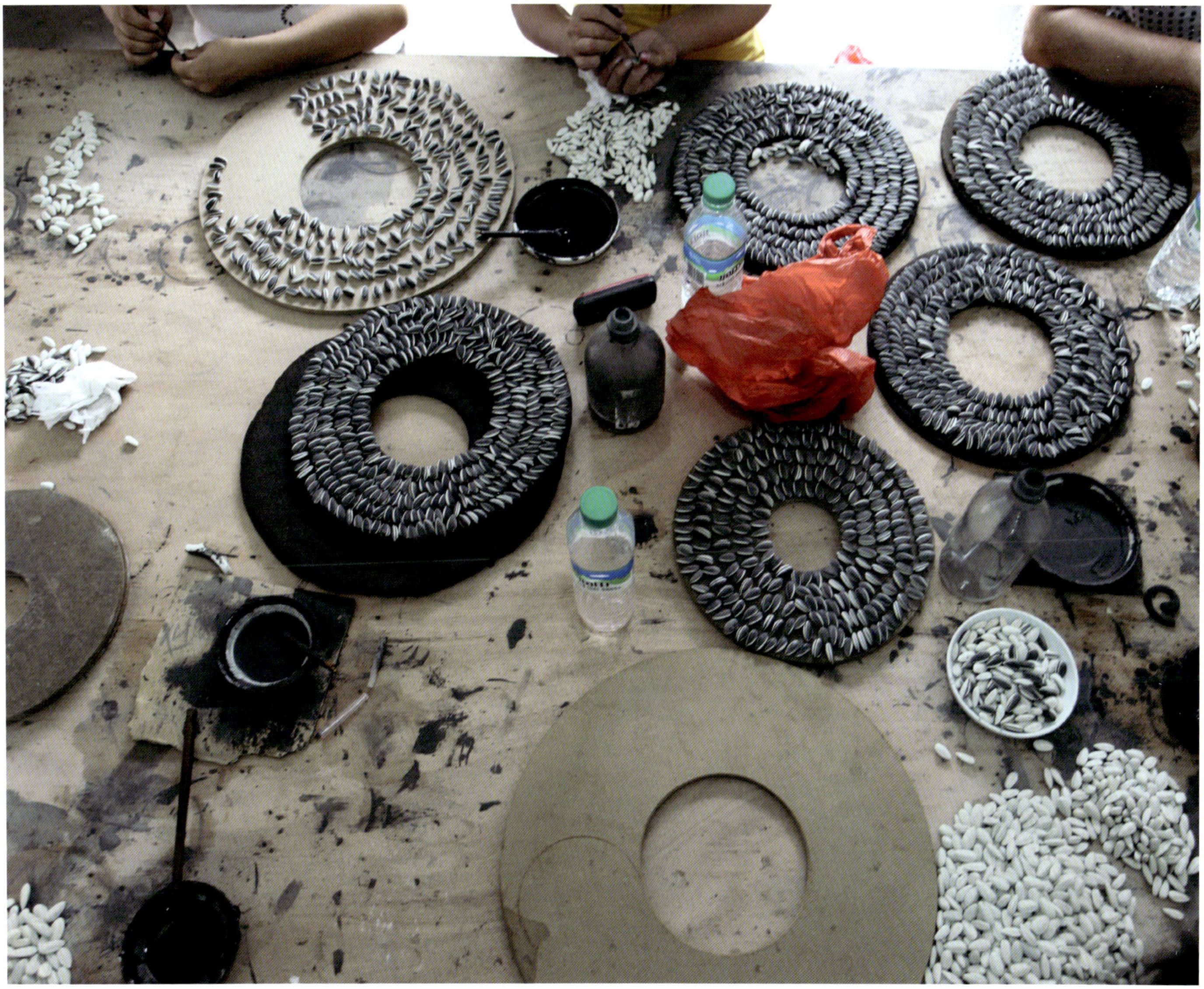

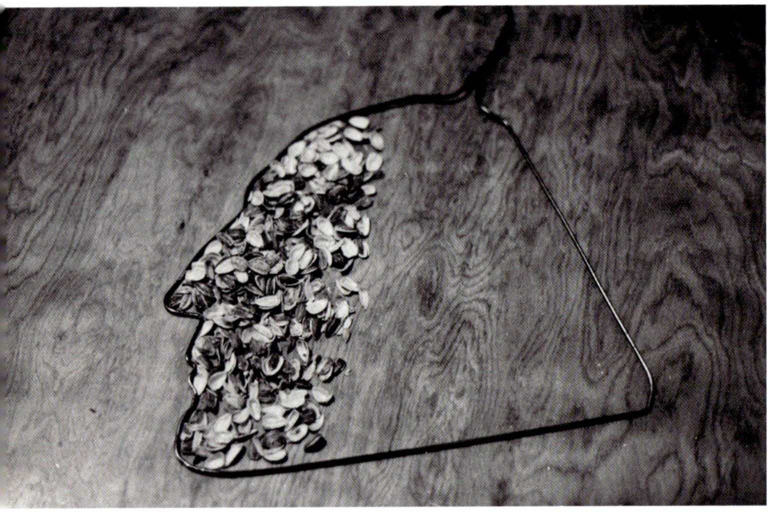

55
Hanging Man and sunflower seeds 1983
Sculpture photographed with seeds, from *New York Photographs, 1983–1993*

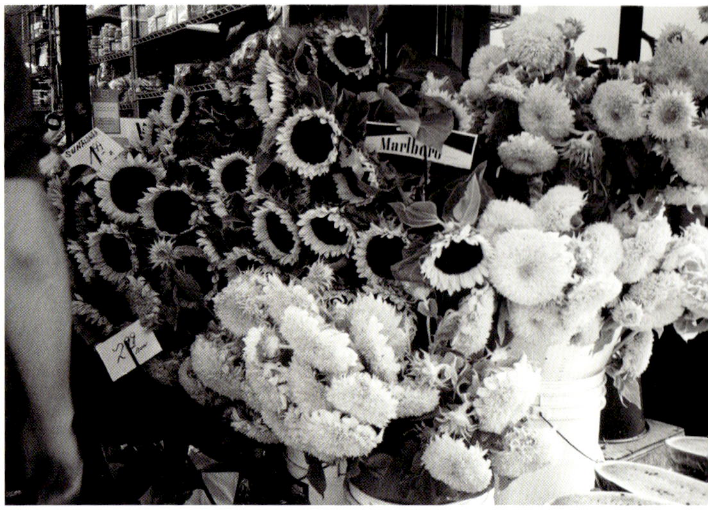

56
Sunflowers in a Shop in Haiti 1992

Previous spread: Production of sunflower seeds in Jingdezhen, southern China, 2010

untouchable or fixed. By dealing with that, you can easily reach the present or use it to raise your own points. Most of the time we can't really figure out the meaning, but we can find a path, and we can go out from there. We can put it in proportion to our own understanding.

MD You said people often mistakenly think you're interested in the traditions of Chinese art. Where do you see your artistic practice in relation to twentieth-century art movements?

AW The struggle of twentieth-century art movements was to find a new definition through a different type of art, and to re-announce our condition. Even at the beginning of the last century, or at the end of the nineteenth century, people already sensed this social change – that modernity was coming. But still nobody could have imagined today's world. Even half a century ago, we couldn't have imagined what's happening today. We're always haunted by the nightmares of before, but we also have to cope with the new condition and I think that's a very slow process. Only what's recognised by society is defined by society. Some ideas that were raised 100 years ago, we only recognise later: 'Oh that guy was very interesting because he raised that question a long time ago.' But most things that are popular today we'll soon forget.

MD That's clearly the case with Duchamp: that it took a long time for him to be recognised. Perhaps there's a similar situation in China now, where it's not easy for ordinary members of society to understand what contemporary art is.

AW Yes, because the original concept is from the West, from the continuous thinking of the development of the West. But China today is also a product of Western modernisation. What we can see on the surface is still the result of the Industrial Revolution. But of course, this society bears a lot of its original character – we normally call it culture – and this has shaped and formed its differences. It's very strong and very different. And people in other cultures are equally confused by what's happening in the world today.

MD I think that's a very good point. It's not that contemporary

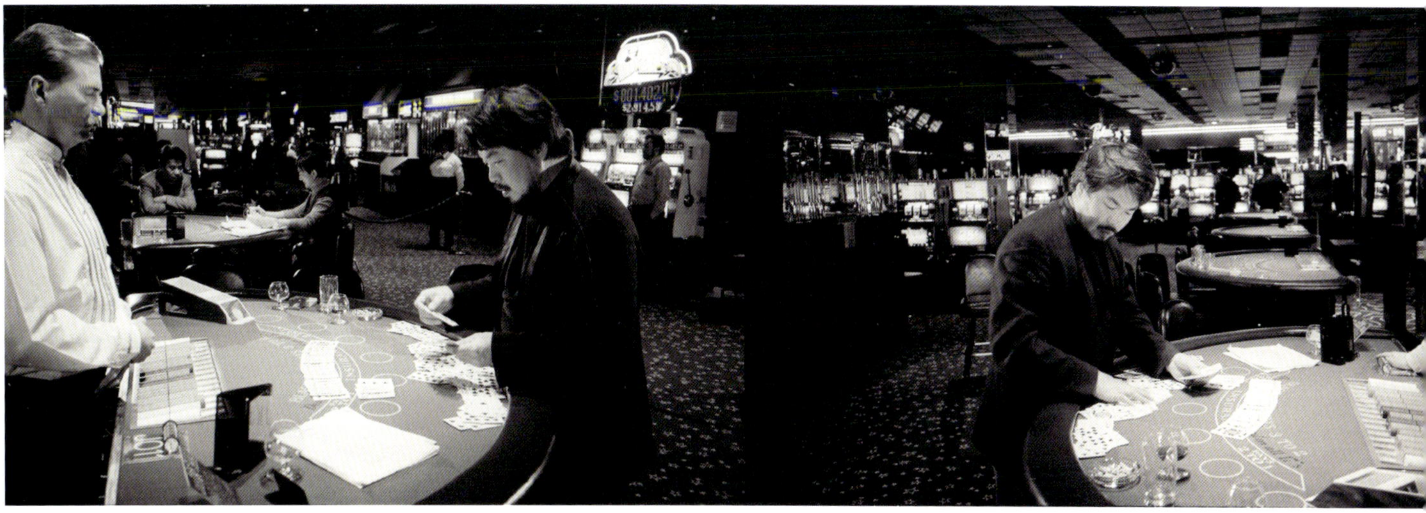

57
Setting up Cards. Atlantic City
1993, from *New York Photographs*,
1983–1993

art is confusing or difficult to understand, but that contemporary life is difficult and confusing.

AW You wake up and realise you're not on land, you're up in the air, or on the bottom of the ocean. The conditions are completely different.

JB As a young artist in New York in the 1980s, you created a sculpture of Marcel Duchamp's profile using a coat hanger. I remember seeing a photograph in one of your books that shows that object on a table with the husks of sunflower seeds piled into the corner of it [fig.55]. In the context of the work for the Turbine Hall, this documentary photograph seems a very resonant image.

AW I'd forgotten about that. It was a photograph that I took in 1983 in New York. That hanger was just always around there. I was an artist then, but nobody else thought so. The rest of the time, I was just eating sunflower seeds and hanging out. Yes, thanks for mentioning that image; many of the things we do today we can find traces of in an earlier time.

JB There's an interesting parallel with Duchamp, who was an exile in America. When you left China for America in the 1980s, was it also as an exile?

AW An exile, but a much lonelier exile. I spent a lot of time at Atlantic City playing cards. [fig.57]

MD And Duchamp played chess.

AW Yes, but my play was for winning. I couldn't afford to lose!

JB How did you feel when you returned to China from New York in the early 1990s, after China had undergone a period of such rapid change?

AW I grew up in the very remote northwest of China, then I had a chance to go to New York, and after twelve years, in 1993, I came back and stayed here – it's been about seventeen years. I couldn't really figure out how it became like it is now, or what it was going to become. If I look back, I think I made the best decision in New York at the time, not doing anything or becoming somebody. But that's also the only condition I could have had. It was a life without clear definition, and just hanging out there with a lot of freedom gave me the possibility not to attach myself to anything. It wasn't until very late, after I came back to China, that I had anything much to do. I called myself an artist, but for five or six years I didn't do any work. I just refused to become, or to accept, some other identity. Now I have the chance to show in Tate, which constantly surprises me. I think it's all some kind of conspiracy you guys made. It's wild!

MD It's an honour for us!

JB Since your return to Beijing, your practice has been an important influence for a younger generation of Chinese artists. Can you talk about this?

AW I've lived a life with a very strong character. When I was born, my family was suffering life-threatening damage, and there were political struggles. Not everybody has this kind of experience. And my earlier learning in New York was a difficult struggle, as it is for all young people who really want to be something; it's not easy. The life of an immigrant or misfit or exile constantly threw me into these kinds of mental struggles. I came back to this nation that I couldn't really recognise and I couldn't really think of as my homeland. China has gone from this very closed society to become a new monster in the world. There's nothing that I can passionately associate with in China

58
In front of Duchamp's Work, Museum of Modern Art 1987 from *New York Photographs, 1983–1993*

because I was so hurt and damaged by the society here and that still hasn't fundamentally changed. Everything's changed but the belief. The system is still there – the Communist system. So all those things put me into a position that's quite unique. Without those things, I think I'd be very different. And then suddenly I became fifty-three! If I want to be truthful to my own condition I have to be very alert and I have to make an effort to make some statement about art as a profession, which is the only thing I can clearly be associated with, and also to support the local community, the younger people, who also want to be artists or to be a little different from the previous generation. That's why I spend so much time on the internet; I think it just needs one sentence or one act and they'll understand the world much better: it might change the meaning of their life.

MD The situation for young artists in China is perhaps difficult because it's so easy to produce things in China compared with other countries, and the ease of production can sometimes be an obstacle to clarity of thought.

AW Yes, in every nation artists face very different problems. But I think that still they have an advantage here because of the ease of making things happen. That means that you have to act with greater frequency. And that means their thinking and their learning will be much faster, because you always learn from your practice. And I think some interesting work will come out of the current situation, because the reality is very strong. But the character of the work is quite strange because now they're producing art for the Western world to look at it. This is because you don't really have open discussions in

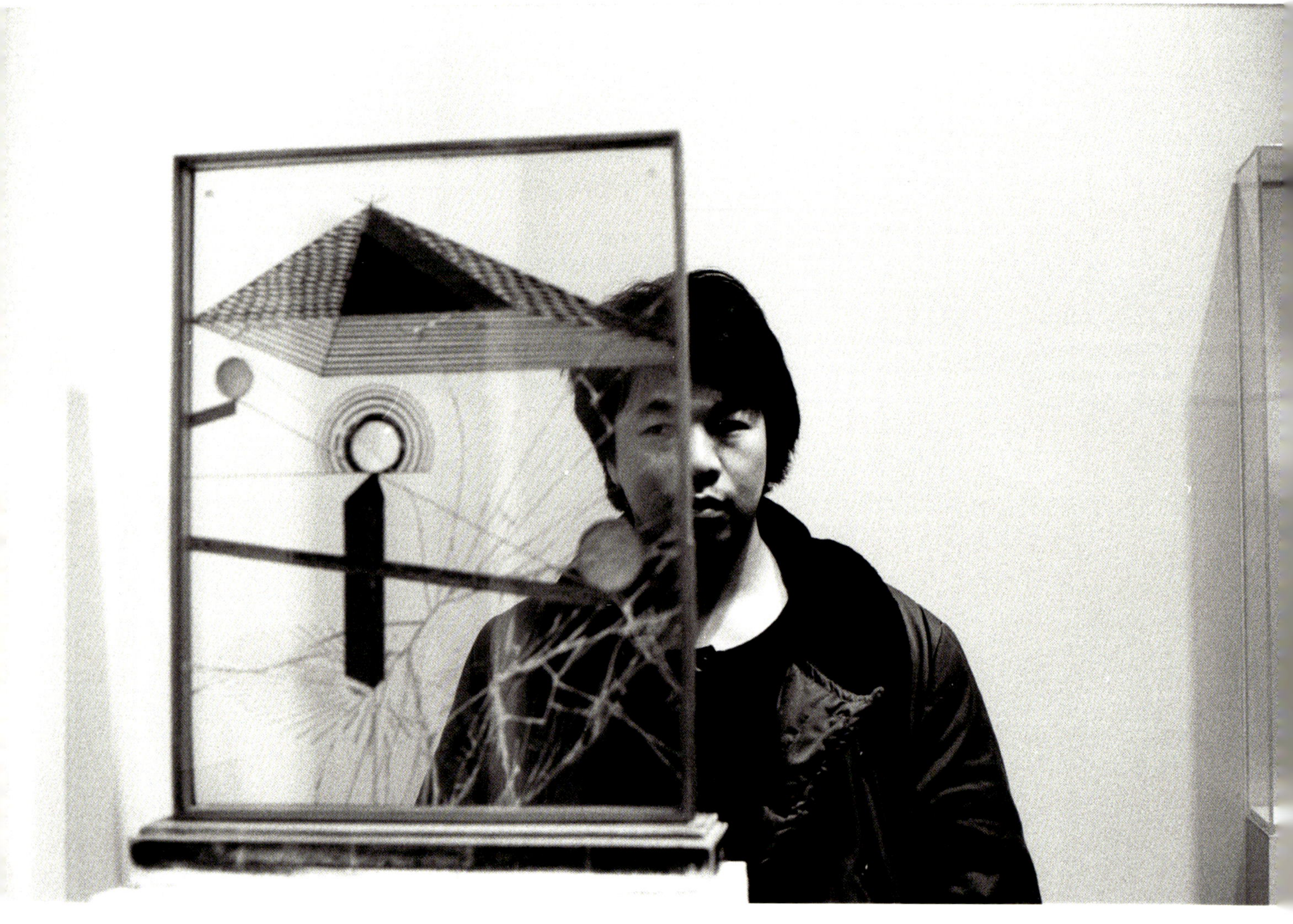

China and you can't associate your work with social struggle. So on the one hand artists are experiencing a big social struggle and change, but on the other hand they're disassociating themselves from it, which is the biggest problem. It's so difficult to find the right language – and it's the same for me – to express your concerns about mass behaviour while at the same time producing individual work that can be effective.

JB You've made certain works that speak much more explicitly in response to those social issues, such as Remembering 2009, one of your responses to the 2008 Sichuan earthquake disaster.

AW Yes, I picked up on the earthquake disaster because it really relates to how a state deals with social and individual matters: the identity of the individuals who died, why the state wants to cover things up, and how to generate people's understanding that they have the right to know about it. It isn't easy to make an example of a civil act, because you have to handle it not so forcefully that the state will crush it. But you have to make it happen, to become an example for other people, so that young people become more conscious and act on that. But we did it very successfully, even though there were a lot of difficulties. We found out about the young students who died in the earthquake – their names, their birthdays, the schools they belonged to, their families, and posted this information on the internet. We made a few programmes that related to it. Then we asked all the people from Twitter to read one name, using a recorder or phone. They sent their voices back to us, and we put these five thousand names together to become a long reading of over two hours. Through this act we received over ten or twenty thousand recordings from people. I always want to design a frame or structure that can be open to everybody: it's very small, people can easily handle it, but when it comes together it becomes so powerful, because the individual realises that there's another person who made the same effort, and there's another and another, and these people can all share the same values and the same effort. Making people in society recognise themselves is very difficult, especially in China. So I'm always trying to think about how to do this. All they had to do was to memorise the name of one dead person, but that small act can became the strongest force or metaphor against the state power. The collected names made it impossible to forget or erase the truth.

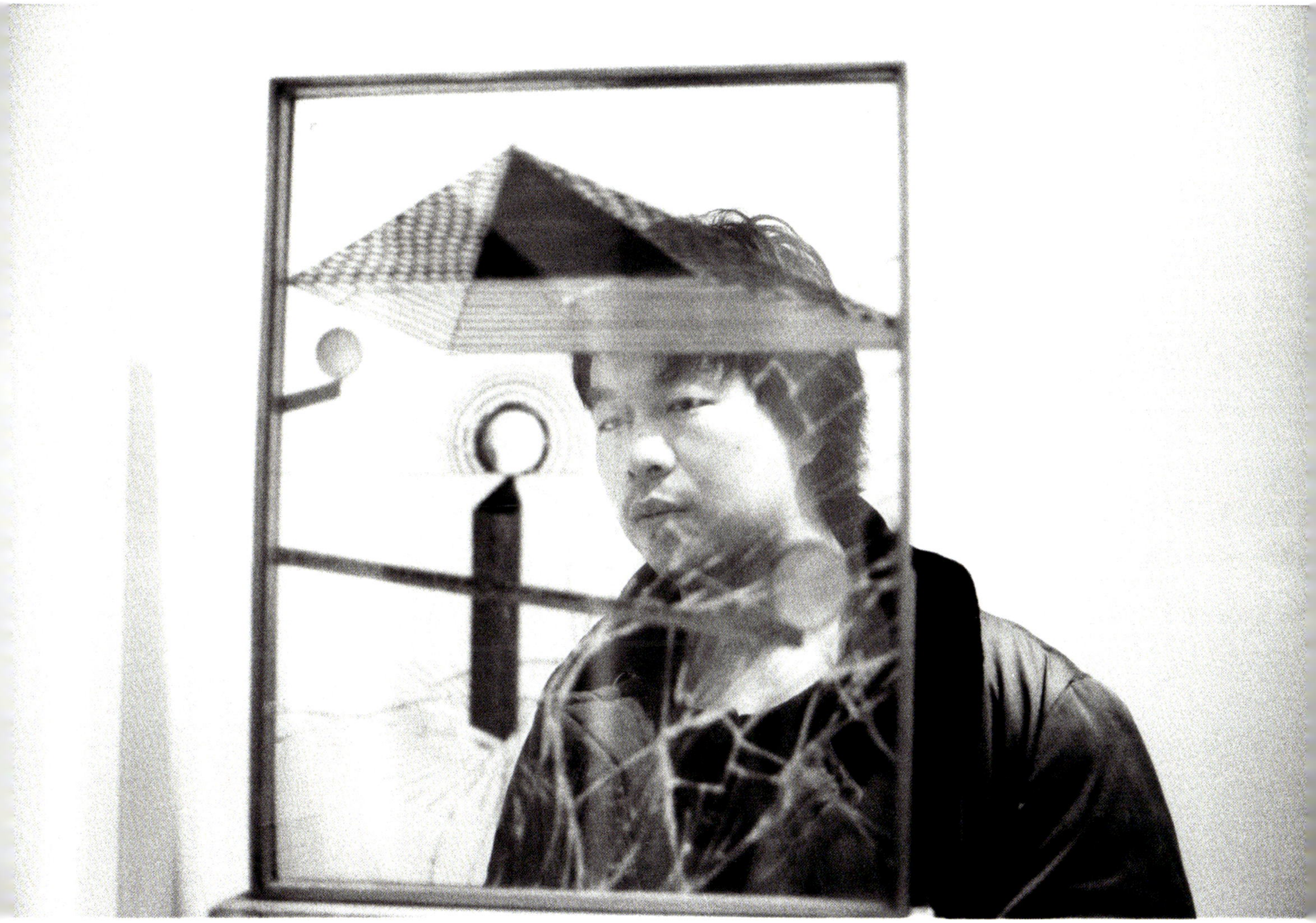

JB You've talked before about this idea of taking personal responsibility in whatever small way.

AW Yes, a small gesture that can identify you in a different way from before you made it is very meaningful for people. And I think that's how art functions in society.

JB This seems to relate back to the idea behind the sunflower seeds: that every single seed is hand-painted and is an individual piece that exists within the whole.

AW Yes, and it's not as if the people making them are putting a readymade thing into a slot like a machine. It's done through your own control of the brush and your own breath and your own bodily gestures. It's such a beautiful act – using fingers and brush. You pick it up and you put on ink – more ink or less ink, lightly or thickly painted. Then you have to turn it over to paint the other side. That's not so easy; we tried it and ruined a few seeds. [laughs]

MD Understanding the process is a very interesting and important part of the project. In relation to what you were saying about responsibility, perhaps the Tate work contrasts the responsibility of the individual with the irresponsibility of the state.

AW The state – or any institutions or groups, which can be cultural or economic or political powers – they always have a tendency to corruption – not financial necessarily, but mental corruption, which takes everything for granted, or accepts conditions that aren't helpful in the development of mental conditions. So only by encouraging individual freedom, or the individual power of the mind, and by trusting our own feelings, can collective acts be meaningful. Otherwise, it's damaging to people. We have to fix it and prove we can have a better society.

JB Often young people start out in a more radical way and become more measured as they develop. It seems as if your practice is going in reverse: starting with smaller individual object-based works in New York and moving on to socially engaged work now. You appear to be becoming more outspoken, more engaged, more radical.

AW I wouldn't say I've become more radical: I was born radical. I can still recall my relationships with my parents, the first authority that we have, and my schools. But of course, at that time there was no vehicle, no possibilities and I wasn't equipped. Now I have a much bigger stage, or at least, my practice has convinced more people to tolerate me. So I don't think I have changed really. Even if my works made in New York look quite conservative, that was a moment when nobody was doing work like that – it was Neo-Expressionism or a more industrial type of working. Now I feel I can speak more freely about my intentions, but I didn't at that time. At that time, I felt as if my life had no meaning, or couldn't have any meaning to others. It wasn't a condition that was very encouraging, and I don't think most people could survive in those conditions. I'm lucky. Today, I have this opportunity so I really appreciate it. But it's taken a very long time. And I'll never forget the difficulties I experienced there. Some people would say, 'Why have you become so active now?' They don't really understand my situation in New York. I was anticipating those demonstrations by homosexuals about AIDS, I was also demonstrating against Desert Storm, which wasn't a popular demonstration in New York City, I was organising the Democratic Students' Movement outside of China, I was doing local demonstrations for years against gentrification in Thompson Square Park. I did it as a photo-report and even had my photographs published in the *New York Times*, *Daily News* and the *New York Post* [fig.59]. Before that, in 1979, I was quite actively involved in the first democratic movement in China, called the Stars group. So, it's not one day's position. But it really takes a long time; it takes a lot of discouragement and a lot of sadness, and you feel powerless and you feel useless and you feel it's not possible. Still today, I often feel unsuccessful – most of the time I feel incapable of making even the smallest move.

MD What a humbling thought that you feel like that about your work.

AW It's true. As my colleagues know, the effort of making work is very great. I spend very little time just doing 'art as

59
Thompson Square Riots 1988, from *New York Photographs, 1983–1993*

art'. Most of the time, we're discussing and focusing on very different matters.

MD Is that perhaps a philosophy that, on the one hand, is indebted to Marcel Duchamp and Conceptualism, and on the other hand to Joseph Beuys?

AW Frankly, I don't understand Joseph Beuys. Since my solo show at Haus der Kunst I've been more appreciated in Germany. Everybody talked about the show. But they think that what I'm doing is a re-announcement of what Beuys was doing. In New York in the 1980s, I think I was more influenced by Andy Warhol or Jasper Johns or Duchamp. Beuys is a little bit mysterious to me. I understand his social sculpture and activism, but not as an influence. If I had to cite somebody who's influential, I'd say it's Duchamp, who takes art as attitude, as lifestyle, as more than art, as mental activity, total involvement. Those things are very nutritious to me.

MD With Beuys there's a mysticism that isn't really so visible in your work.

AW Yes, because I try not to see art as a secret code. I try to make it at least have a very simple appearance, very easy to do. Everybody can do it. It's more a mental adjustment.

MD It sounds easy, but that mental adjustment can be very difficult.

AW Yes. It's like Buddhist practice. A Buddhist would say, first you think a mountain is a mountain, a river is a river. Then you become more learned and you realise a mountain isn't so simple: it's not just a mountain, it's not just a river. Then, if you practice to an even higher degree, you start to realise a mountain is a mountain, a river is a river. So it's difficult. It's an argument that has to be proved through practice. It's like examining how you fall down; it's very difficult to analyse how it happens.

[Ai Weiwei takes a mobile phone call]

AW That was the Public Security Bureau. They want to talk to me.

MD About anything in particular?

AW I asked if there's anything they're particularly interested in and they said, 'No, no, no, we just want to see you.' I said 'OK.' June 4th is coming. Twenty-one years ago on the 4th of June, the students' movement was crushed. So every year at this particular time they're very nervous. They probably want to know if I have anything planned!

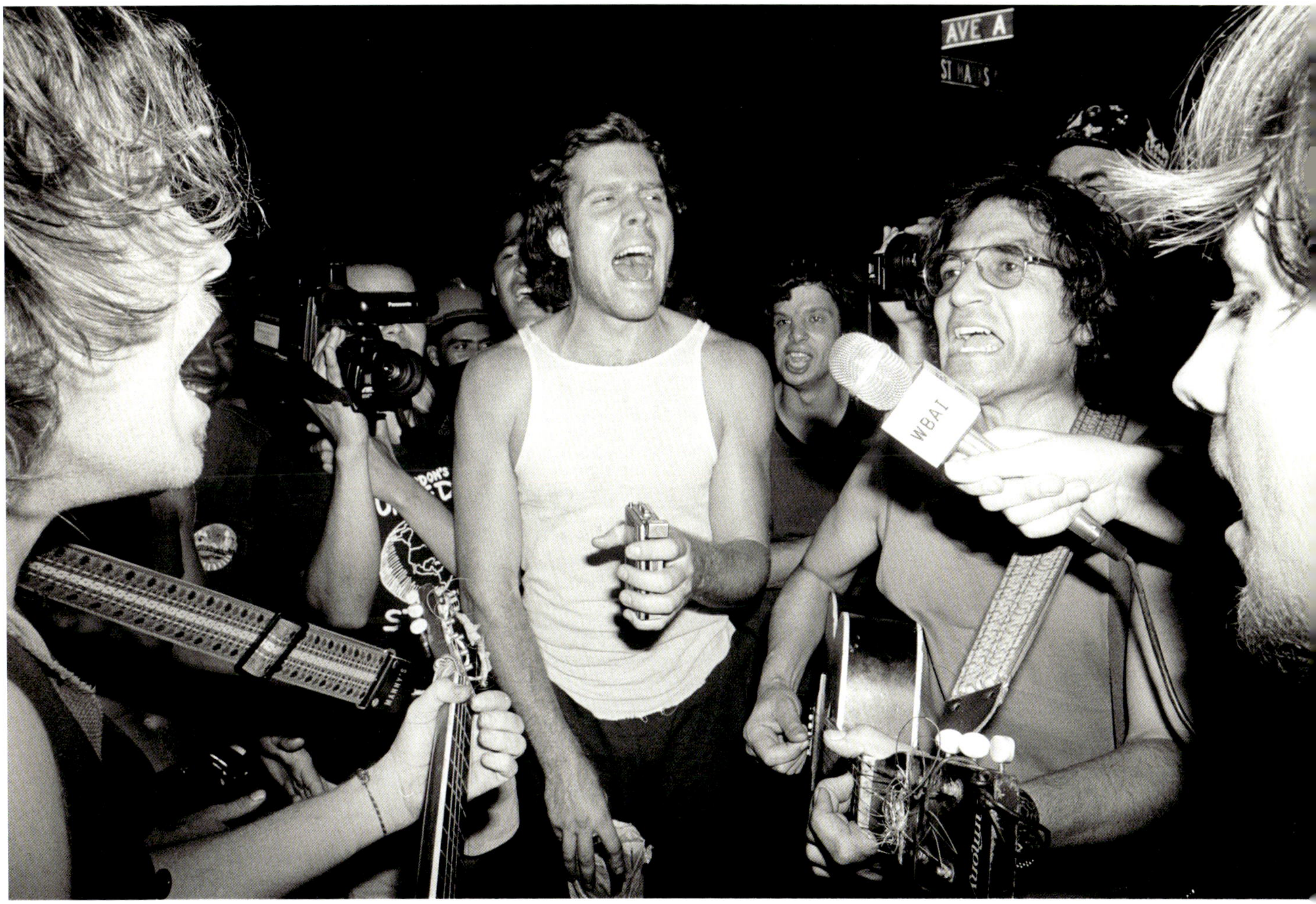

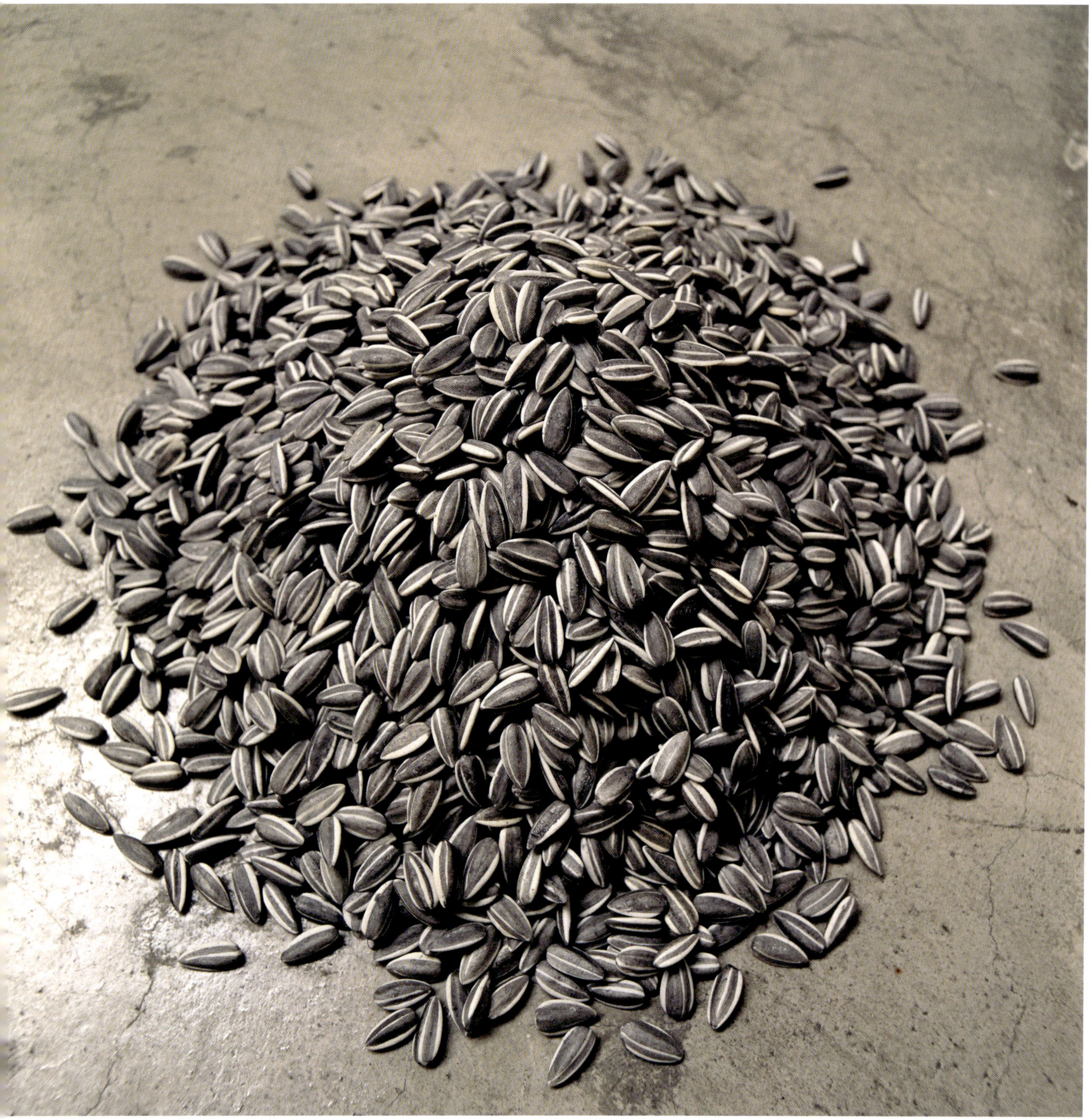

Sunflower seeds, Ai Weiwei's studio, 2010

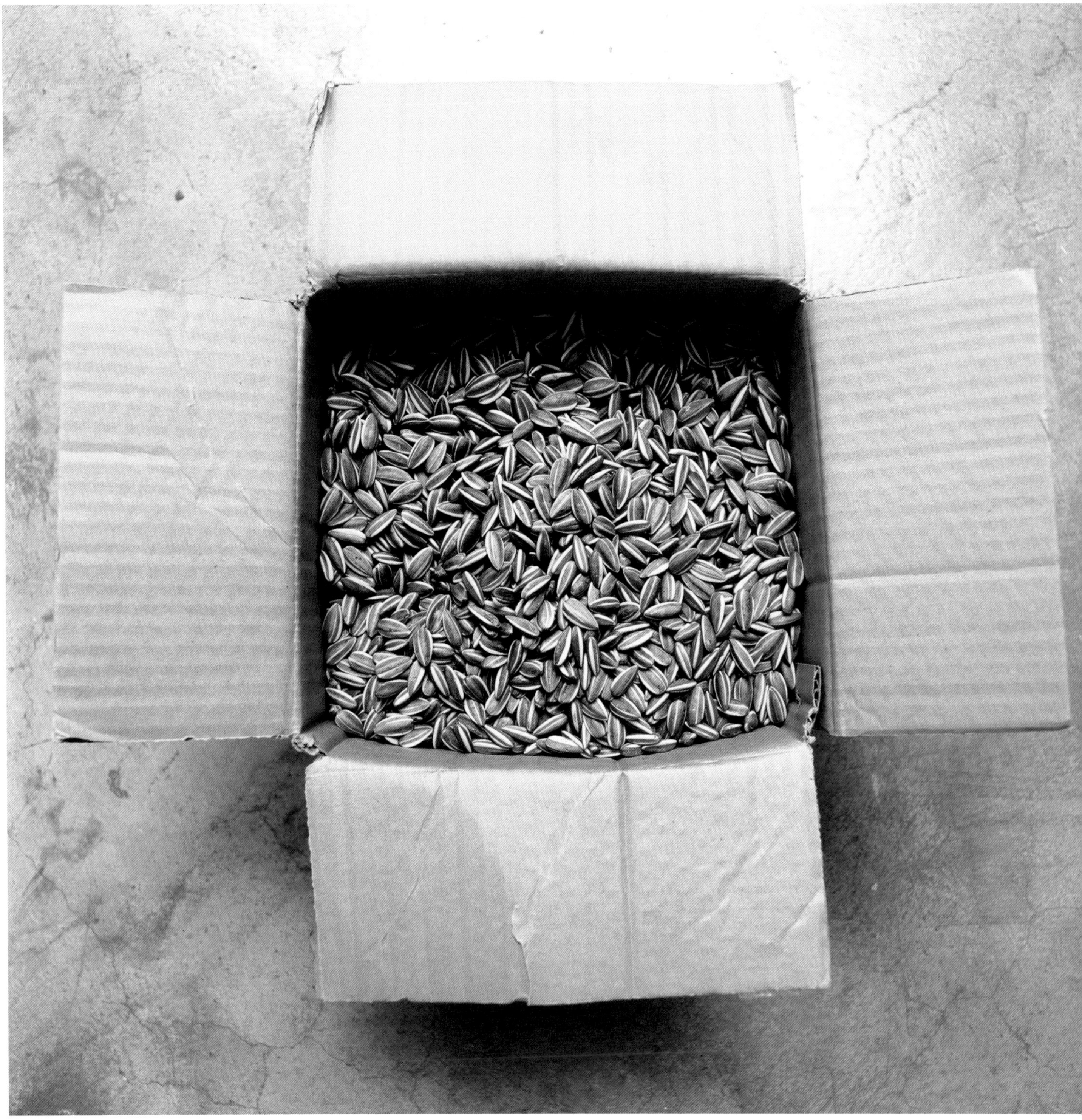

Sunflower seeds, Ai Weiwei's studio, 2010

SUNFLOWER SEEDS: MAKING

Sunflower Seeds is an accumulation of the repeated effort of many individuals. Over 100 million porcelain sunflower seeds have been made by hand by specialists working in the city of Jingdezhen in southern China. Historically, the region is famed for the production of the highest quality Imperial porcelain. The same traditional methods of production – which have a history of over 1,200 years – have been used now in the making of the sunflower seeds. The whole process takes some twenty to thirty steps: from the processing of the clay, moulding, firing to 1,300°C, painting of the objects and firing again at 800°C. In preparation for the Unilever commission, Ai began experimenting over two and a half years ago, working with small teams of crafts people in small-scale workshops. Gradually numbers increased, until 1,600 artisans were carefully and skilfully working to produce the seeds.

The images on the following pages show the various steps involved in the production of the seeds.

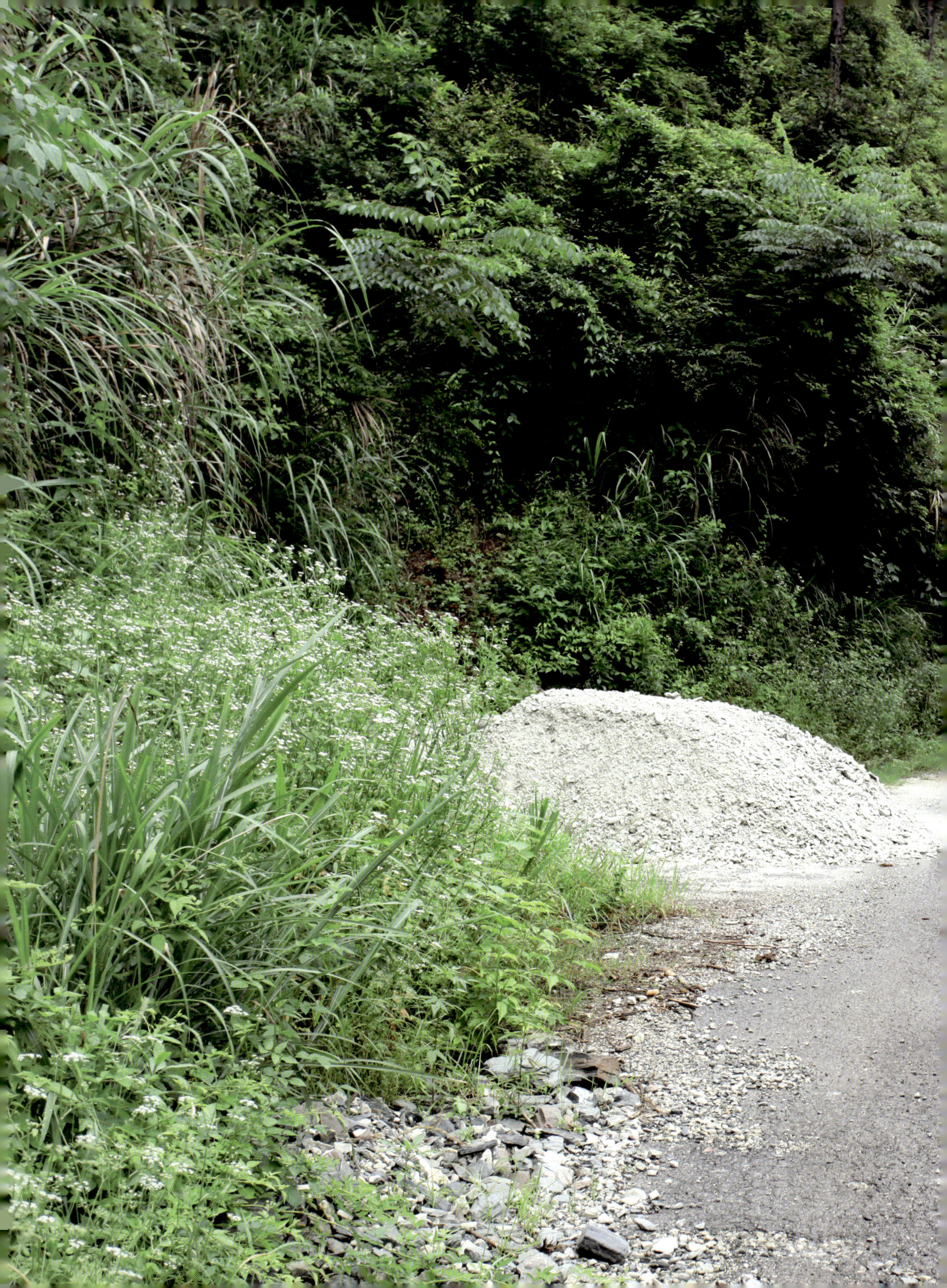

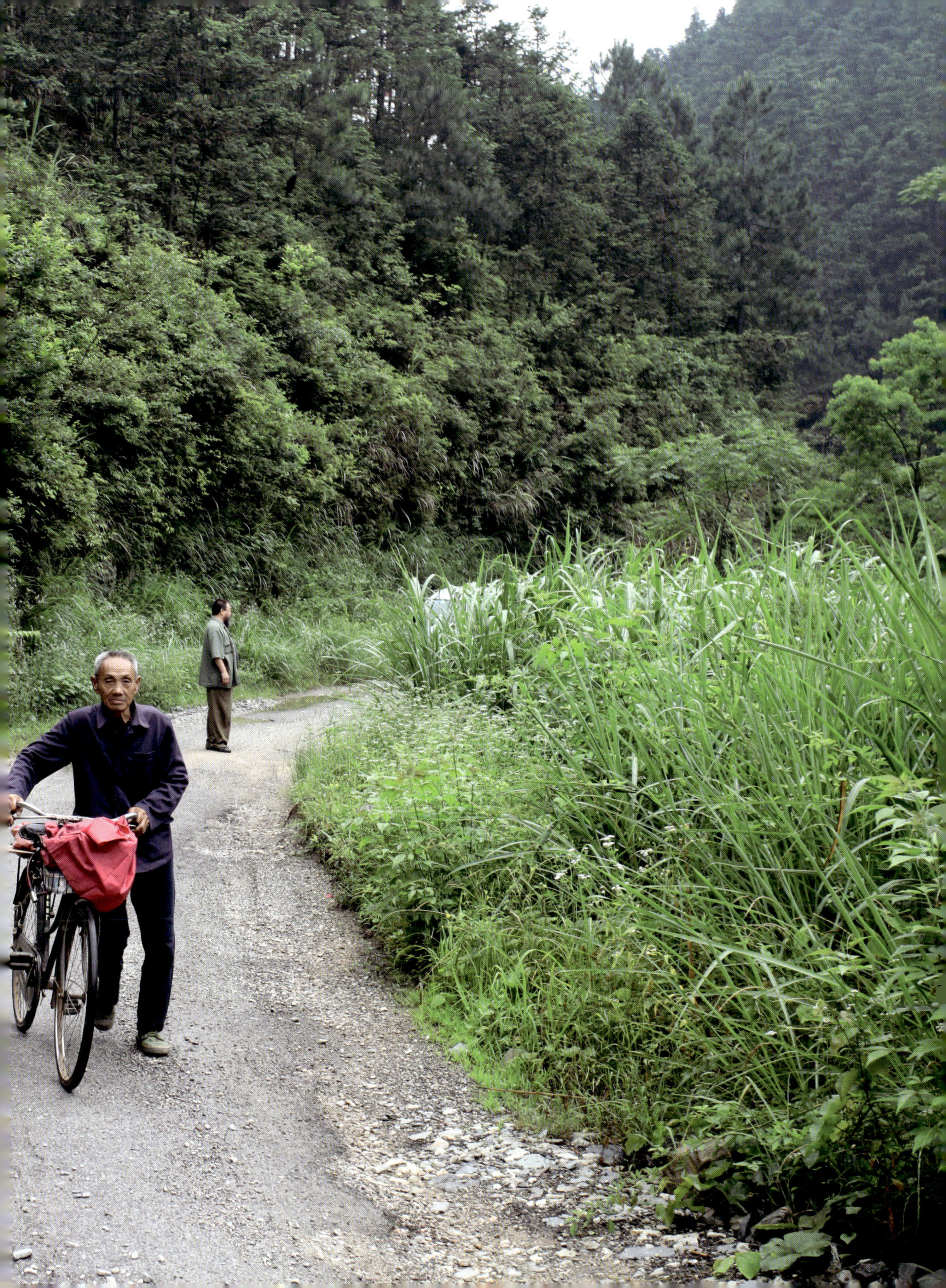

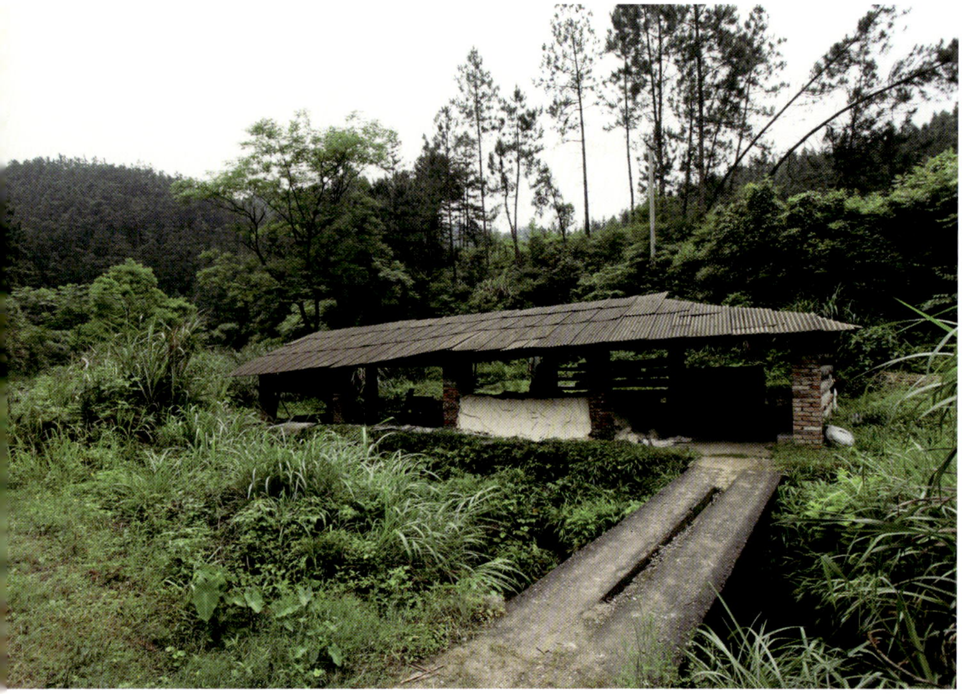

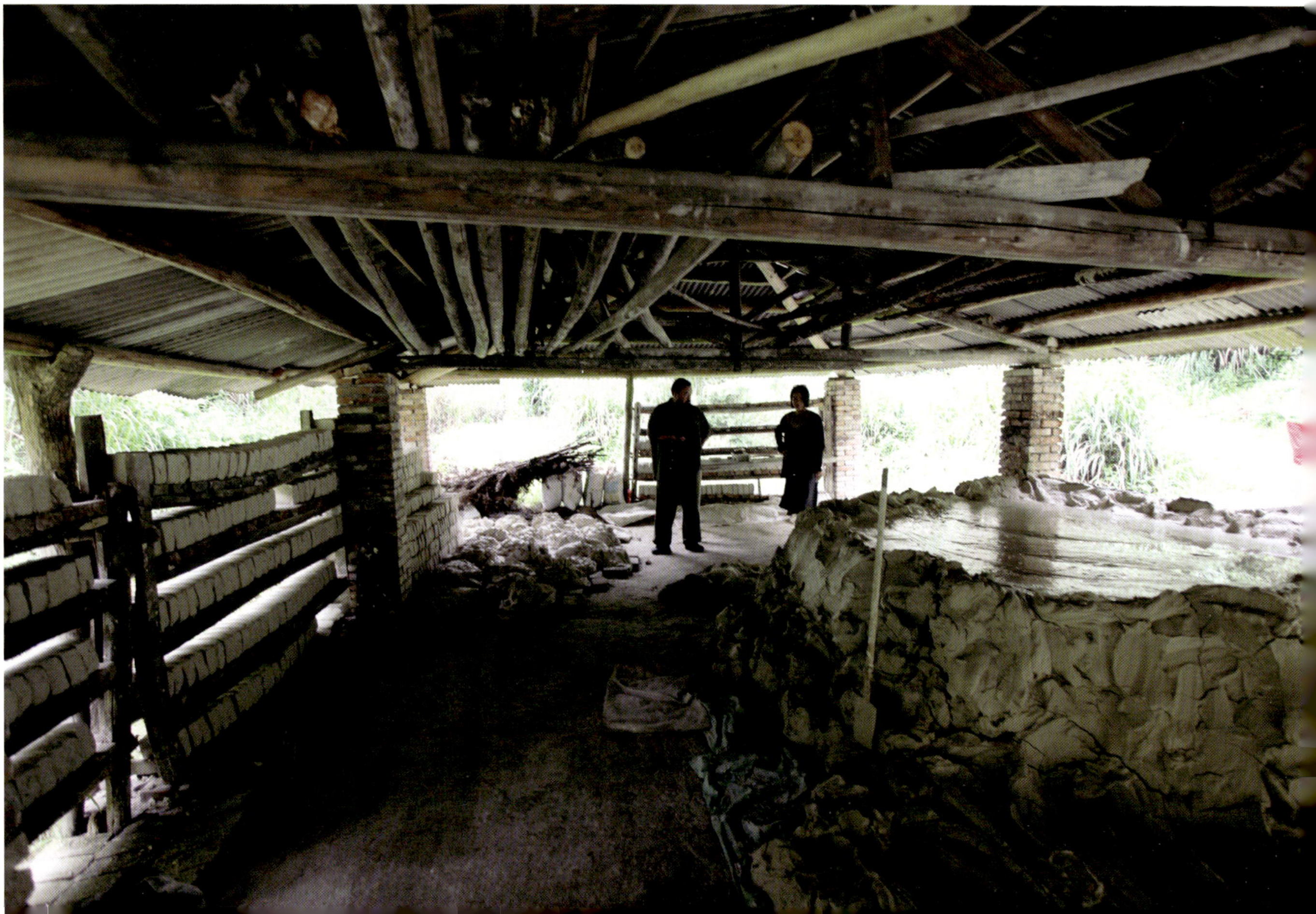

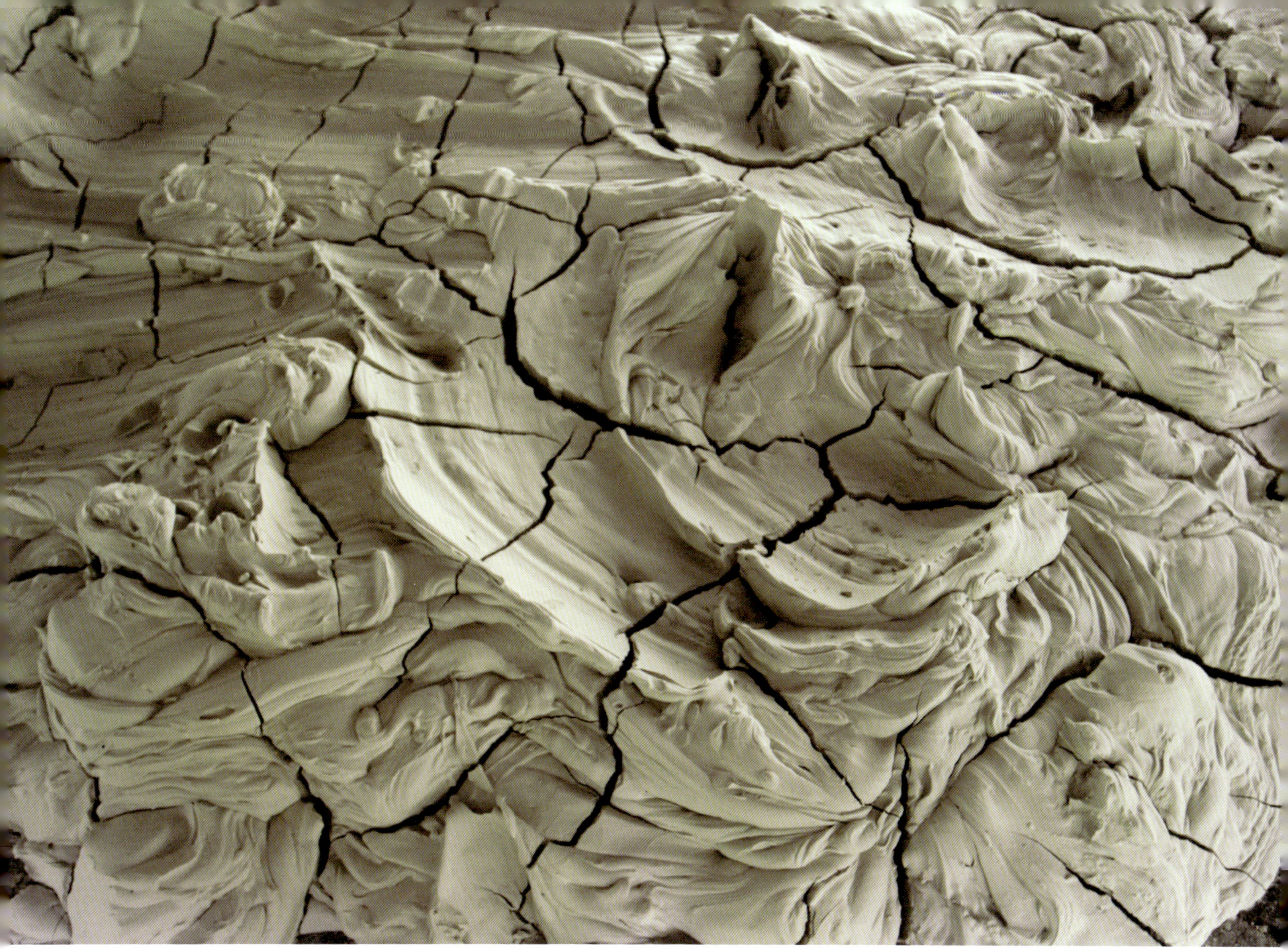

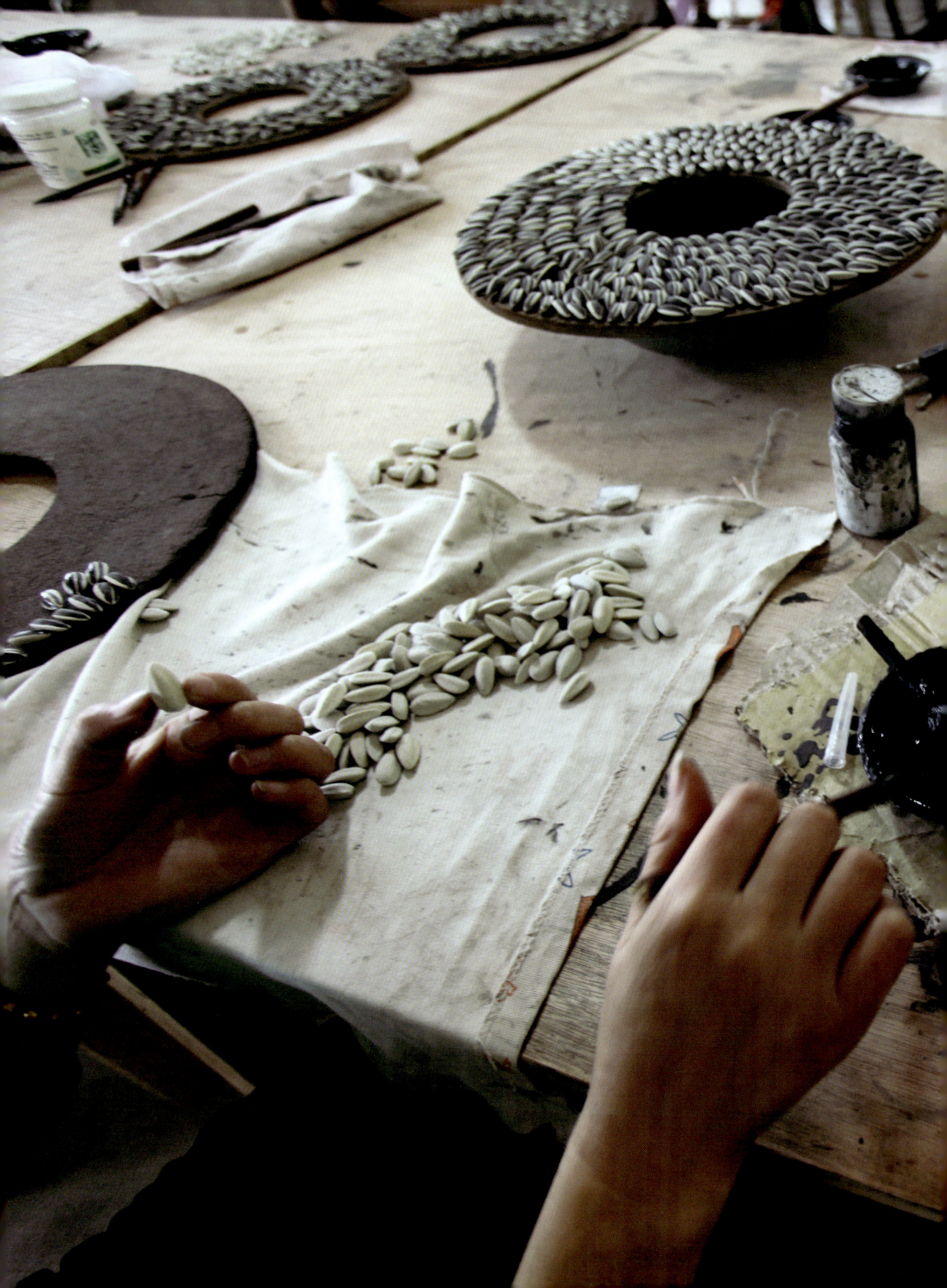

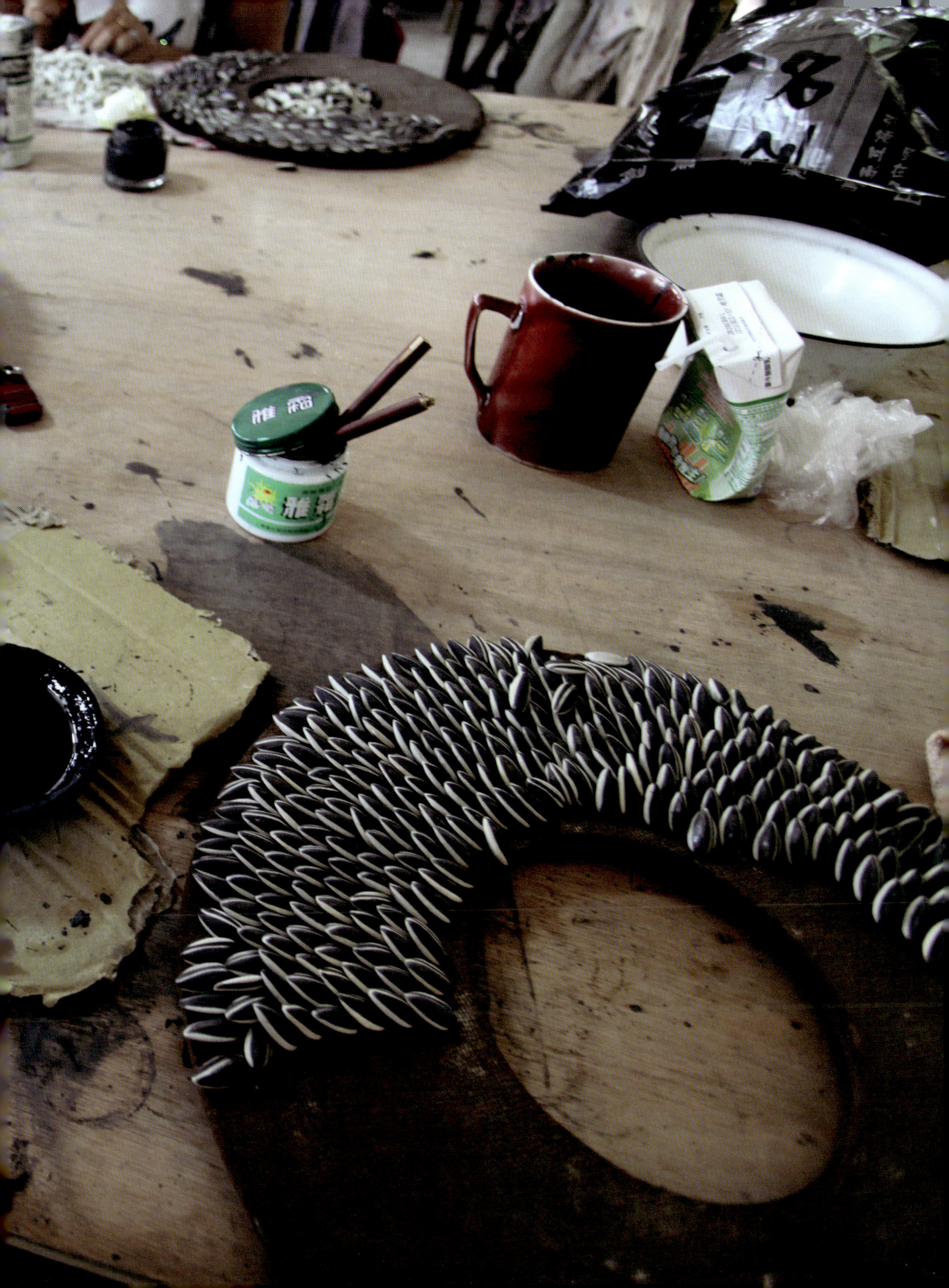
雅霜

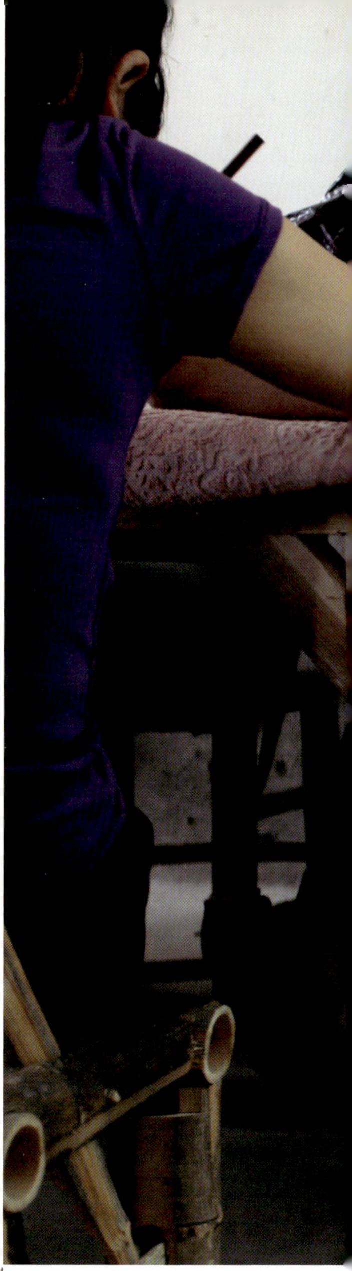

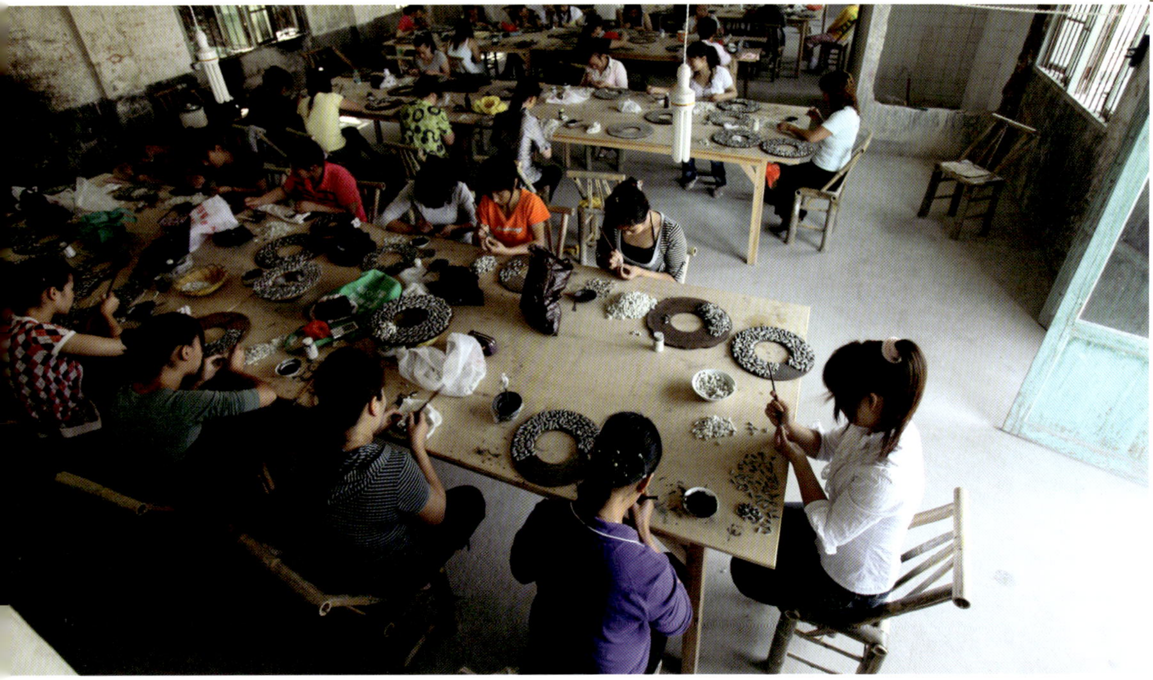

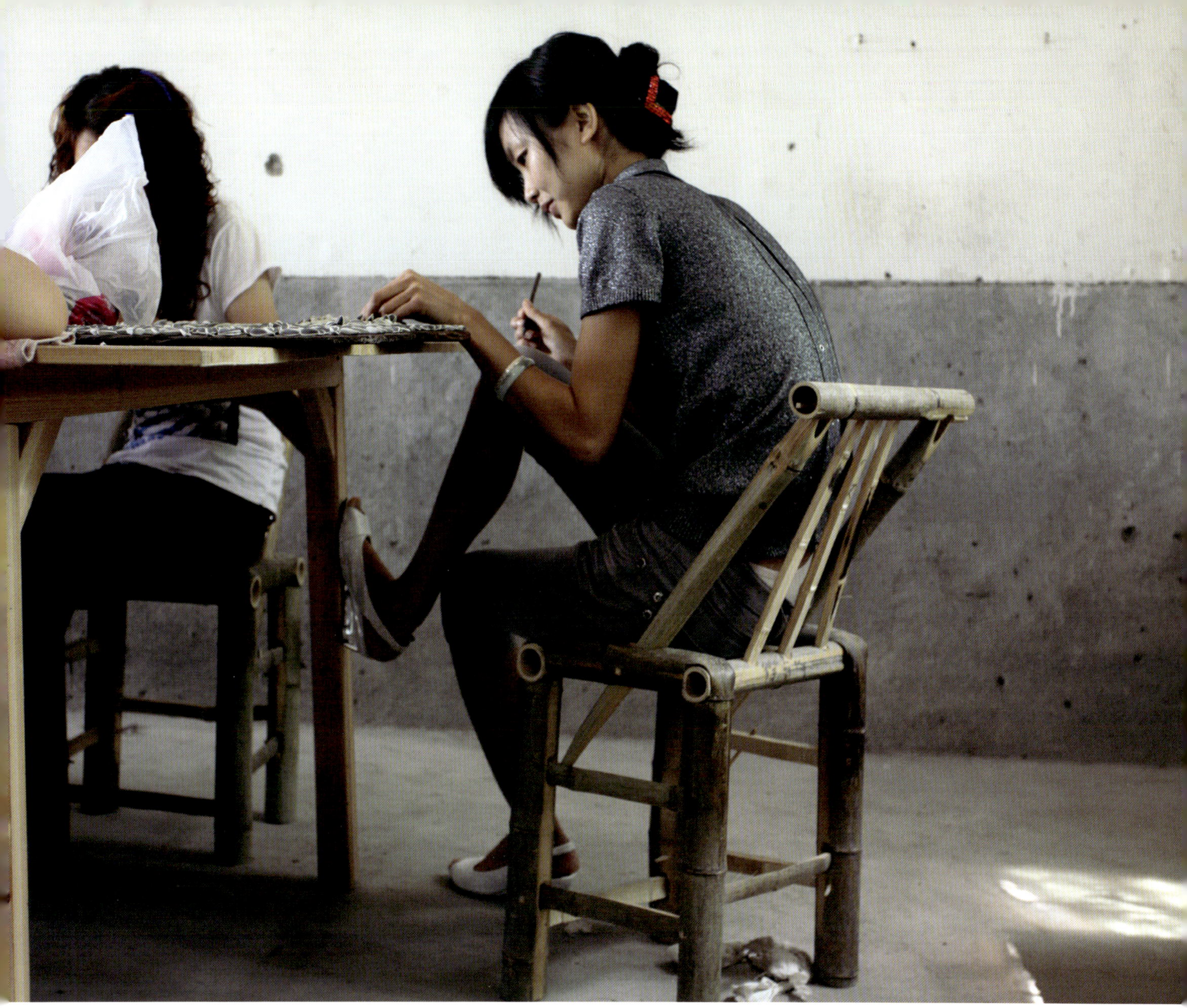

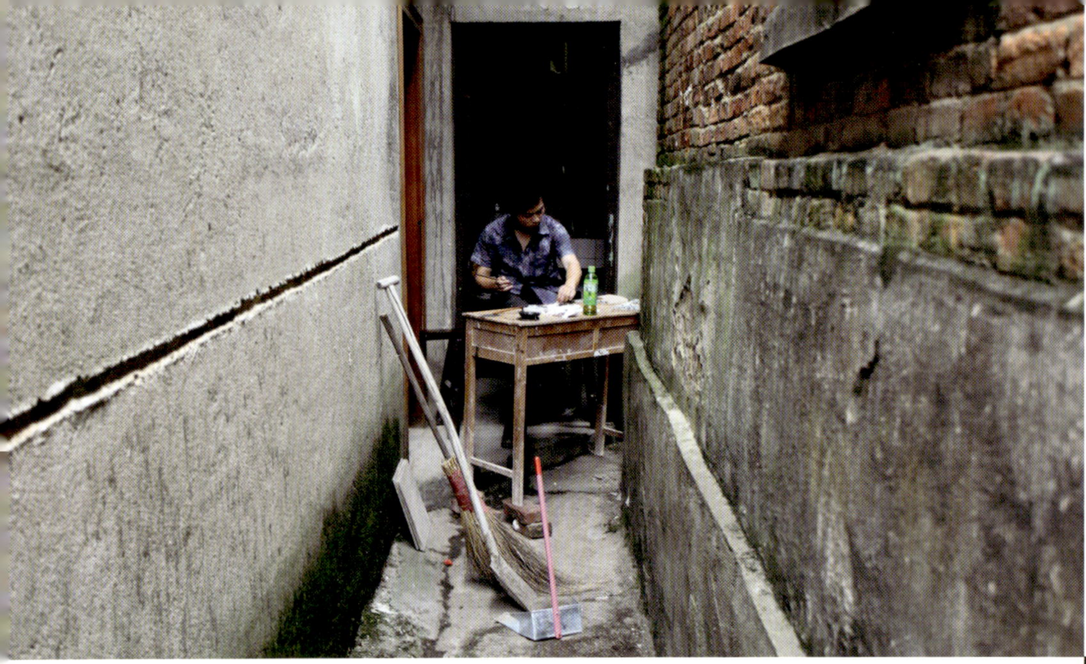

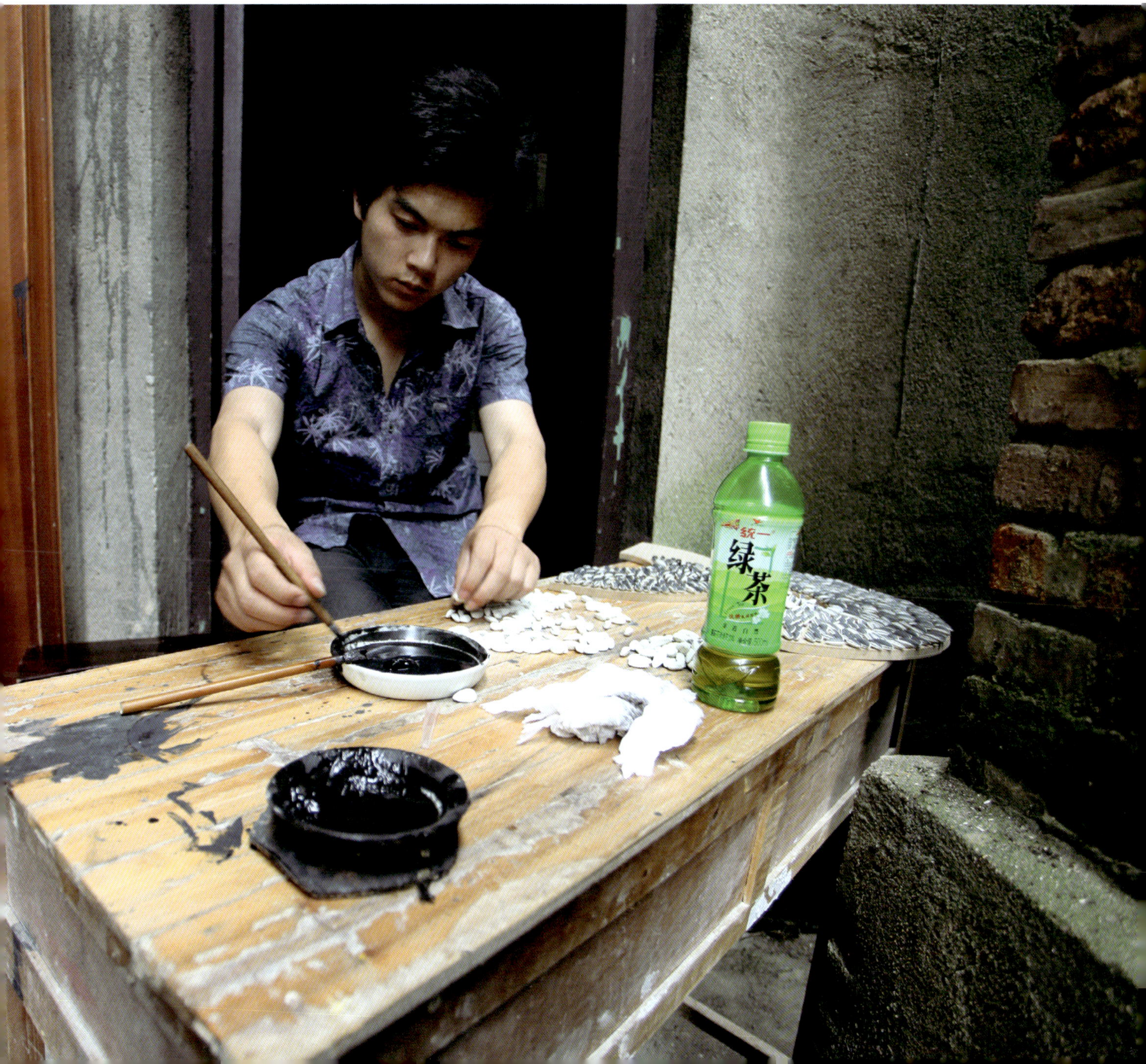
统一
绿茶

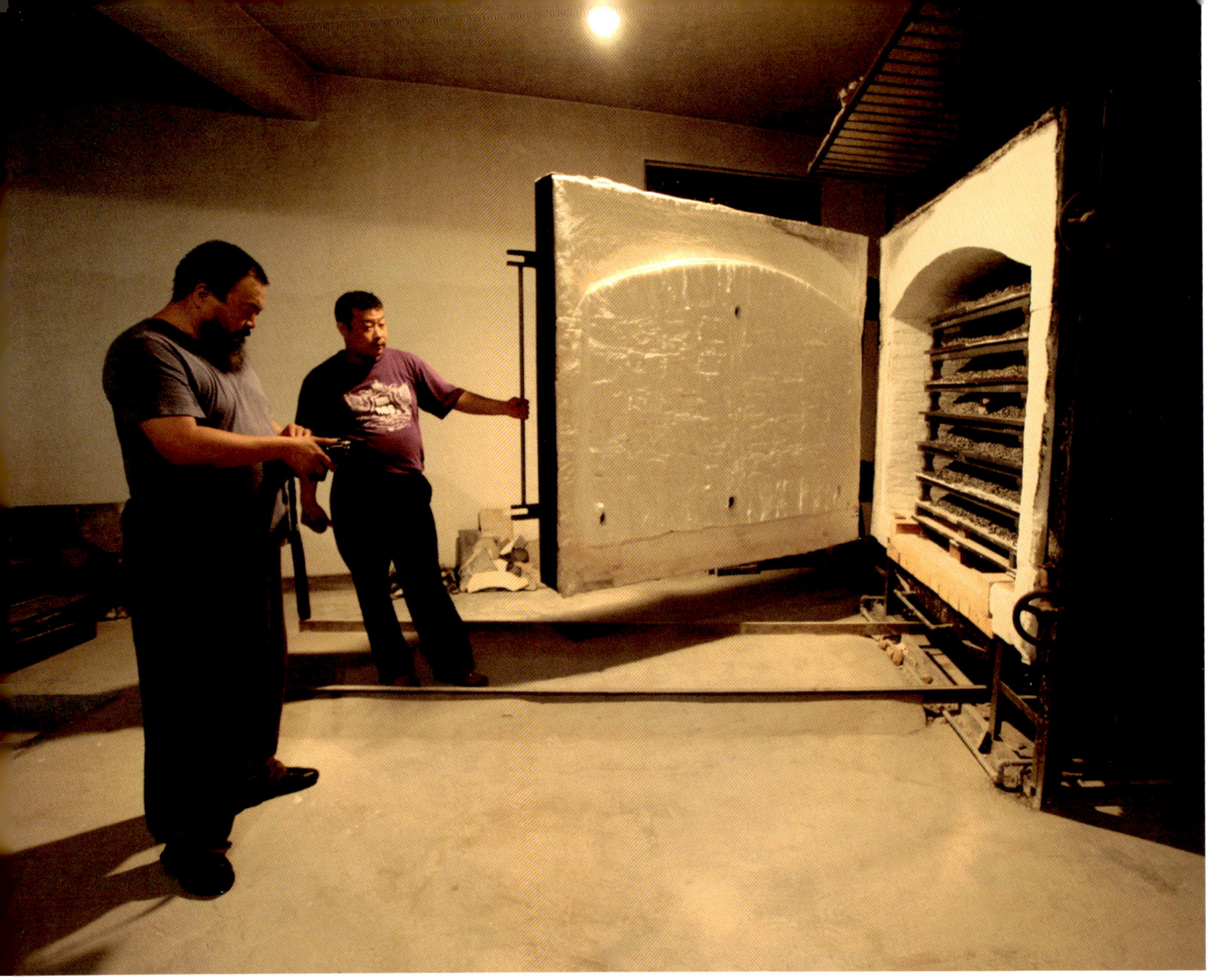

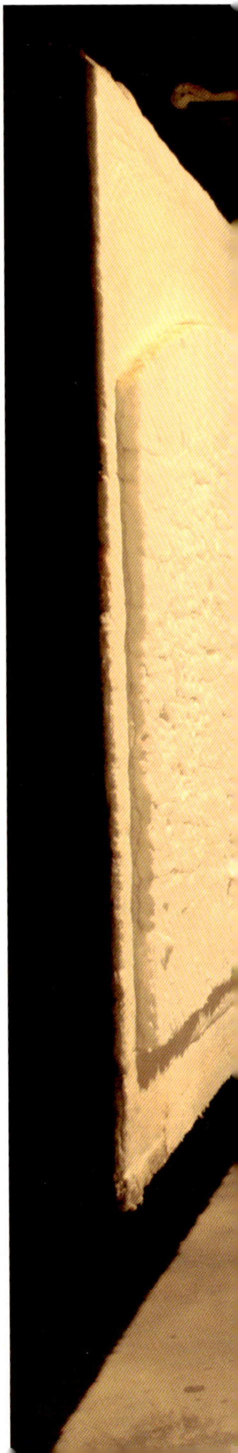

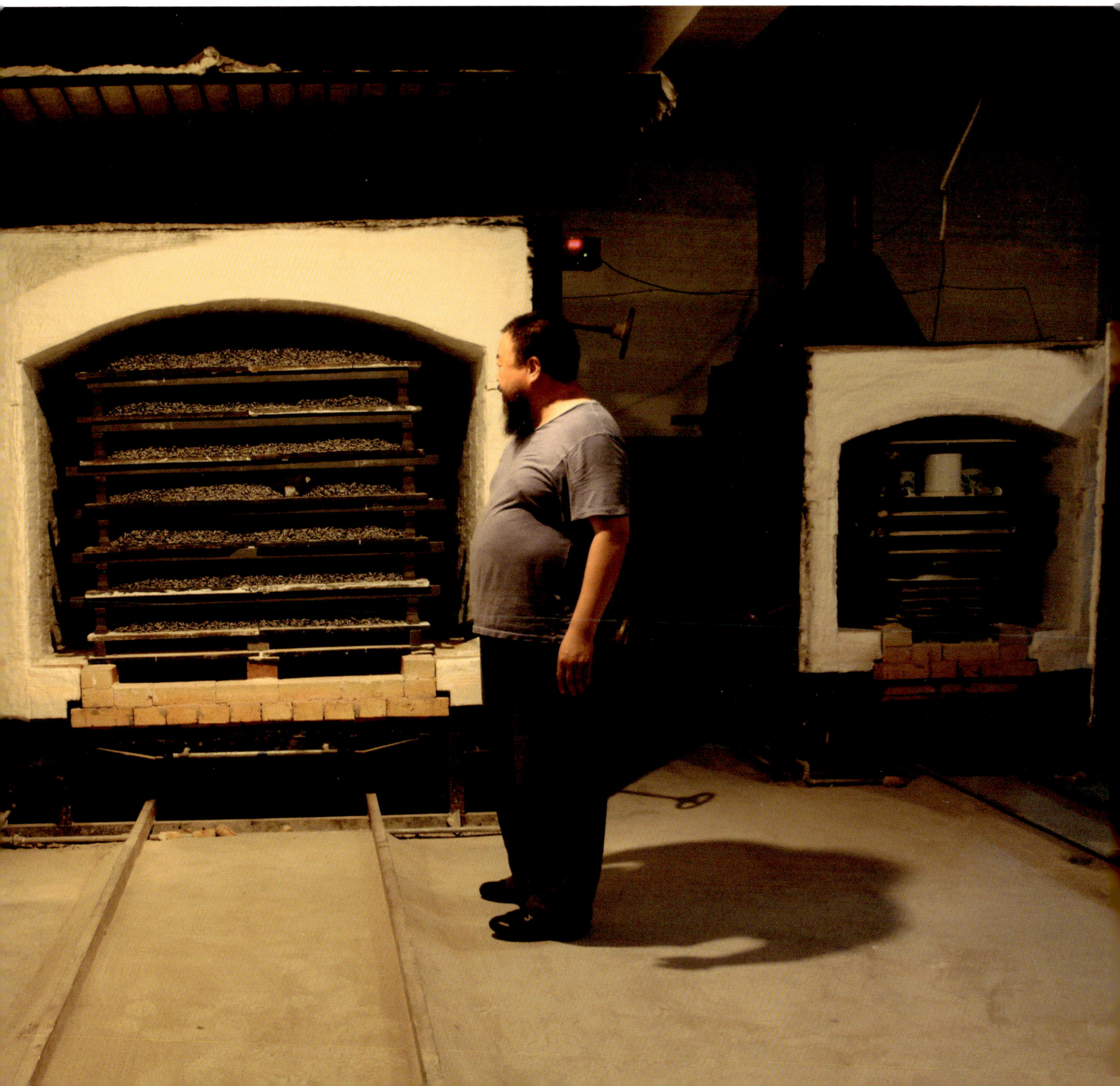

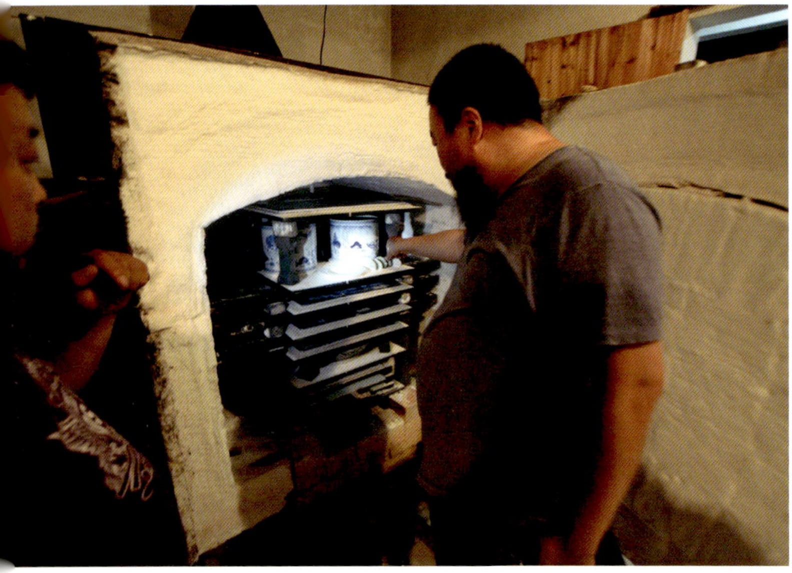

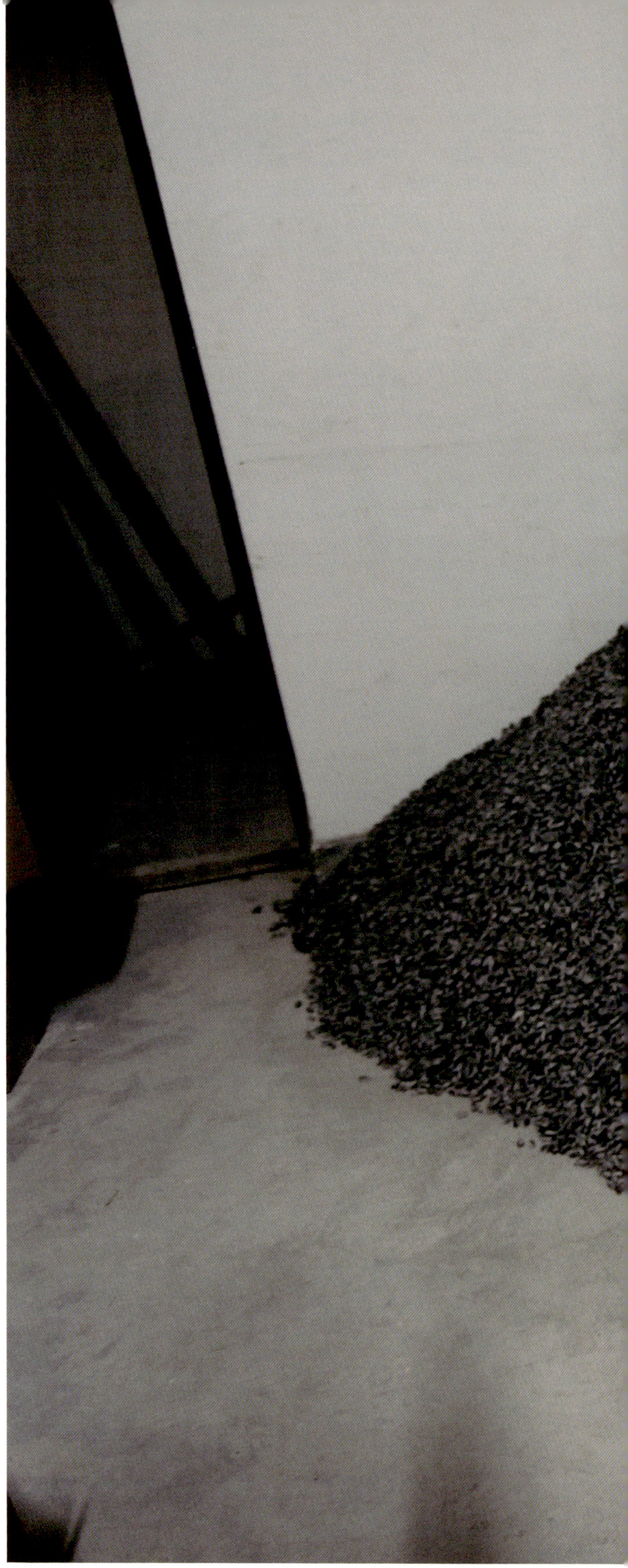

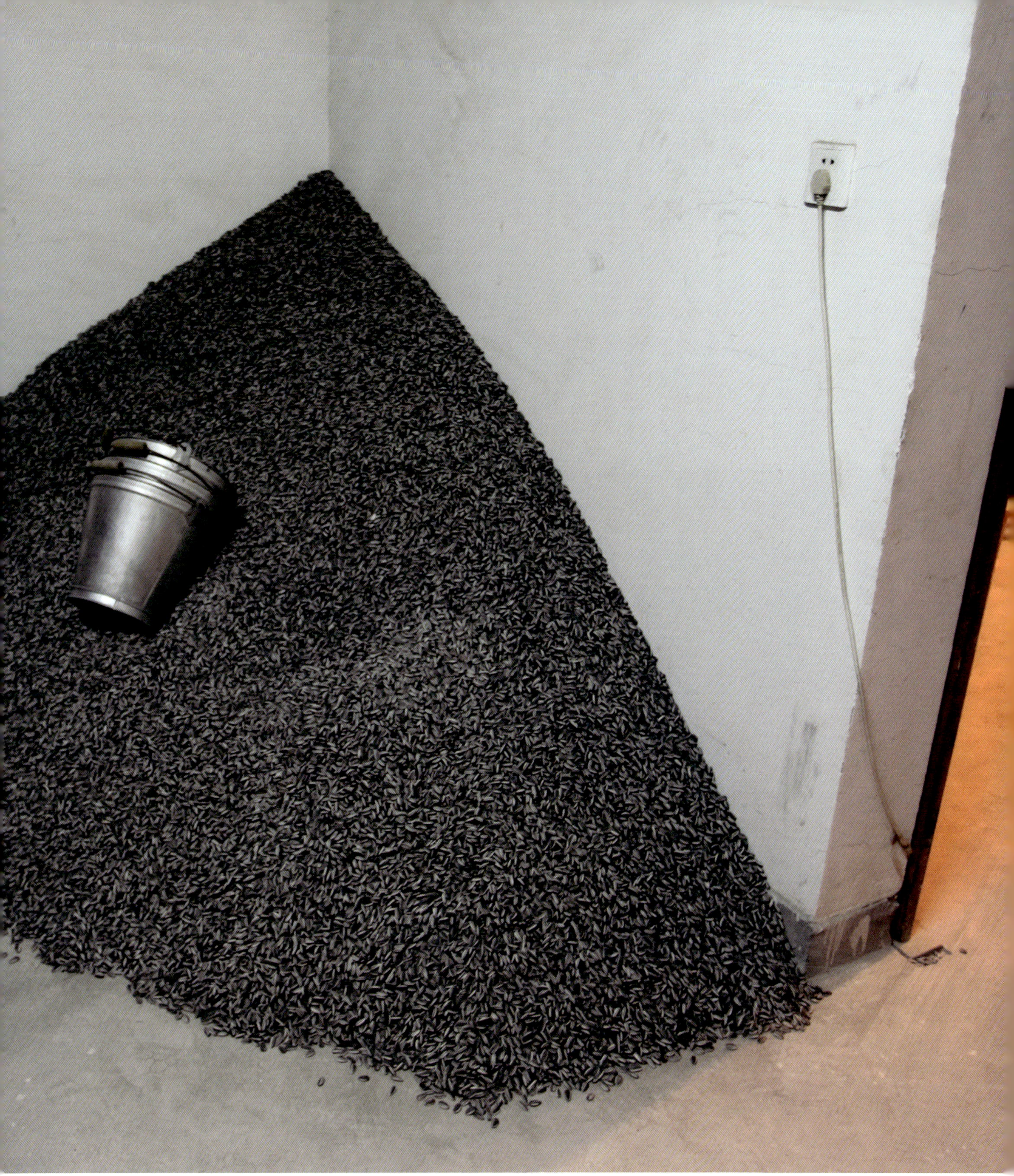

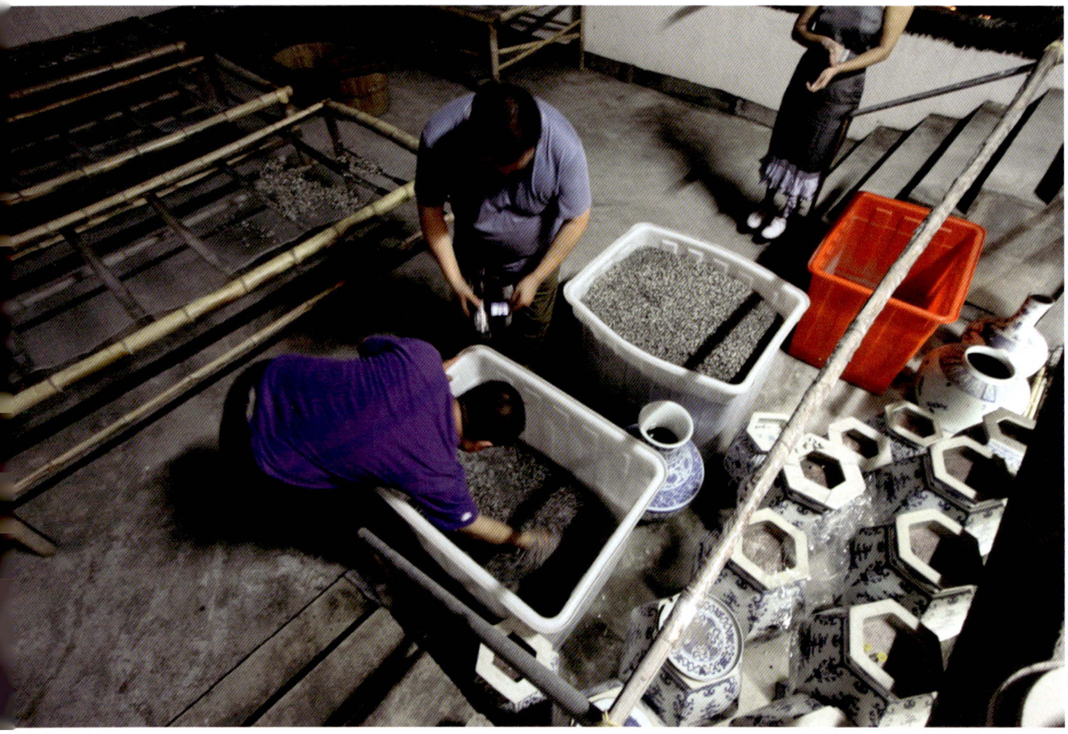

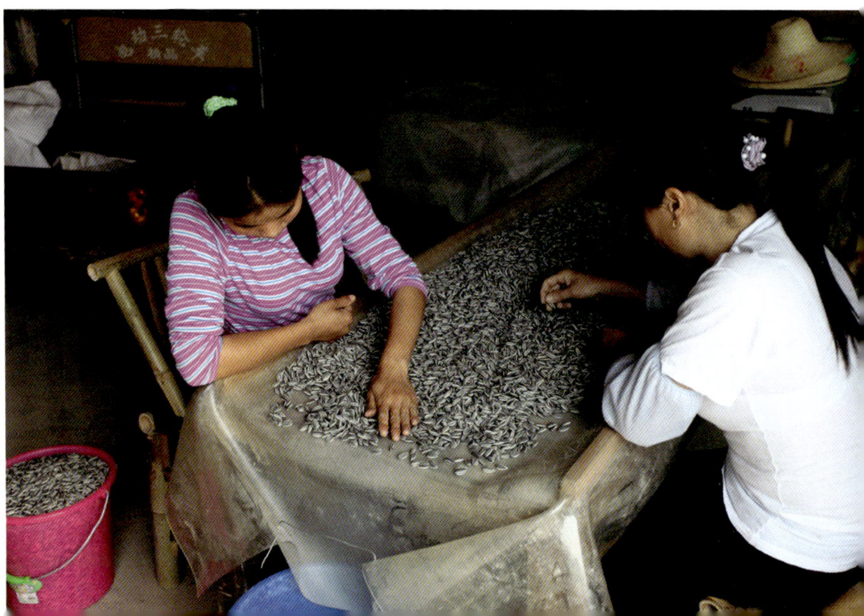

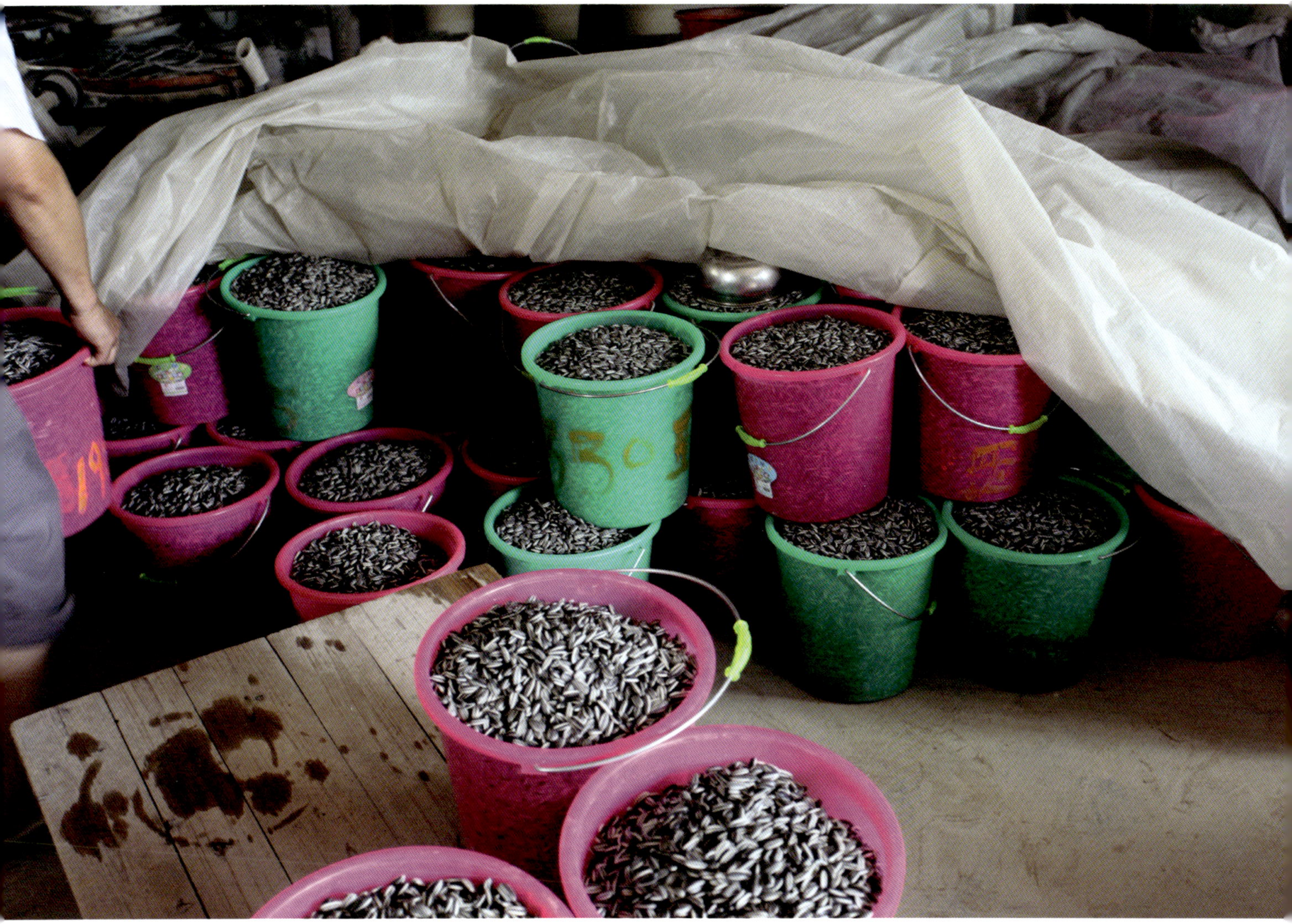

SUNFLOWER SEEDS: INSTALLATION

Over 100 million porcelain sunflower seeds have been made, forming a mass that weighs over 150 metric tonnes, with a total volume of 100 cubic metres.

After transportation by sea, the sunflower seeds were systematically installed at Tate Modern, and the surface raked to create a flat landscape of 1,000 square metres covering the east end of the iconic Turbine Hall.

The images on the following pages document the installation of the sunflower seeds and the final exhibited work.

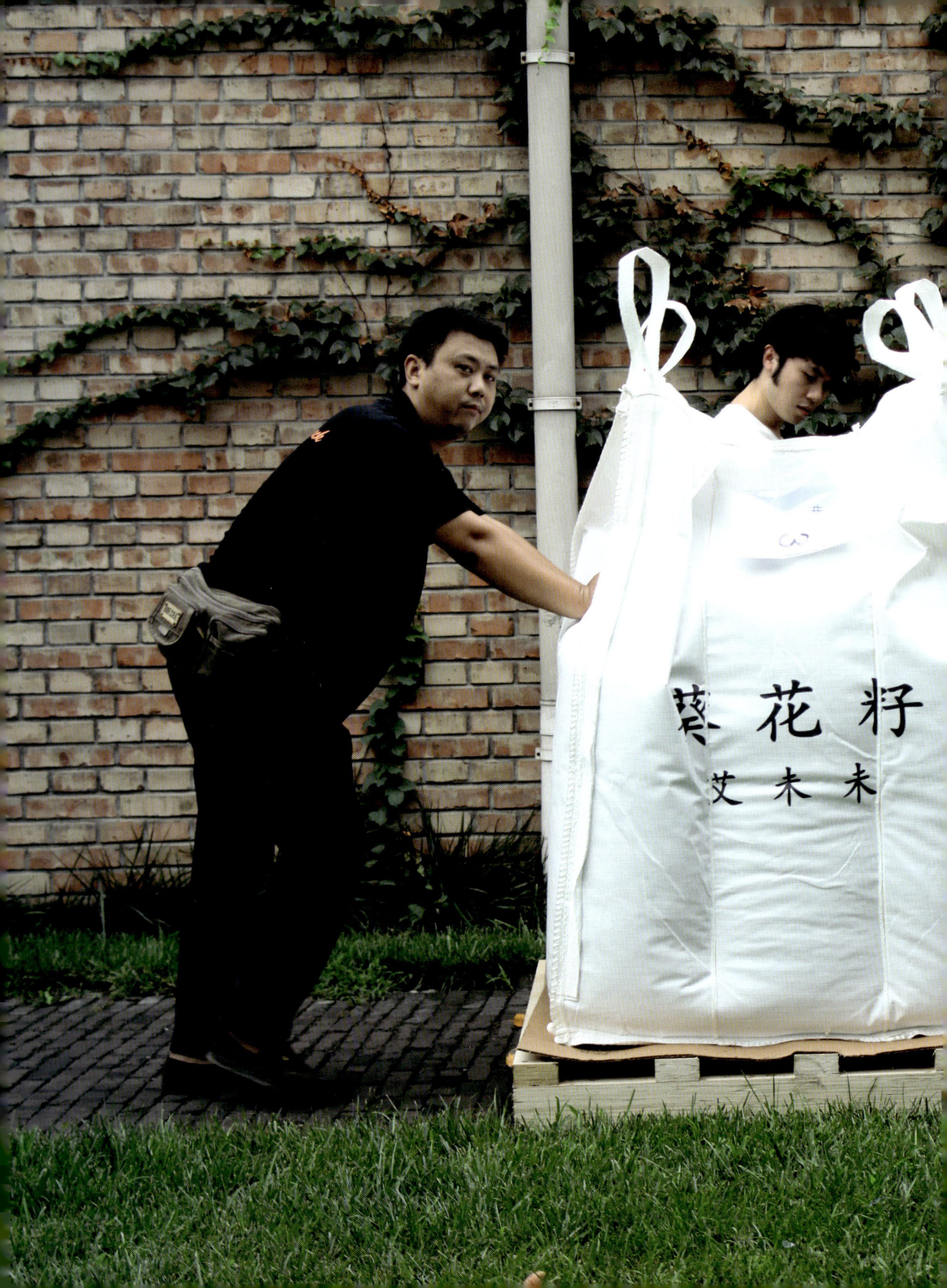
葵花籽
艾未未

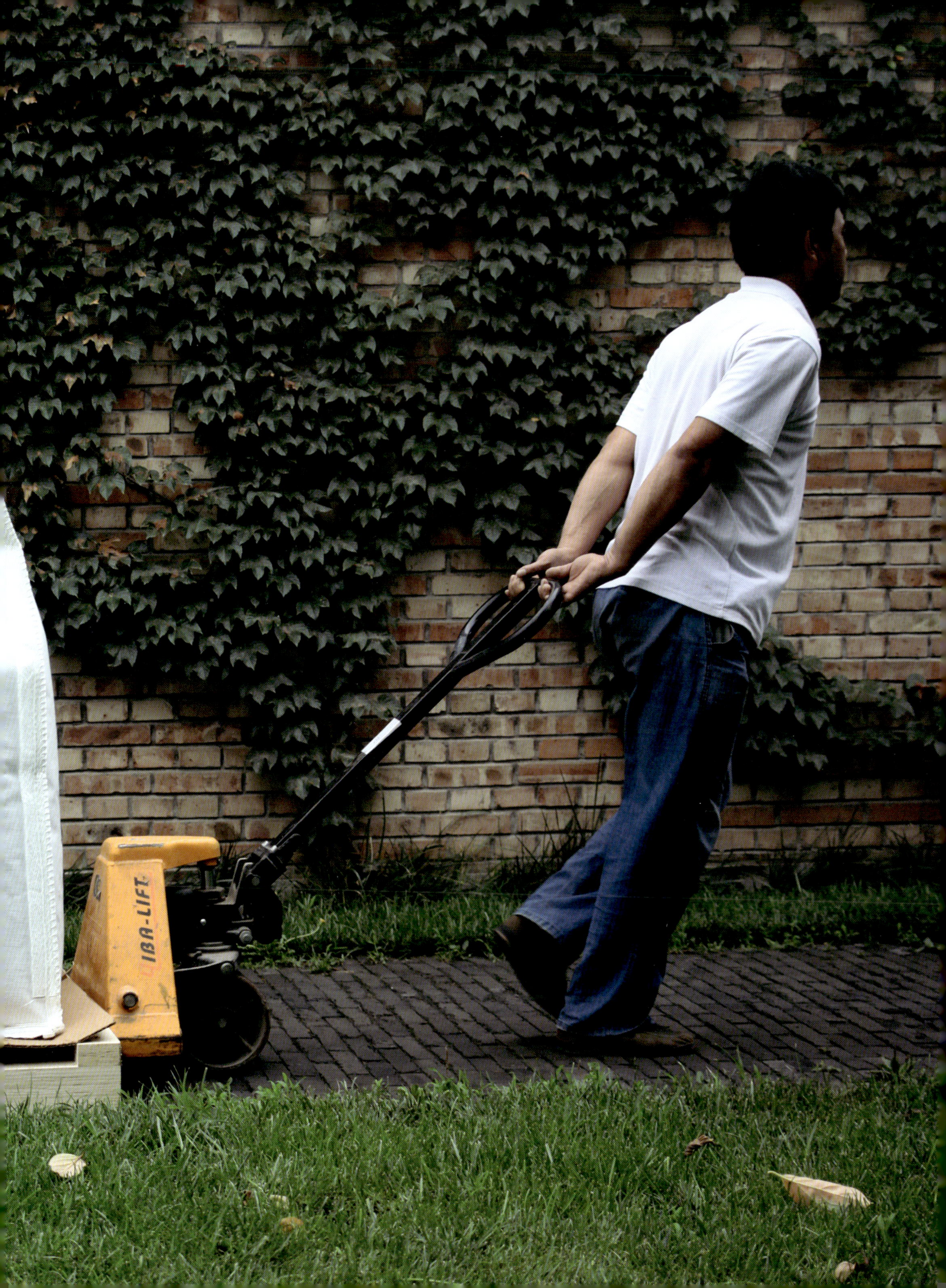
IBA-LIFT

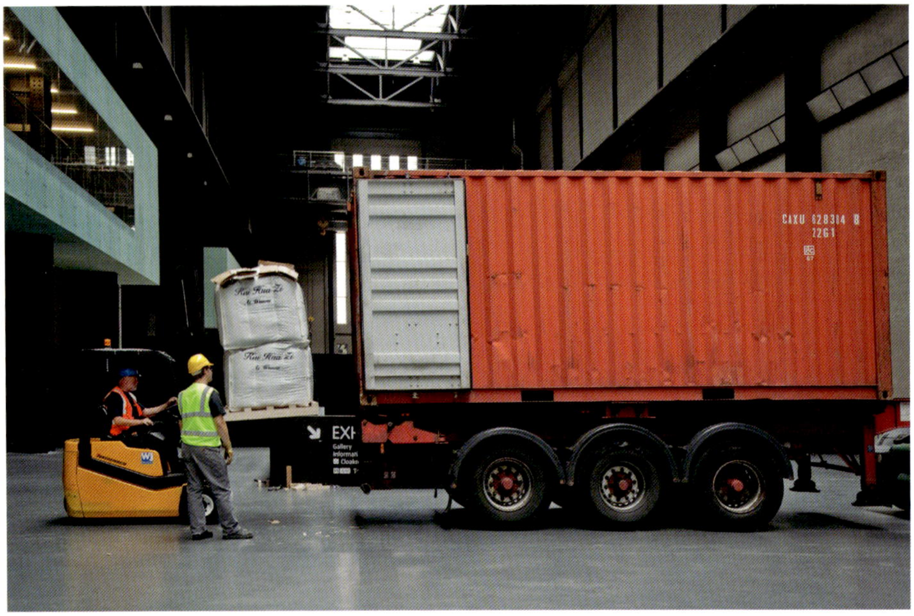

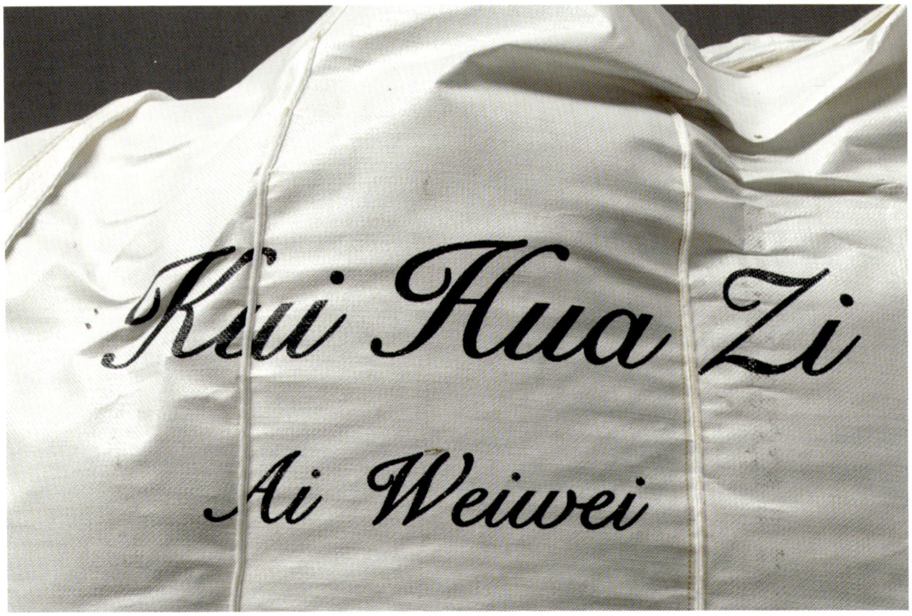
Kui Hua Zi
Ai Weiwei

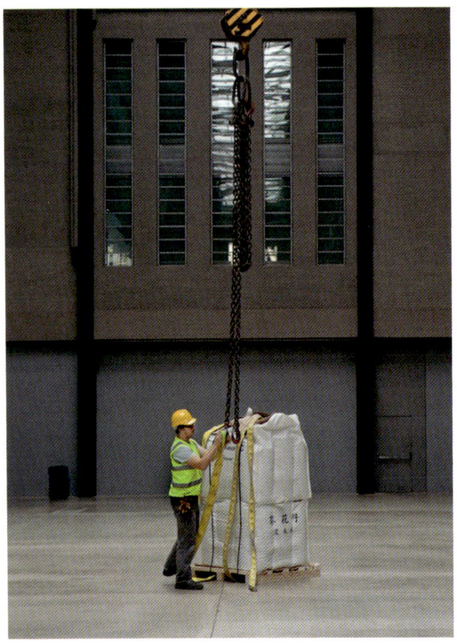

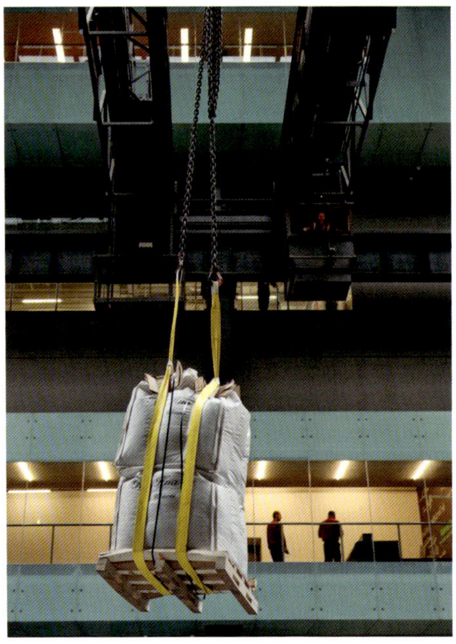

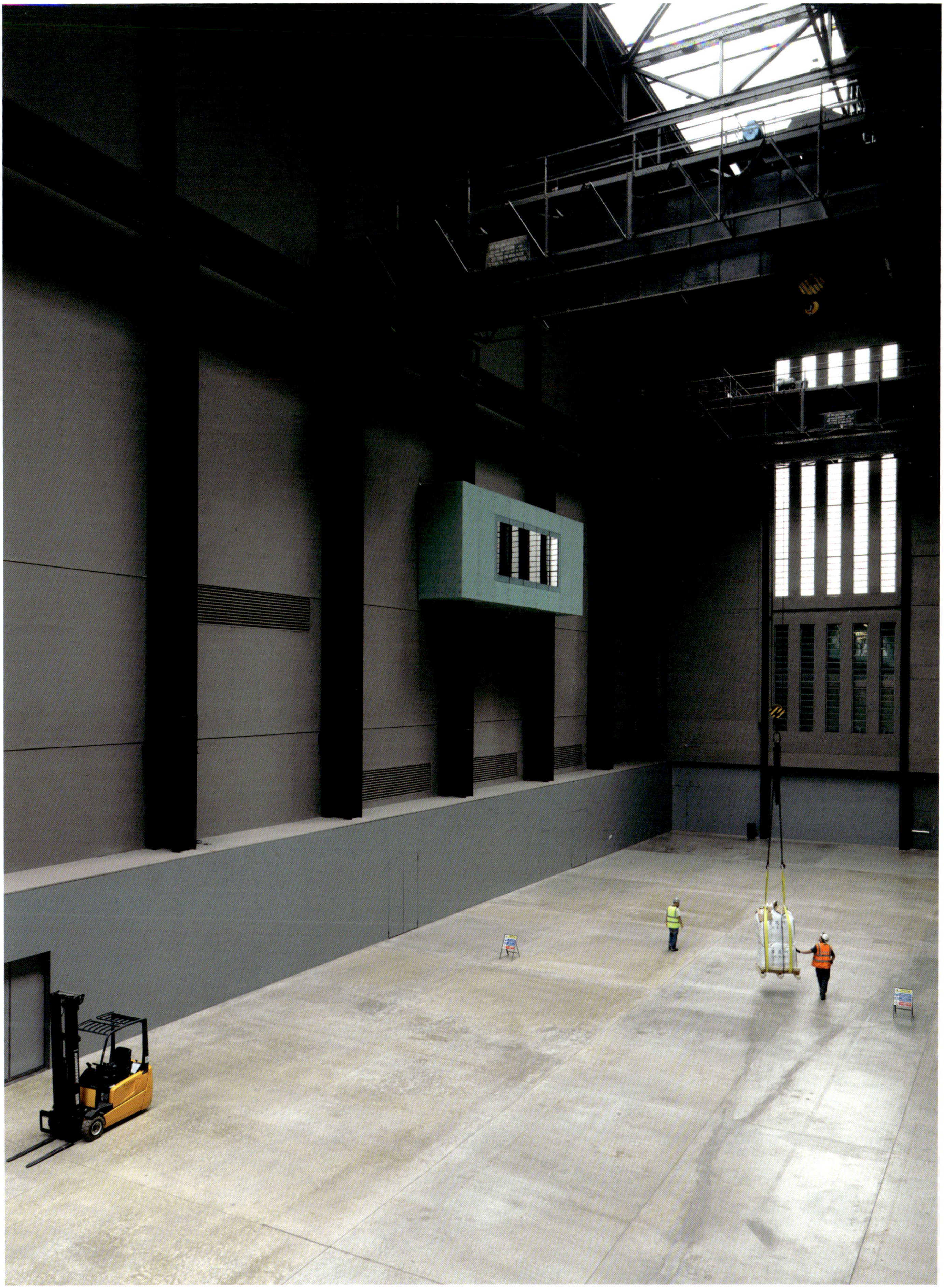

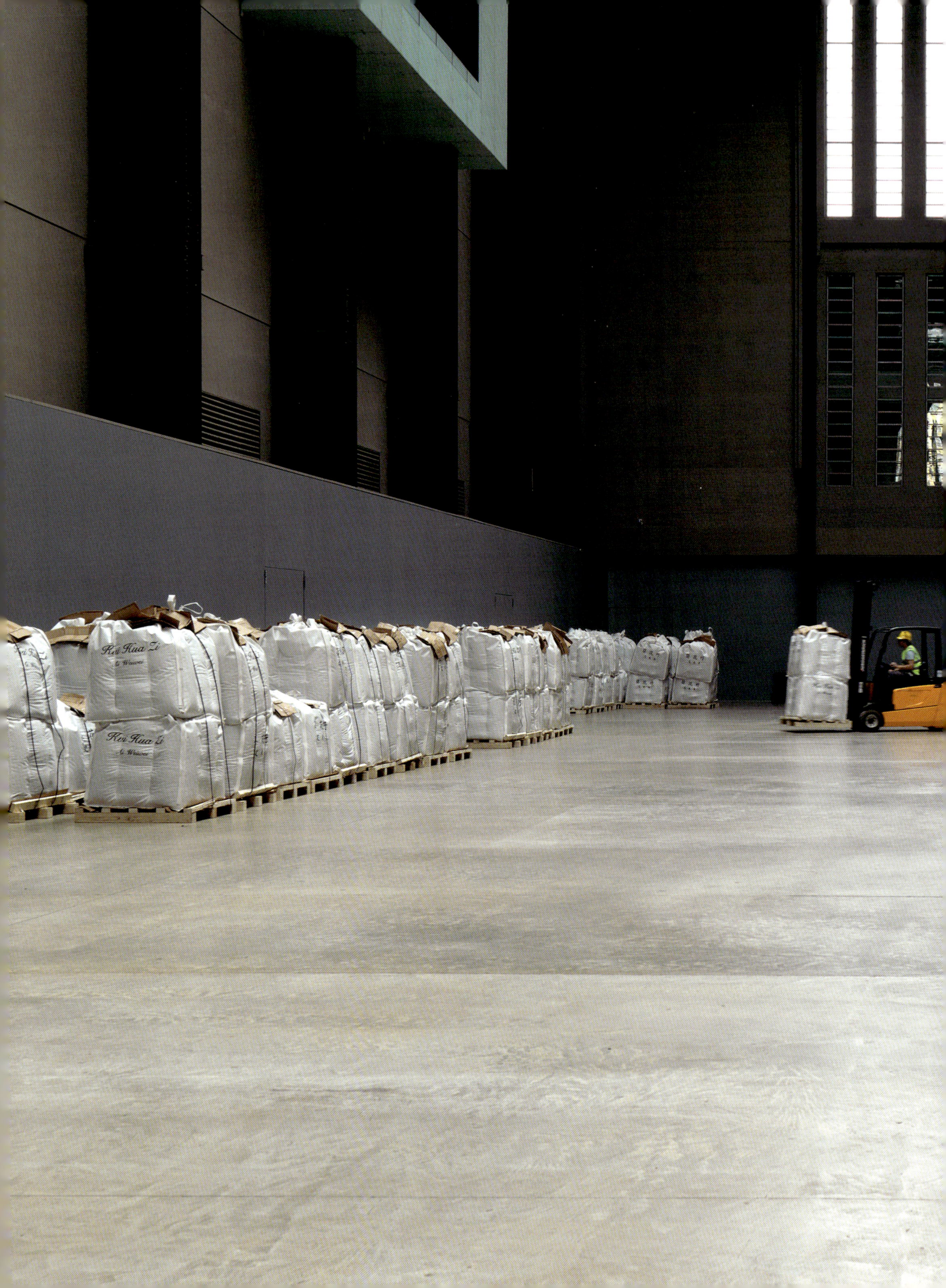

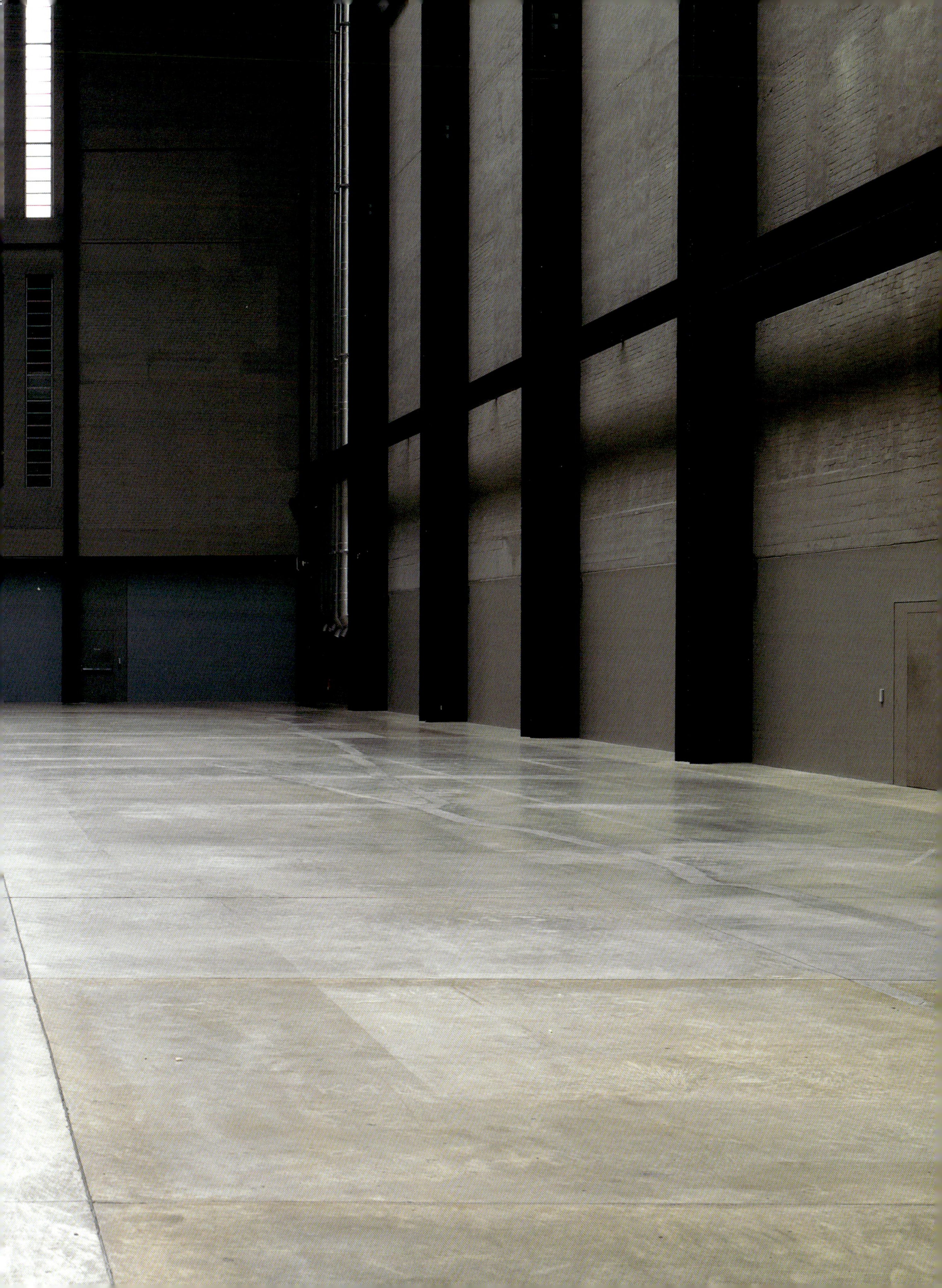

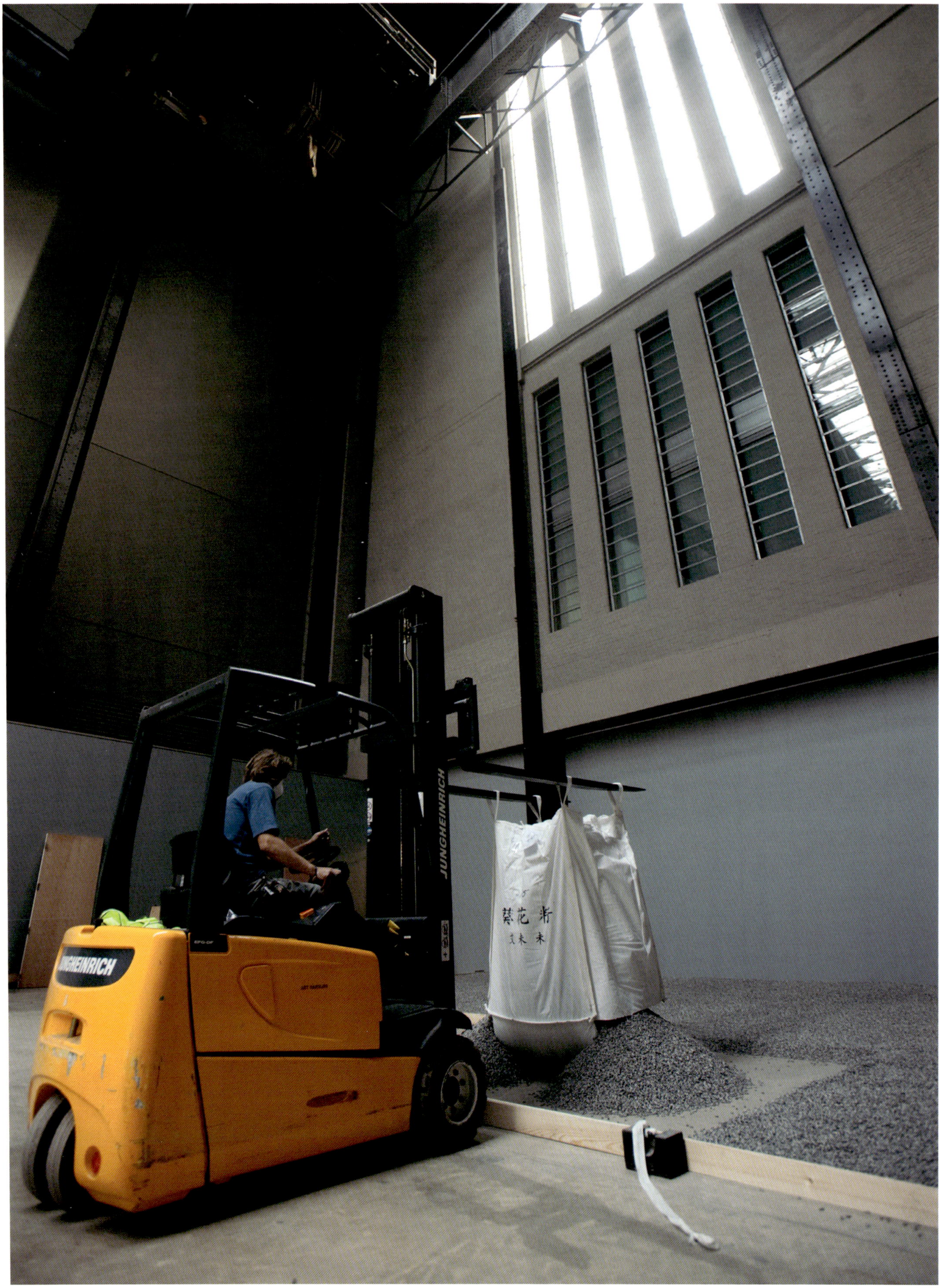
JUNGHEINRICH

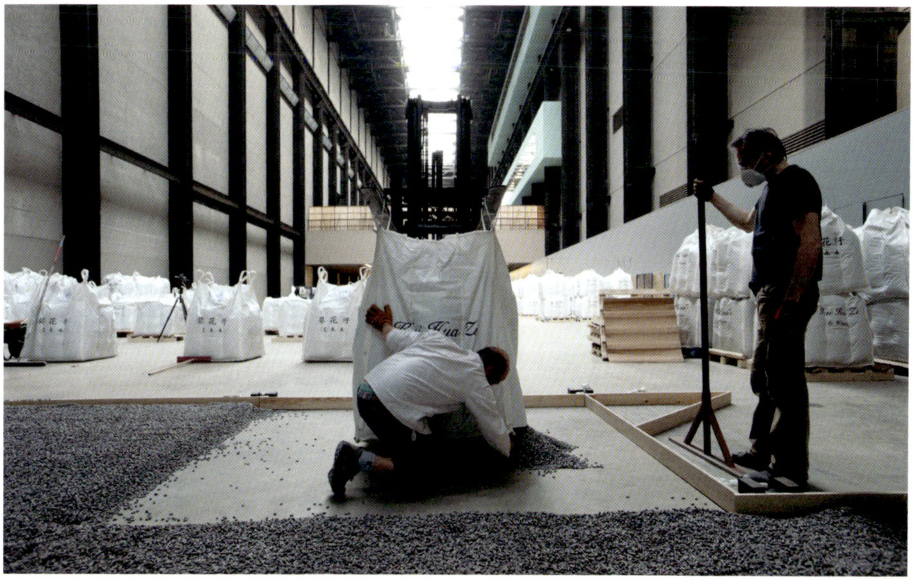

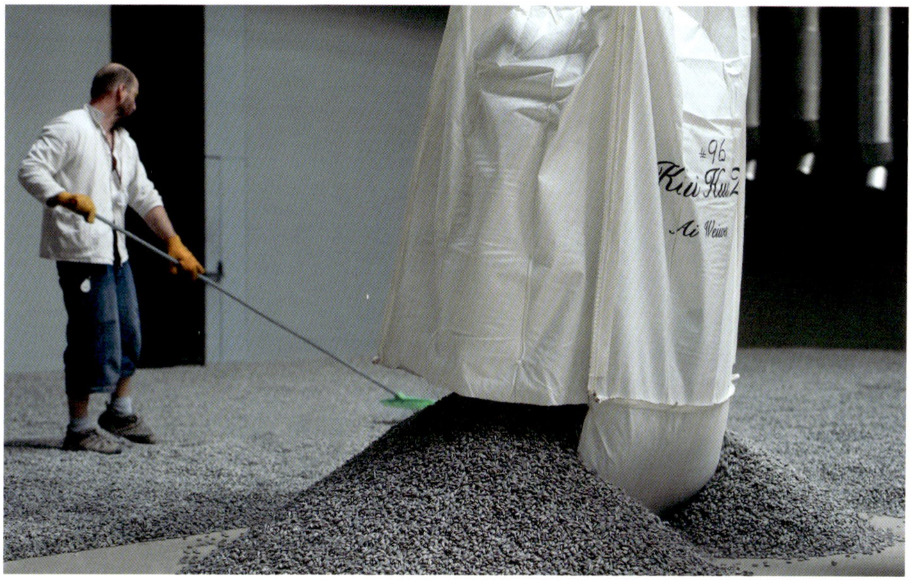
#96

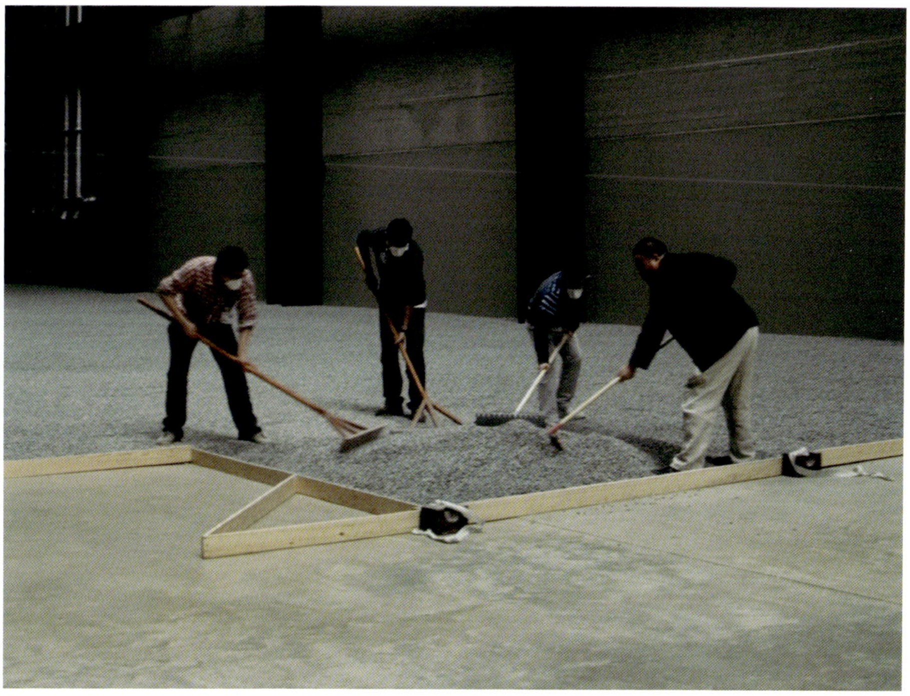

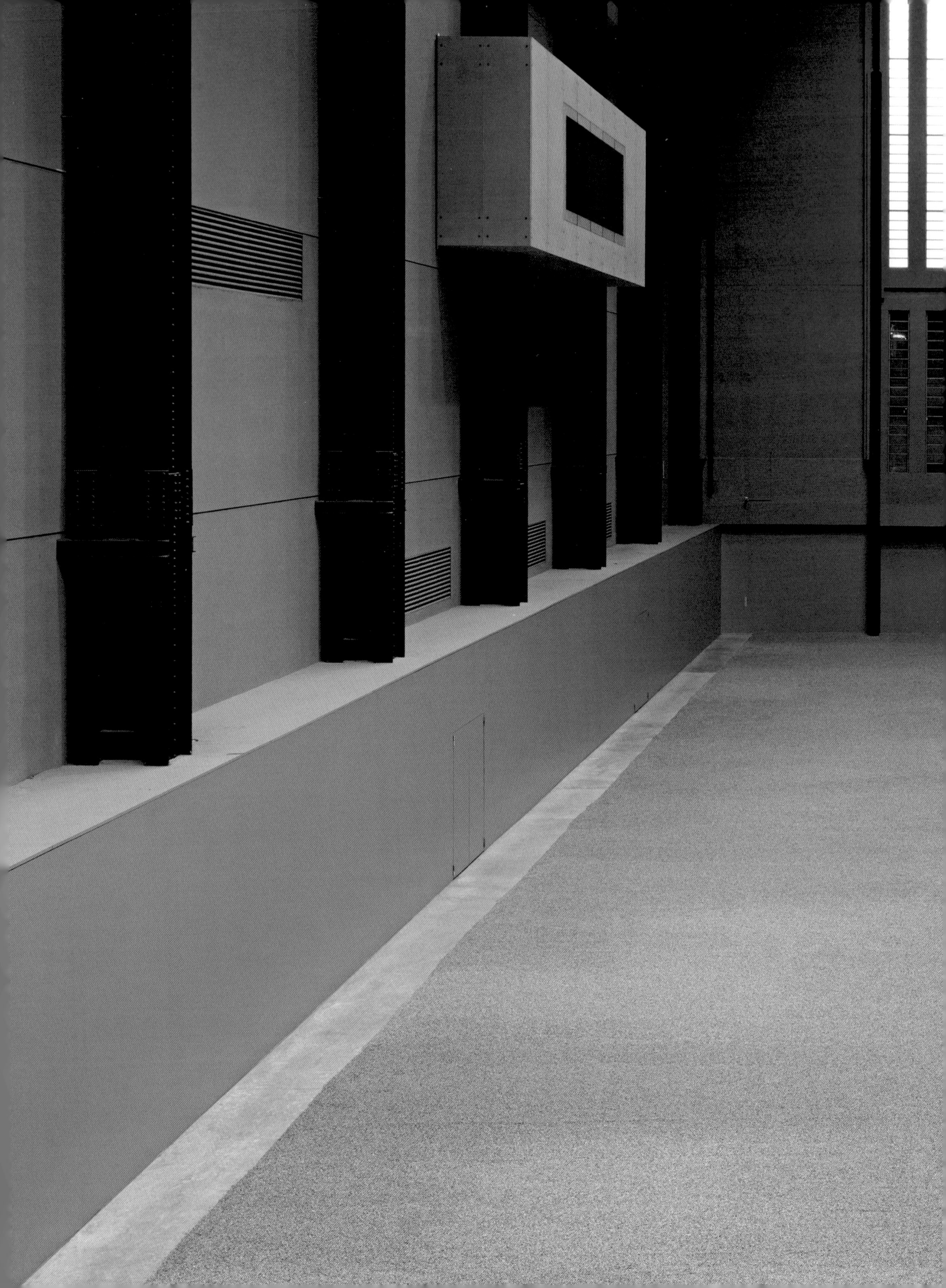

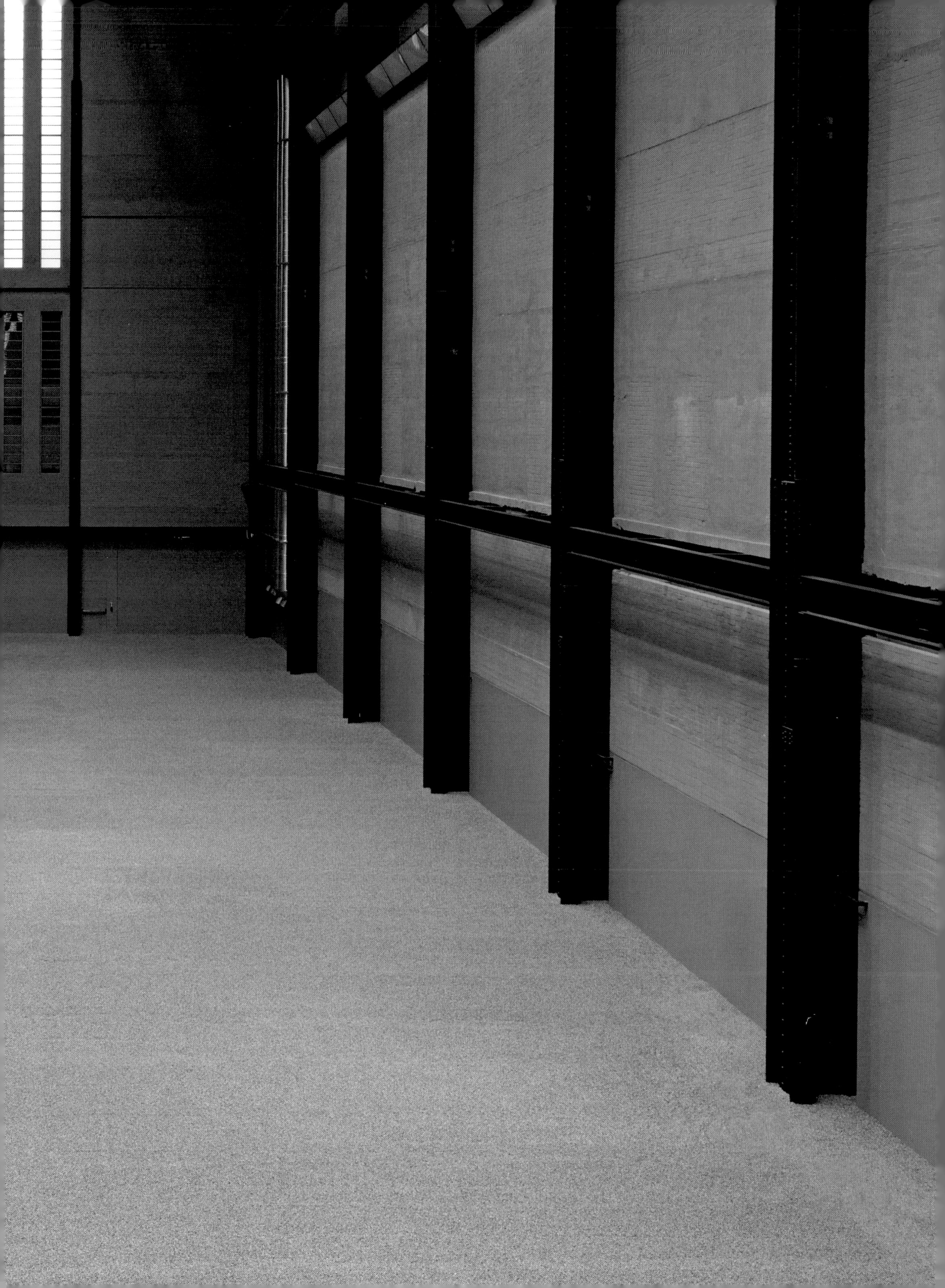

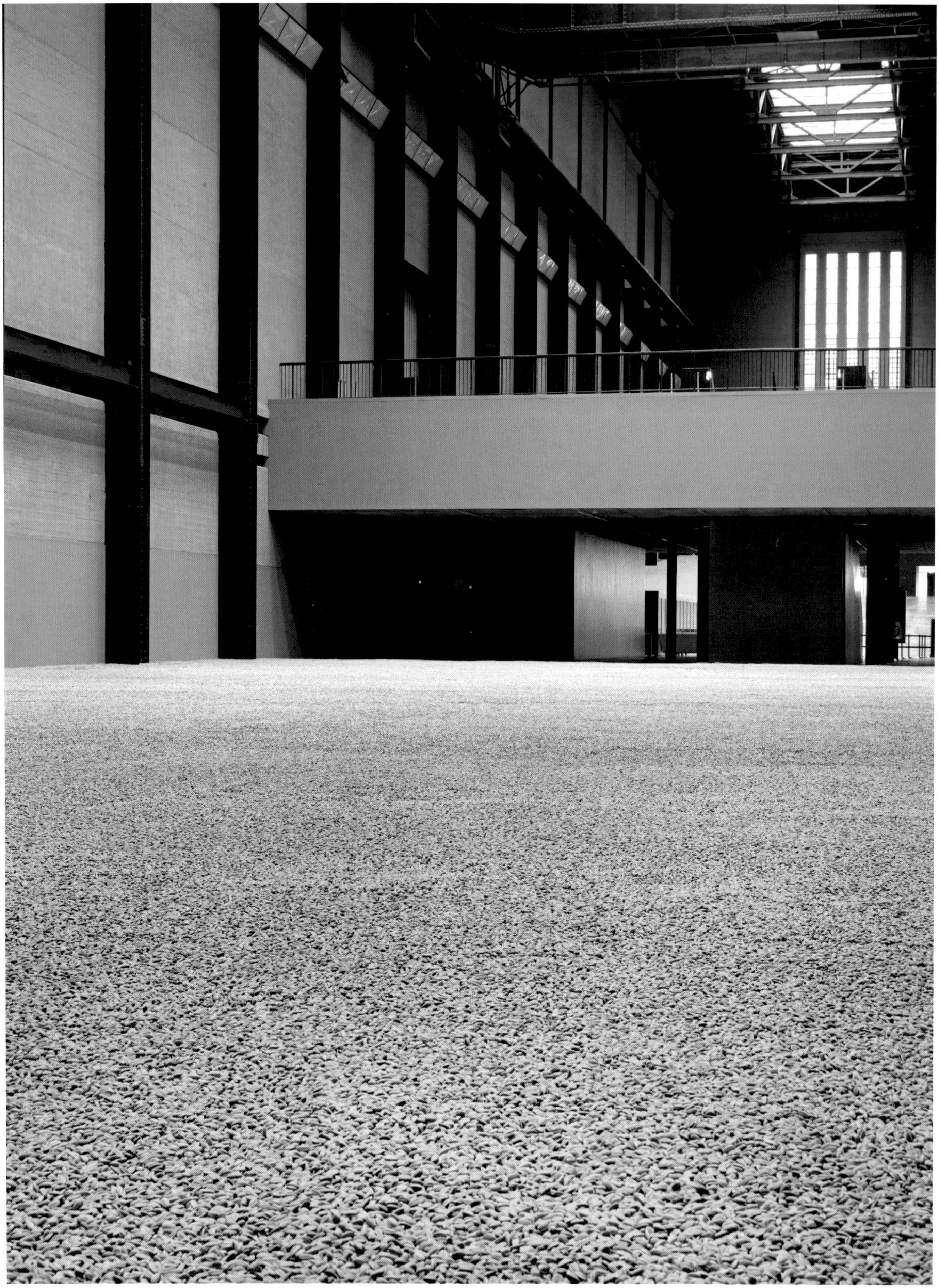

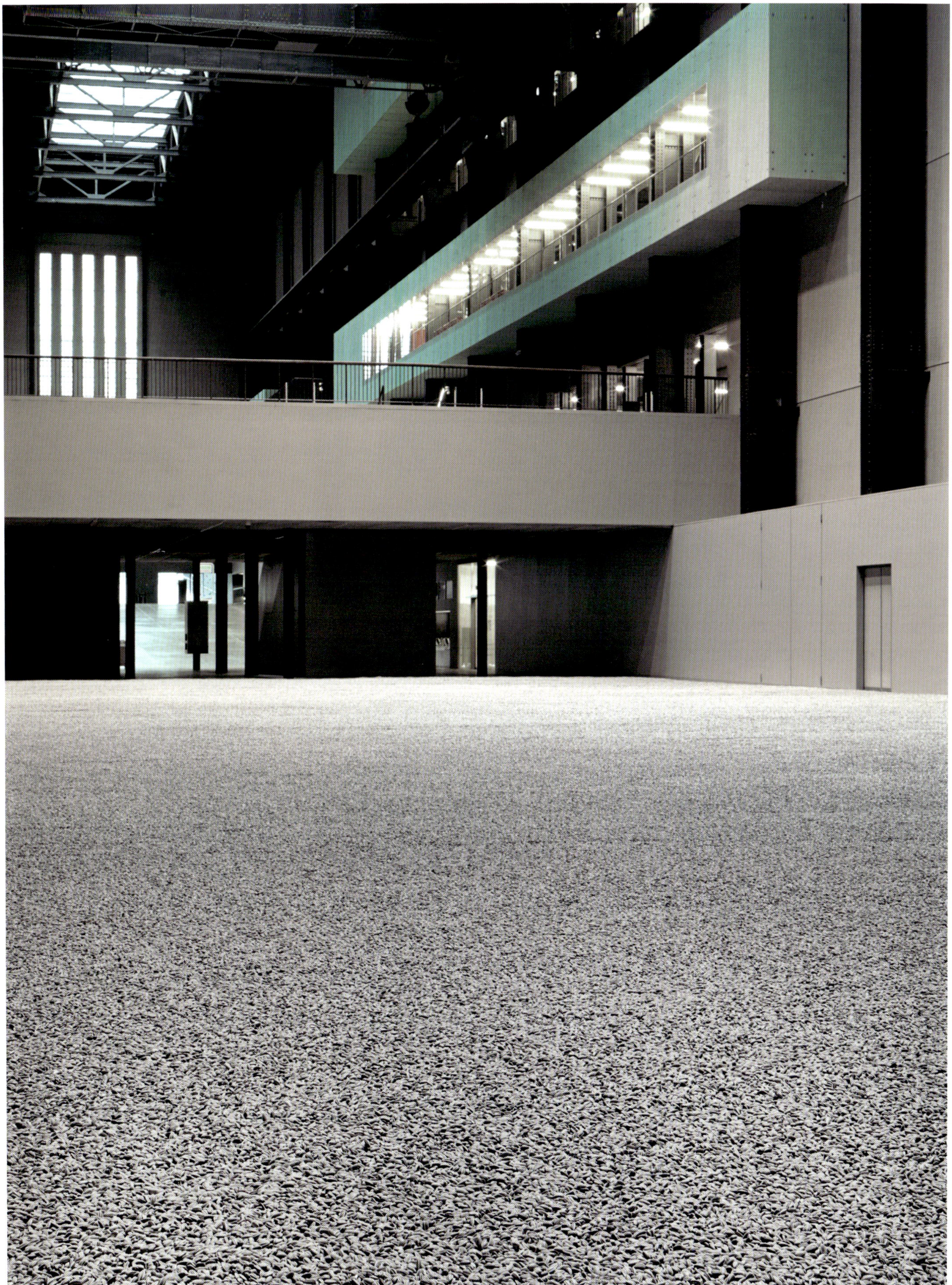

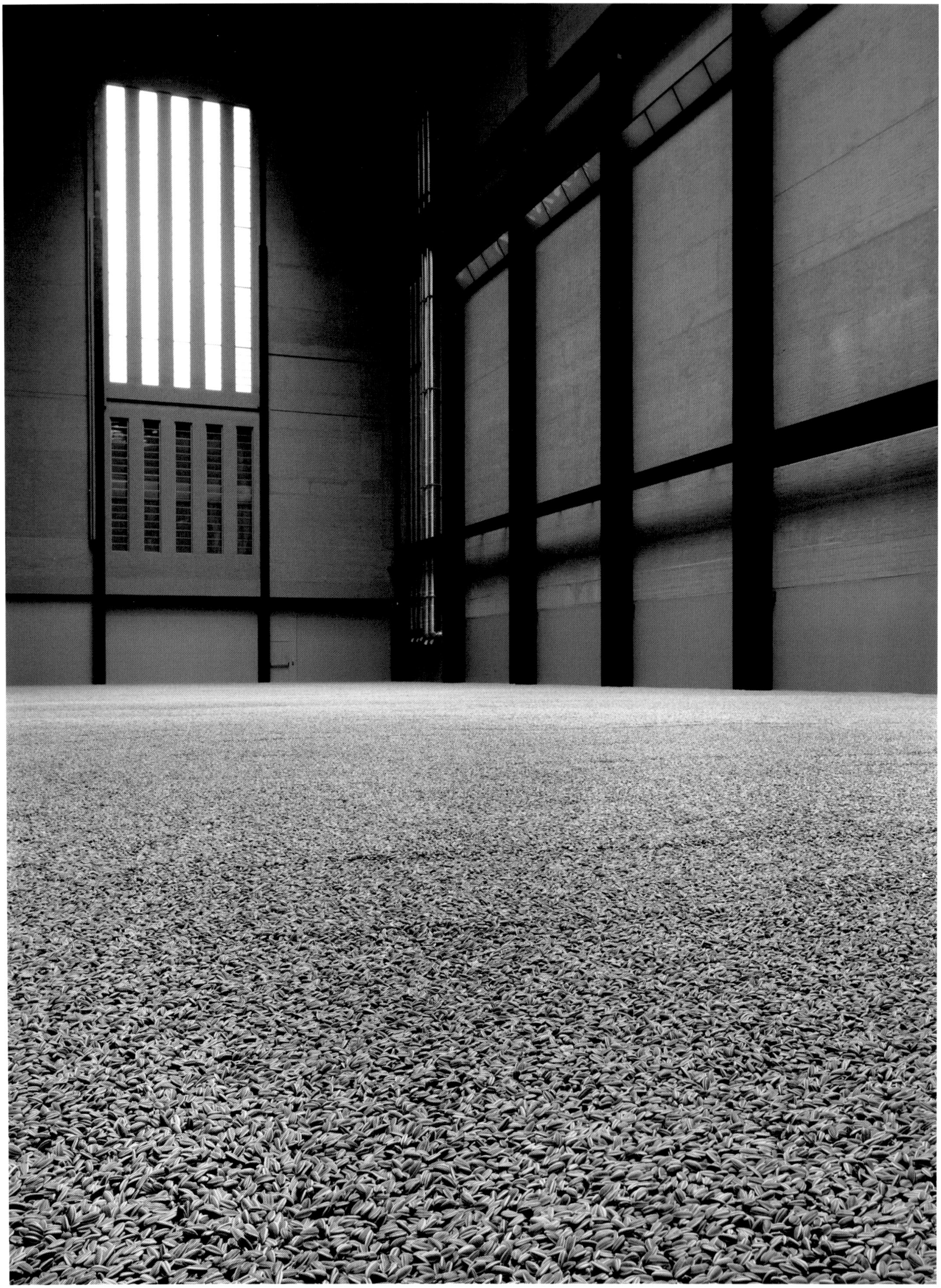

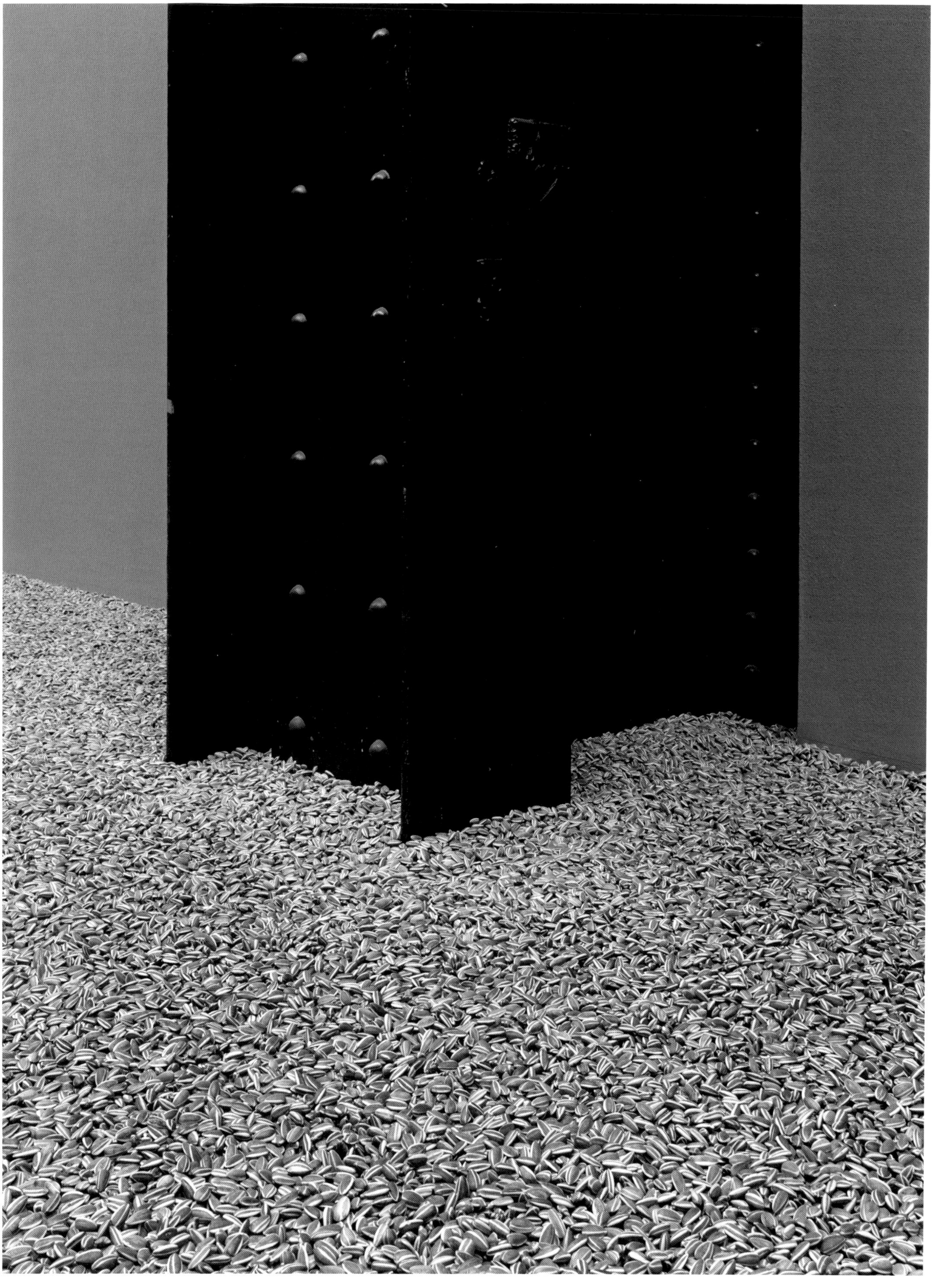

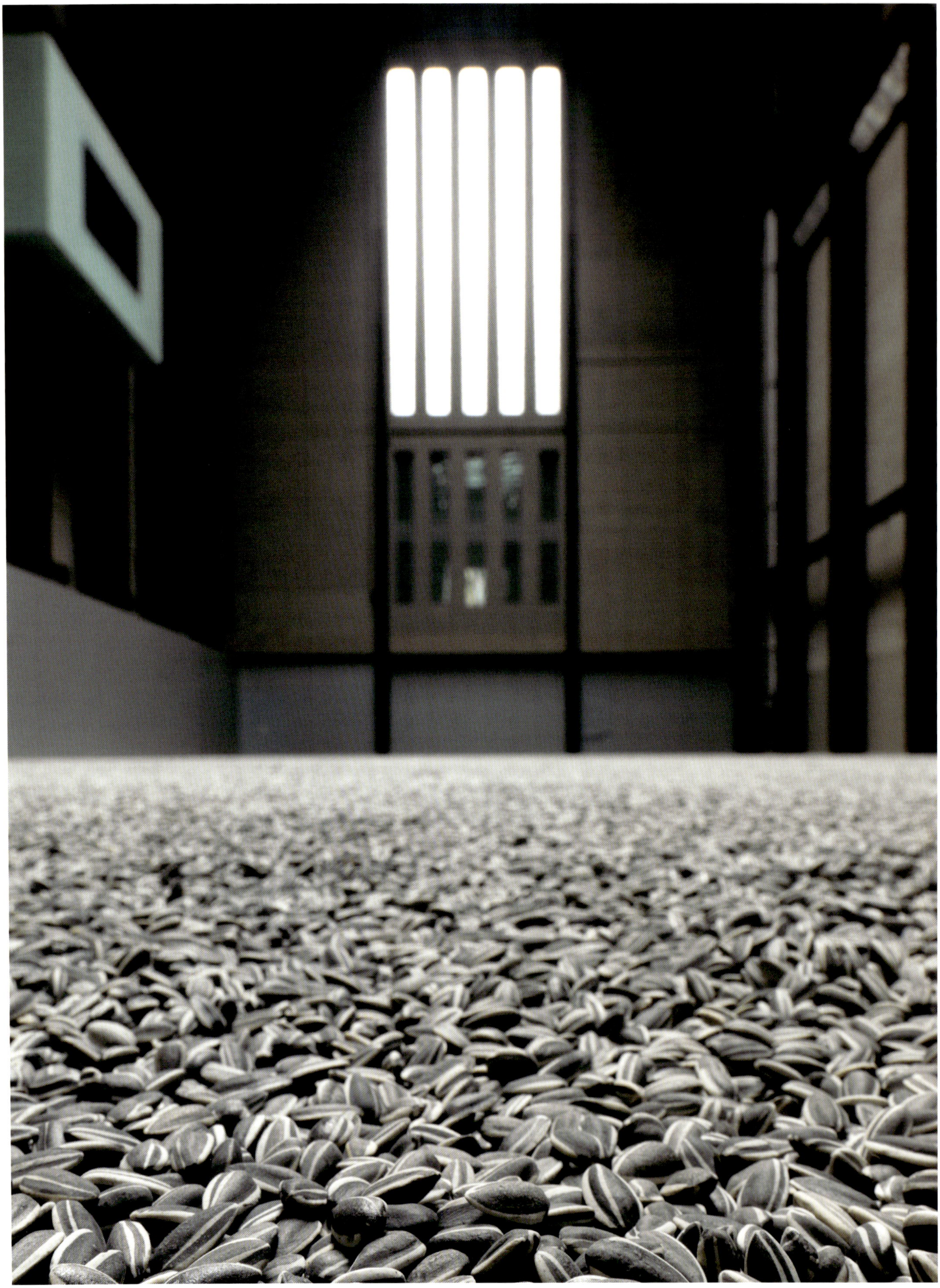

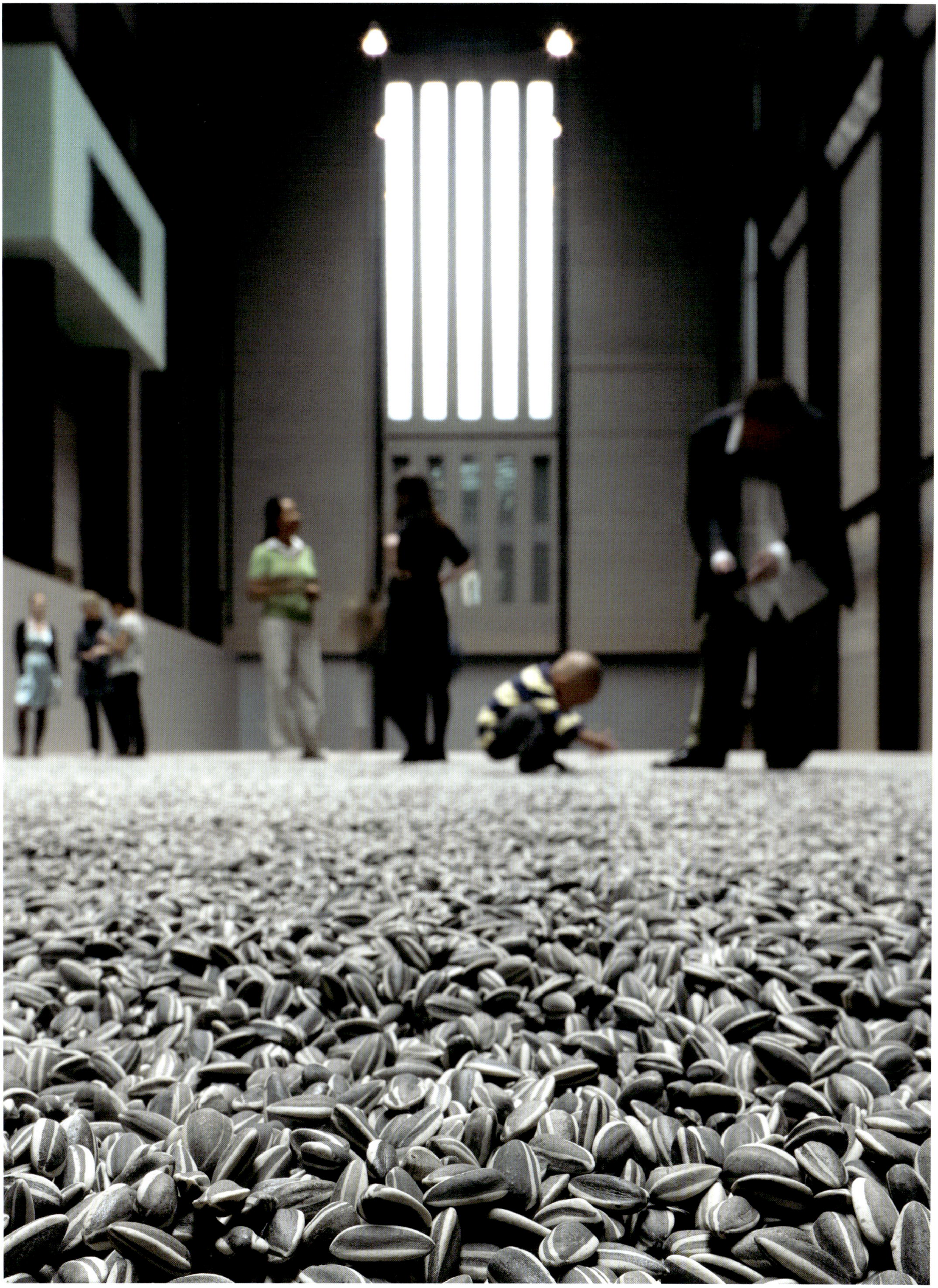

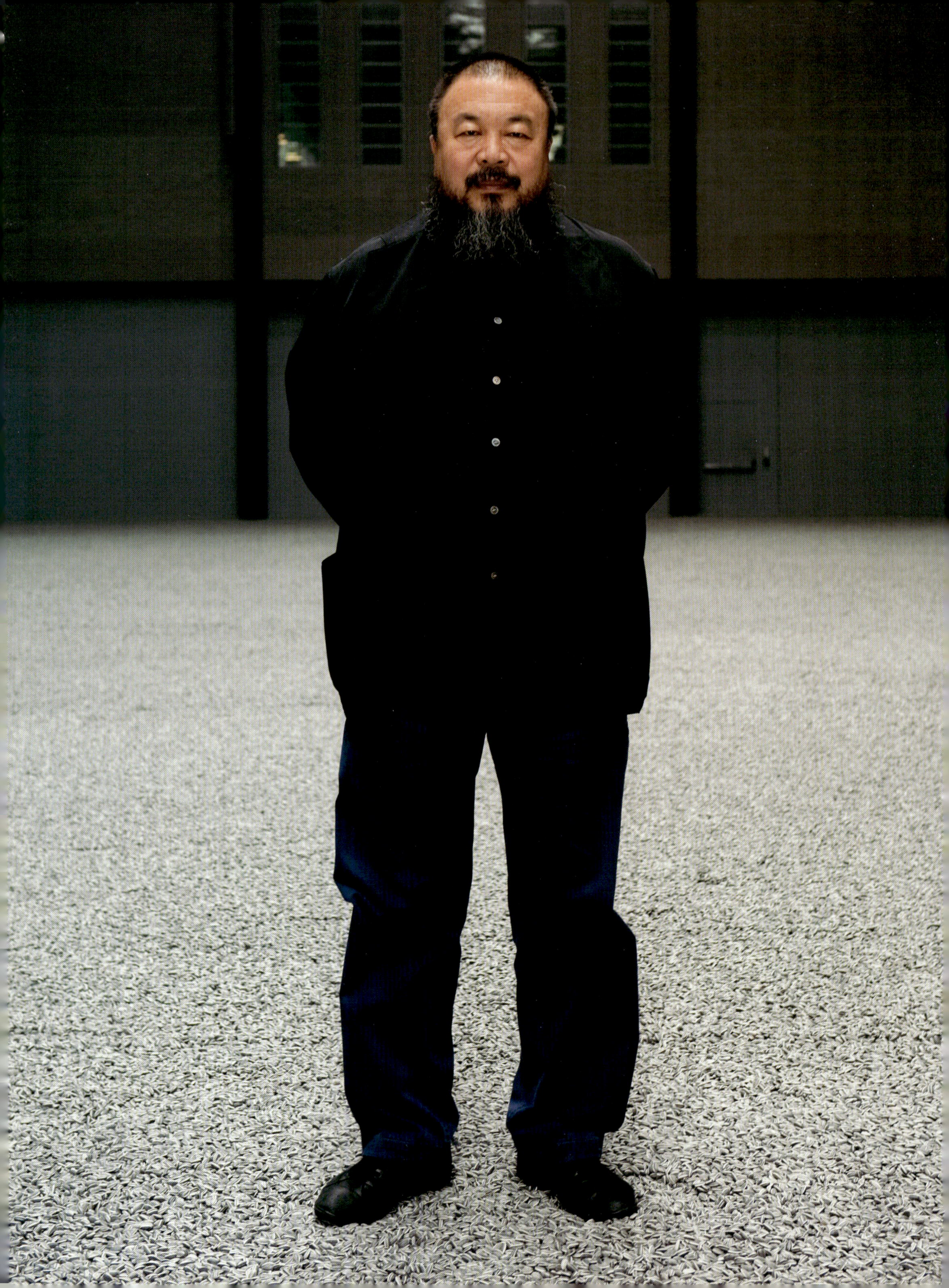

AI WEIWEI
艾未未

1957 Born in Beijing, China. Lives and works in Beijing.

SELECTED ACTIVITIES

2010 Co-Director of 2011 Gwangju Design Biennial, Gwangju, South Korea
Design for Comme de Garçons Aoyama Store, Tokyo, Japan
Digital Activism in China: A discussion with Jack Dorsey (co-founder of Twitter) and Richard MacManus, The Paley Media Center, New York
Talk with Nobel Prize winner Herta Müller at the international culture festival *Litcologne*, Cologne, Germany. **1978** Enrolled at the Beijing Film Academy. Co-founder of Stars, the avant-garde art group.

2008 Curator of the architecture project Ordos 100.
'Citizen Investigation' project, researching information about the students who died in the earthquake in Sichuan on 12 May 2008.

2007 Documenta 12, Kassel, Germany: for his project *Fairytale* he invited 1,001 Chinese citizens to Kassel.

2003–2008 Commissioned to design Beijing's 2008 Olympic Stadium together with architects Herzog & de Meuron.

2003 Founded the architecture studio FAKE Design, Beijing.

2002 Curator of the project Jinhua Architectural Art Park, Jinhua, China.

2000 Co-curator, with Feng Boyi, of the exhibition *Fuck Off*, Shanghai, China.

1999 Moved to Chaochangdi in north-east Beijing. Built the studio-house, his first architectural project.

1997 Co-founder and Artistic Director of China Art Archives & Warehouse (CAAW), Beijing.

1994–1997 Published *Black Cover Book* (1994), *White Cover Book* (1995) and *Grey Cover Book* (1997).

1993 Returned to Beijing.

1981–1982 Moved to the United States, living mainly New York. Attended Parsons School of Design, New York.

SELECTED AWARDS

Honorary doctorate degree, Faculty of Politics and Social Science, University of Ghent, Belgium, 2010

GQ Men of the Year 2009

The *Art Review* 'Power 100' 2009, ranked 43

Chinese Contemporary Art Award, 2008

SOLO EXHIBITIONS

2010 *A Few Works from Ai Weiwei*, Alexander Ochs Galleries, Berlin, Germany
The Unilever Series: Ai Weiwei, Turbine Hall, Tate Modern, London, UK
Hurt Feelings, Galerie Christine Koenig Galerie, Vienna, Austria
Ai Weiwei, Galerie Urs Meile, Lucerne, Switzerland
Dropping the Urn: Ceramics 5000 BCE – 2010 CE, Museum of Contemporary Craft, Portland, USA; previously at Arcadia University Gallery, Glenside, USA
Ai Weiwei, Haines Gallery, San Francisco, USA
Barely Something, Stiftung DKM, Duisburg, Germany

2009 *With Milk_find something everybody can use*, Mies van der Rohe Pavilion, Barcelona, Spain
World Map, Faurschou Gallery, Beijing
So Sorry, Haus der Kunst, Munich, Germany
According to What?, Mori Art Museum, Tokyo
Ways Beyond Art, Ivory Press Space, Madrid, Spain
Four Movements, Phillips de Pury, London
Ai Weiwei: New York Photographs 1983–1993, Three Shadows Photography Art Centre, Beijing

2008 *Ai Weiwei,* Albion Gallery, London
Ai Weiwei, Hyundai Gallery, Seoul, Korea
Under Construction, Sherman Contemporary Art Foundation, Campbelltown Arts Center, Sydney, Australia
Illumination, Mary Boone Gallery, New York
Go China! Ai Weiwei, Groninger Museum, Groningen, The Netherlands

2007 Galerie Urs Meile, Beijing-Lucerne, Lucerne, Switzerland
Travelling Landscapes, AedesLand, Berlin

2006 *Fragments*, Galerie Urs Meile, Beijing-Lucerne, Beijing

2004 Kunsthalle Bern, Berne, Switzerland
Caermersklooster – Provinciaal Centrum voor Kunst en Cultuur, Ghent
Robert Miller Gallery, New York

2003 Galerie Urs Meile, Beijing-Lucerne, Lucerne

1988 *Old Shoes: Safe Sex*, Art Waves Gallery, New York

1982 Asian Foundation, San Francisco

GROUP EXHIBITIONS

2010 29th São Paulo Biennial, Brazil
Venice Architecture Biennale, Italy
Passages: Travels in Hyperspace, LABoral Centre of Art and Industrial Creation, Gijon, Asturias, Spain
The Big Bang, White Rabbit Gallery, Sydney
Une Idée, une forme, un entre: Poesie Politique du corporel, Migrosmuseum, Zürich, Switzerland
The Flower of May, Gwangju Museum of Art and Kunsthalle Gwangju, Gwangju, South Korea
Taking a Stance: 8 Critical Attitudes in Chinese and Dutch Architecture and Design, OCAT Art & Design Gallery, Shenzhen, China; previously at Today Art Museum, Beijing; Dutch Culture Center, Shanghai
Regionale 10, Liezen, Austria
The Problem of Asia, Chalk Horse, Sydney
Marcel Duchamp and the Forestay Waterfall, Salle Davel, Cully, Switzerland *Lost and Found,* Neugerriemschneider, Berlin
Rem(a)inders, Galleria Continua, Beijing*The State of Things. Brussels / Beijing* (curator), National Art Museum, Beijing (2010); previously at Bozar Palais des Beaux-Arts, Brussels, Belgium (2009)
Acconci Studio + Ai Weiwei: A Collaborative Project, Para/Site Art Space, Hong Kong
Until Now: Collecting the New (1960–2010), Target Gallery, Minneapolis Institute of Arts, Minneapolis, USA
Radical Conceptual, Museum of Modern Art, Frankfurt am Main
Contemplating the Void, Guggenheim Museum, New York

2009 *Beg, Borrow and Steal,* Rubell Family Collection, Miami, USA
Fascination with the Foreign: China – Japan – Europe, The Hetjens Museum, Düsseldorf, Germany
Garbage, AfterGallery, projectroom, Moscow, Russia
Attitude, Shit-art Center, Zhengzhou, China
Pete and Repeat: The Works from the Zabludowicz Collection, 176, London
Void of Memory, Kimusa of Platform 2009, Seoul, Korea
Fairytale, Herzliya Museum of Contemporary Art, Herzliya, Israel
I want to talk to you, T.art Center, Beijing
The Big World: Recent Art from China, Chicago Cultural Center, Chicago, USA
Map Games: Dynamic of Change, Centre for Contemporary Arts (CAOS), Terni, Italy
United Technologies, Lismore Castle, Lismore, Ireland
The Making of Art, Kunsthalle Schirn, Frankfurt am Main
Action – Camera: Beijing Performance Photography, Morris and Helen Belkin Art Gallery, Vancouver, Canada
Mahjong: Contemporary Chinese Art from the Sigg Collection, The Peabody Essex Museum, Salem, USA (2009); previously at The University of California, Berkeley Art Museum & Pacific Film Archive, Berkeley, USA (2008); as *Mahjong - Chinesische Gegenwartskunst aus der Sammlung Sigg*, Museum der Moderne, Salzburg, (2007); Hamburger Kunsthalle, Hamburg, Germany (2006); Kunstmuseum Bern, Berne, Switzerland (2005)

2008 *Earthquake*, Art Channel, Beijing
China: Construction / Deconstruction. Chinese Contemporary Art, Museu de Arte de São Paolo, São Paolo
Out There: Architecture Beyond Building, Biennale Architecture, 11th International Architecture Exhibition, Venice, Italy
Liverpool Biennial International 08: *Made Up*, Tate Liverpool, Liverpool, UK
Super Fengshui: UCCA Site Commissions, Ullens Center for Contemporary Art, Beijing
Reconstruction # 3: The Artists Playground, Sudeley Castle, Gloucestershire, UK
China Power Station: Part III, Musée d'Art Moderne Grand-Duc Jean, Luxembourg
Branded and on Display, Tufts University Art Gallery, Medford, USA; previously at Scottsdale Museum of Contemporary Art, Scottsdale, USA; Salt Lake City Art Center. Salt Lake City, USA (2008); Kannert Art Museum, University of Illinois, Champaign, USA; Ulrich Museum of Art, Kansas State University, Wichita, USA (2007)
Second Lives: Remixing the Ordinary, Museum of Arts and Design, New York
Hypallage –The Post-Modern Mode of Contemporary Chinese Art, OCT Art & Design Gallery, Shenzhen
Half-Life of a Dream: Contemporary Chinese Art from the Logan Collection, San Francisco Museum of Modern Art, San Francisco
Selections from the Hara Museum's Permanent Collection, Hara Museum of Contemporary Art, Tokyo
China. The City exp(l)osed, Institut Français d'Architecture & du Patrimoine, Paris, France
Map Games: Dynamic of Change, Today Art Museum, Beijing
China Gold: Chinese Contemporary Art, Musée Maillol, Paris
Interval of Silence, RedStar Gallery, Beijing
Body Media, Duolun Museum of Modern Art, Shanghai; previously at Tang Contemporary Art, Beijing
Delirious Beijing, PKM Gallery, Beijing
Community of Tastes, Iberia Center for Contemporary Art, Beijing
New Vista: The Phenomenon of Post-Tradition in Contemporary Art, White Space Gallery, Beijing
Red Aside: Chinese Contemporary Art of the Sigg Collection, Fundació Joan Miró, Barcelona, Spain
The Real Thing: Contemporary Art from China, Institut Valencia d'Art Modern (IVAM), Valencia, Spain (2008); previously at Tate Liverpool, Liverpool (2007)

2007 Sixth Shenzhen Contemporary Sculpture Exhibition *A Vista of Perspectives*, OCT Contemporary Art Terminal, Shenzhen
Origin Point: Star Star Group. Retrospective Exhibition, Today Art Museum, Beijing
EI – Entity Identity – Beijing Series. Western Concepts – Chinese Drafts, Stedelijk Museums' Hertogenbosch, MB's-Hertogenbosch, The Netherlands
Fortunate Objects: Selections from the Ella Fontanals Cisneros Collection, CIFO – Cisneros Fontanals Art Foundation, Miami
Inspired by China: Contemporary Furnituremakers Explore Chinese Traditions, Museum of Fort Lauderdale, Fort Lauderdale, USA; previously at Peabody Essex Museum, Salem, USA (2006)
China Now, Cobra Museum, Amsterdam, The Netherlands
Get It Louder, SOHO Shangdu, Beijing
Something New Pussycat, Klara Wallner Galerie, Berlin
Energies – Synergy, Foundation De 11 Lijnen, Oudenburg, Belgium
Chinese Video: Chord Chances in the Megalopolis, Morono Kiang Gallery, Los Angeles, USA
Documenta 12, Kassel, Germany
Contemporary Art Exhibitions of Kogo Art Space, Kogo Art Space, Hangzhou, China
Metamorphosis: The Generation of Transformation in Chinese Contemporary Art, Tampere Art Museum, Tampere, Finland
Thermocline of Art. New Asian Waves, ZKM – Zentrum für Kunst und Medientechnologie, Karlsruhe, Germany
Art from China – Collection Uli Sigg, Centro Cultural Banco do Brasil, Rio de Janeiro, Brasil
China Welcomes You... Desires, Struggles, New Identities, Kunsthaus Graz, Graz, Austria
The Year of the Golden Pig: Contemporary Chinese Art from the Sigg Collection, Lewis Glucksman Gallery, Cork University College, Cork, Ireland
Money, Beijing Today Gallery, Beijing
Forged Realities, Universal Studios, Beijing
Project *We Are the Future*, 2nd Moskow Biennial of Contemporary Art, Art Centre Winzavod, Moskow, Russia
A Continuous Dialogue, Galleria Continua, San Gimignano, Italy
What about Sculpture? Chambers Fine Art, New York

2006 *Art in Motion: Chinese Contemporary Art Meets BMW Art Cars*, Museum of Contemporary Art Shanghai, Shanghai
This Is Not For You: Sculptural Discourses, Thyssen-Bornemisza Art Contemporary, Vienna
Detours: Tactical Approaches to Urbanization in China, Eric Arthur Gallery, Faculty of Architecture, Landscape and Design, University of Toronto, Toronto, Canada
China Now. Faszination einer Weltveränderung, Sammlung Essl, Kunst der Gegenwart, Klosterneuburg / Vienna
MoCA Envisage / Entry Gate: Chinese Aesthetics of Heterogeneity, Museum of Contemporary Art Shanghai, Shanghai
The 5th Asia-Pacific Triennial of Contemporary Art, Queensland Art Gallery, Queensland, Australia
Zones of Contact, 15th Biennial of Sydney, Sydney
Territorial. Ai Weiwei und Serge Spitzer, Museum für Moderne Kunst, Frankfurt am Main
Altered, Stitched and Gathered, P.S. 1 Contemporary Art Center, Long Island City, New York
China Power Station I, Serpentine Gallery, London
Herzog & de Meuron. No 250. Eine Ausstellung, Haus der Kunst, Munich
Fill in the Blanks, China Art Archives & Warehouse, Beijing
Busan Biennial 2006, Busan Museum of Modern Art, Busan, Korea
Misleading Trails, Samek Art Gallery, Bucknell University, Lewisburg, USA; previously at Schick Art Gallery, Skidmore College, Saratoga Springs, USA; Boyden Gallery, St Mary's College of Maryland, St Mary's City, USA
Cityscapes 'Beijing Welcomes You'. Ein Stadtmodell von Lu Hao sowie Fotografien von Ai Weiwei, Kunsthaus Hamburg, Hamburg
A Continuous Dialogue, Galleria Continua, Beijing
China Contemporary: Architecture, Art and Visual Culture, Netherlands Architecture Institute, Rotterdam, The Netherlands
Black and Blue, Robert Miller Gallery, New York
Antique Modernity: Breaking Traditions, Ethan Cohen Fine Arts, New York
2006 Beaufort Outside, Museum of Modern Art, Ostend, Belgium
China zwischen Vergangenheit und Zukunft / Between Past and Future – New Photography and Video from China, Haus der Kulturen der Welt, Berlin; previously at Nasher

Museum of Art at Duke University, Durham, USA; Santa Barbara Museum of Art, Santa Barbara, USA
Regeneration: Contemporary Chinese Art from China and the US, Williams College Museum of Art, Williamstown, USA (2006); previously at Arizona State University Art Museum, Tempe, USA; University Art Gallery, University of California San Diego, La Jolla, USA; Ben Maltz Gallery, Otis Otis College of Art & Design, Los Angeles, USA (2005); David Winton Bell Gallery, List Art Center Brown University, Providence, USA; Samek Art Gallery, Bucknell University, Lewisburg, USA; Jean Paul Slusser Gallery, University of Michigan, Ann Arbor, USA (2004)

2005 The 2nd Guangzhou Triennial, Guangdong Museum of Art, Guangzhou, China
Misleading Trails, Fine Arts Gallery, Vanderbilt University, Nashville, USA; Charlotte and Philip Hanes Art Gallery, Wake Forest University, Winston-Salem, USA; University of North Texas Art Gallery, Denton, USA; Altgeld Gallery, Northern Illinois University, DeKalb, USA
Between Past and Future: New Photography and Video from China, Victoria and Albert Museum, London; previously at Seattle Art Museum, Seattle, USA (2005); Museum of Contemporary Art Printemps Chicago and The David and Alfred Smart Museum of Art, Chicago, USA; International Center of Photography, New York (2004)
Xianfeng! Beeldhouwkunst von de Chinese avant-garde / Chinese Avant-Garde Sculpture, Museum Beelden aan Zee, Scheveningen, The Netherlands
Convergence at E116'/N40, Platform China Contemporary Art Institute, Beijing
A Strange Heaven: Contemporary Chinese Photography, Tennis Palace Art Museum, Helsinki, Finland
1st Monpellier Biennial of Chinese Contemporary Art, Montpellier, France
Cina. Prospettive d'Arte Contemporanea / China: As Seen by Contemporary Chinese Artists, Provincia di Milano, Spazio Oberdan, Milan, Italy
Herzog & de Meuron: An Exhibition, Tate Modern, London; as *No 250. An Exhibition. Beauty and Waste in the Architecture of Herzog & de Meuron*, previously at Netherlands Architecture Institute, Rotterdam, The Netherlands (2005); as *Herzog & de Meuron: No.250. Eine Ausstellung*, Schaulager, Basel, Switzerland (2004)

2004 *Silknet: Emerging Chinese Artists*, Galerie Urs Meile Beijing-Lucerne, Lucerne
Persona3, China Art Archives & Warehouse, Beijing
Le Printemps de Chine, CRAC ALSAC, Altkirch, France
Piss Off, Museum of New Art, Pontiac, USA
The 9th International Architecture Exhibition, The Venice Biennial, Venice, Italy
Misleading Trails, China Art Archives & Warehouse, Beijing
On the Edge: Contemporary Chinese Photography & Video, Ethan Cohen Fine Arts, New York
Chinese Object: Dreams & Obsessions, Salvatore Ferragamo Gallery, New York
Modern Style in East Asia, Beijing Tokyo Art Projects, Beijing

2003 *New Zone: Chinese Art*, Zacheta National Gallery of Art, Warsaw, Poland
A Strange Heaven: Contemporary Chinese Photography, Galerie Rudolfinum, Prague, Czech Republic
Junction. Chinese Contemporary Architecture of Art, Lianyang Architecture Art Museum, Shanghai

2002 *Cement: Marginal Space in Contemporary Art*, Chambers Fine Art, New York
China: Tradition und Moderne, Museum Ludwig Galerie Oberhausen, Oberhausen, Germany
Art from a Changing World, Ludwig Forum for International Art, Henie Onstad Kunstsenter, Hoevikodden, Norway
1st Guangzhou Triennale 2002, Guangdong Museum of Art, Guangzhou, China

2001 *Take Part II*, Galerie Urs Meile, Beijing-Lucerne, Lucerne
Tu Mu: Young Chinese Architecture, Aedes Galerie, Berlin
Take Part I, Galerie Urs Meile, Beijing-Lucerne, Lucerne

2000 *Fuck off*, EastLink Gallery, Shanghai
Portraits, Figures, Couples and Groups, BizArt, Shanghai
Our Chinese Friends, ACC Galerie and Galerie der Bauhaus-Universität (in collaboration with Galerie Urs Meile, Beijing-Lucerne), Weimar, Germany

1999 *Innovations Part I*, China Art Archives & Warehouse, Beijing
d'Apertutto, La Biennale di Venezia, 48. Esposizione Internationale d'Arte, Venice, Italy
Modern China Art Foundation Collection, Caermersklooster – Provinciaal Centrum voor Kunst en Cultuur, Ghent
Concepts, Colors and Passions, China Art Archives & Warehouse, Beijing

1998 *Double Kitsch: Painters from China*, Max Protetch, New York

1997 *A Point of Contact: Korean, Chinese, Japanese Contemporary Art*, Daegu Art & Culture Hall, Daegu, Korea

1996 *Begegnung mit China*, Ludwig Forum für Internationale Kunst, Aachen, Germany

1995 *Configura 2. Dialog der Kulturen*, Angermuseum, Galerie am Fischmarkt, Erfurt, Germany
Change: Chinese Contemporary Art Exhibition, Goteborg Museum, Goteborg, Sweden

1993 *Chinese Contemporary Art: The Stars 15 Years*, Tokyo Gallery, Tokyo

1989 *The Stars: Ten Years*, Hanart Gallery, Hongkong; previously at Hanart Gallery, Taipei, Taiwan; Paris, France

1987 *The Star at Harvard: Chinese Dissident Art*, Fairbank Center for East Asian Research, Harvard University, Cambridge, USA

1986 *China's New Expression*, Municipal Gallery, New York
Avant-Garde Chinese Art, Albany University Art Museum, New York

1980 Second *Star Exhibition*, National Art Museum of China, Beijing

1979 First *Star Exhibition*, outside the National Art Museum of China, Beijing

ARCHITECTURAL WORKS

2008 Ordos 100, Ordos, Inner Mongolia, China (curator, urban planning, landscape design; under construction)
Alexander Ochs Gallery, Berlin (interior renovation; unrealised)
The Great Pyramid, Dessau, Germany (unrealised)
The Dog House, Tokyo (unrealised)

2007 Fairytale 1001 Dormitory for the project *Fairytale 1001* at Documenta 12, Kassel, Germany (temporary construction)
241 Caochangdi, Caochangdi, Beijing
Red Brick Art Galleries, Caochangdi, Beijing
Naga (interior design), in collaboration with EXH, Beijing
Undercover Villa, Ordos, Inner Mongolia
Lage Restaurant, Shanghai
Kerry Center Auction House, Beijing
Art Farm, in collaboration with HHF, New York
Jiangnanhui, Hangzhou, Zhejiang, China
Kunming Art Valley, Kunming, Yunnan, China (unrealised)

2006 Three Shadows Photography Art Centre, Caochangdi, Beijing
Tsai Residence, in collaboration with HHF, New York
Shulang Factory, Yantai, Shandong, China

2005 Jinhua Architectural Art Park, Jinhua, Zhejiang (curator of landscape design)
Courtyard 104, Galerie Urs Meile, Caochangdi, Beijing
Tree House, in collaboration with HHF, Lijiang, Yunnan
Cola House, Hangzhou, Zhejiang, China
Qingdao Creative Media Institute of Beijing Film Academy, in conjunction with Herzog & De Meuron
Bian Bian Shopping Street, Jiuzhaigou, Sichuan, China (unrealised)
Club House of Water Villa, Lijiang, Yunnan, China (unrealised)
Memorial for Mountain Climbers, Huangshan, Anhui, China (unrealised)
Qingdao, Shandong, China (unrealised)

2004 National Stadium for 2008 Summer Olympics, Beijing
Neolithic Pottery Museum, Jinhua Architectural Art Park, Jinhua, Zhejiang
Courtyard 105, Caochangdi, Beijing
Go Where Restaurant, Beijing
Nine Boxes, Beijing
Cuo House, Beijing
Six Rooms, Nanjing, Jiangsu, China (interior under construction)
Ya Bar, Beijing (space design; demolished)
2008 Summer Olympics, Beijing (landscape design, unrealised)

2003 Ai Qing Middle School, Jinhua, Zhejiang (landscape design)
Ai Qing Cultural Park, Jinhua, Zhejiang (landscape design)
Commercial and Cultural Centre of Jingdong New District, Jinhua, Zhejiang, in collaboration with Herzog & De Meuron (unrealised)
Songshan Lake Culture and Exhibition Centre, Dongguang, Guangzhou, Guangdong (unrealised)

2002 Yiwu River Bank, Jinhua, Zhejiang (landscape design)
Anter Automotive Factory, Huaiyin, Jiangsu, China
Shanghai University of Visual Art, Shanghai (unrealised)

2001 Commune by the Great Wall, Beijing (landscape design)
Bar Jia 55, Beijing
Boao Villa, Haikou, Hainan, China (concept design, unrealised)

2000 Soho Contemporary City, Beijing (landscape design)
In Between, Soho Contemporary City, Beijing (installation)
China Art Archives and Warehouse, Caochangdi, Beijing

1999 Ai Weiwei Studio House, Caochangdi, Beijing

ARTIST'S ACKNOWLEDGEMENTS

I would like to express my gratitude to the following people who have made this project possible. First is my workshop in Jingdezhen, including Liu Weiwei and the team of 1,600 people who expended extensive time, skill, energy and patience in the production of this work. I would also like to thank the members of FAKE Design for their ongoing accomplishments. I am most grateful to Tate's Director Nicholas Serota and his curatorial team, including Sheena Wagstaff, Juliet Bingham, and Marko Daniel, for their invaluable expertise. I also thank Unilever for facilitating this commission as part of The Unilever Series. In particular, I wish to thank Uli and Rita Sigg and Chris Dercon for their continued support.

Last but not least, I thank all my friends who have continuously supported my commitment to art. I also thank all the people active on the Internet, and in particular my supporters on Twitter.

Ai Weiwei